PROJECT MANAGEMENT BASICS

PROJECT MANAGEMENT BASICS

A Step by Step Approach

ROBERT L. KIMMONS

Kimmons-Asaro Group Limited, Inc.
Houston, Texas

CRC Press
Taylor & Francis Group
Boca Raton London New York

CRC Press is an imprint of the
Taylor & Francis Group, an **informa** business

First published 1990 by Marcel Dekker, Inc.

Published 2019 by CRC Press
Taylor & Francis Group
6000 Broken Sound Parkway NW, Suite 300
Boca Raton, FL 33487-2742

© 1990 by Taylor & Francis Group, LLC
CRC Press is an imprint of Taylor & Francis Group, an Informa business

First issued in paperback 2019

No claim to original U.S. Government works

ISBN 13: 978-0-367-45080-9 (pbk)
ISBN 13: 978-0-8247-8391-4 (hbk)

**Visit the Taylor & Francis Web site at
http://www.taylorandfrancis.com**

**and the CRC Press Web site at
http://www.crcpress.com**

Library of Congress Cataloging-in-Publication Data

Kimmons, Robert L.
    Project management basics: a step by step approach/Robert L. Kimmons.
        p.   cm.
    Includes bibliographical references and index.
    ISBN 0-8247-8391-3
    1. Industrial project management.   I. Title.
HD69.P75K56   1990
658.4'04--dc20
                                        90-3505
                                         CIP

Preface

Project management has reached a certain maturity. It is recognized by businesses and the public as a viable, and in many cases the only effective, approach to completing difficult and complex assignments. In recent years, the number of applications served by project management has increased sharply, and these numbers continue to grow. *Management by project* has come into its own.

When I started my working life after graduation from the University of Illinois in 1947, I headed on a bearing leading me ultimately into the profession of project management. I did not foresee then that someday there would be a career called *project management*. Certainly I did not start out to become a project manager, and my steps in becoming one were not a part of a well organized effort. My early ambitions tended toward being a mining engineer working in Latin America. Through a series of circumstances, I became a civil engineer instead and worked for many years in Venezuela and Mexico. Along the way, I became a project manager.

My career paralleled the development of modern project management, but there was no possible way that I could have access to the present knowledge of project management. My own learning experiences were optimized by a continual trial and error process. The idea of using these experiences— identifying goals, setting strategies and developing plans to achieve these goals, scheduling and monitoring progress toward the goals, and applying corrective action when new problems arose— did not become clear until many years later. I realize that my employers paid a high price for my training.

The project manager must keep in mind the *continuity* of the project management process. This process is applicable to almost any effort imaginable, and it works substantially in the same way with many different types of endeavors. The single key element is understanding the *sequential* nature of the steps in the project management approach, and the need to follow them.

Where does a project manager go for guidance today? All of us owe a great debt to our mentors, for it is here that the great preponderance of real learning occurs. Recently I identified forty men and women who have markedly expanded my knowledge and capabilities as a project manager. But this "on the job" training, however important it may be, cannot be the entire answer because it takes too long. A person cannot devote forty years just learning to be a project manager; there needs to be a way to accelerate the instruction.

Today there are various books on the subject of project management. Many of them are focused upon particular facets only. By some authors, project management is looked upon solely as scheduling or as estimating and cost control of the work. This book challenges these arbitrary limitations.

In writing this book I have tried to distill much of what I have learned on the job and from others over the years and to put it into a format which is simple, readable, comprehensive, and easy to use. Frequently project managers do not need to learn certain things as much as they need to be reminded of something they already know. They need a key word to focus on rather than pages of explanation. This book tries to run through the life of a project manager and to present those things which will undoubtedly be met repeatedly over the years. I have tried to point out the predicaments, to highlight the trouble spots, and to place strategically located red flags where disasters have been encountered previously. Although the book contains the basics of project management, it goes further. The material is presented in a condensed and graphic format conducive to rapid perusal and allows for a free-wheeling thought process by the reader in applying what the book says to his own projects.

ACKNOWLEDGMENTS

To my forty mentors, without whose patience and persistence my education in running projects would have been impossible.

To the sponsoring companies and, most particularly, to the participants in my Workshops on Project Management. Their active intervention has kept me current, while confirming that we are still attempting to resolve many of the same problems.

To the Construction Industry Institute at the University of Texas in Austin for their well-structured and well-managed success in identifying and resolving project management problems.

To the Project Management Institute in Drexel Hill, Pennsylvania, for it s efforts in promoting project management internationally and in compiling the Project Management Body of Knowledge (PMBOK).

To my wife, who has mastered the art of "managing the project man-ager." Florence has been the source of constant support, but would be the first to say that "it isn't easy."

To all of these, and also to the new project mangers who will be meeting these challenges in the future, this book is dedicated with all of the excitement that is part of the project management profession.

Robert L. Kimmons

Contents

1 PROJECT MANAGEMENT

OBJECTIVES

Project Management includes the application of simple, but not always obvious, rules of common sense to uncommon and complex situations, with deadlines and tight budgets. Project work is stressful. It will be less so for those who understand the project management process.

The material for this book has been carefully prepared to present the fundamental state of the art of project management in a clear and understandable form. The emphasis is on the effective transmission of practical and usable information, concentrating on presenting **why** an experienced project manager does the things he does and **how** he does them. To organize the material to be most usable, one page is supplied for each topic. Each page can stand alone. The written material is arranged in a logical sequence following the progression of the project manager's primary concerns on a real life project.

THE PROFESSION OF PROJECT MANAGEMENT: To properly set the stage the book begins with a discussion of **what project management is, where it can be used,** and the **benefits of the project management approach**.

PROJECT MANAGEMENT TECHNOLOGY: This concept of a technology peculiar to project management is explored.

TOOLS FOR THE PROJECT MANAGER: The importance of a comprehensive project plan is stressed. A great deal of detail on developing a project plan is given. Project scheduling and budgeting are presented as being determined and set by the plan. The integration of these two elements for better project monitoring is explained. The project manager controls the outcome of the project by continually analyzing status and implementing corrective action. An explanation is given of how accurate and timely status reports to the right people can materially affect the project results.

MAJOR RESONSIBILITIES: The project manager has the responsibility of managing the interfaces between many disciplines involved. Engineering, Procurement, and Construction are the principal ones along

1

with their many components. Three of these areas that need individual reinforcement are the **materials management function, management of the construction effort,** and **subcontract administration.** The major risks in most facility-related projects lie in the work done at the jobsite. The close out of a project is often neglected or done half-heartedly. A key to doing this important task is advance planning.

MANAGEMENT SKILLS: Because of their heavy experience and involvement in technical matters, the emphasis of most project managers may be mostly on the "project" aspects rather than on the "management" perspectives. Fundamentals of some of the key managerial skills are reviewed in the book and presented with particular emphasis on their use in a project environment.

FUTURE YEARS: The final page is devoted to a look into the future and what project managers must anticipate in dealing with the challenges that lie ahead.

CHARACTERISTICS OF THE PROJECT MANAGEMENT APPROACH

The project management approach is characterized by four principal components:

1. Defined goals
2. Designated resources
3. Specific organization
4. Prescribed methodology

DEFINED GOALS: Project management requires that objectives, targets and goals be spelled out in terms of **what** is to be done, **how** it is to be done, and **why** it is to be done. Strategy for reaching these goals and planning for project execution are the cornerstones of the process. The quality of the completed work and the safety provisions for execution and operation are fundamental considerations.

DESIGNATED RESOURCES: One or more of the resources required to do the work on a project are usually limited. The resources that are usually considered are:

1. **TIME** is controlled against the project schedule.

2. **MONEY** is controlled against the project budgets.

3. **PERSONNEL** are controlled against the project staffing plan.

4. **EQUIPMENT** is controlled against the project budget or against the equipment utilization plan.

Project management requires that the total utilization of resources to be used in doing the work be predicted accurately at an early date. The rate at which the resources will be expended is also established well in advance.

SPECIFIC ORGANIZATION: Although the form and type of project organization may vary considerably, good project management calls for a **definitive assignment of responsibility and authority** for completing the project work.

PRESCRIBED METHODOLOGY: Project management requires a definition of what is to be done. It identifies resource needs, establishes baselines for performance and quality, monitors results, prescribes corrective actions to maintain or exceed baseline performance, and reports on job status regularly.

Project management is characterized by its need for a **special kind of a manager**...a manager who is proficient in a discipline pertinent to the project work, skilled in the methodology of project management, and a competent manager in a project environment.

DEFINITION OF PROJECT MANAGEMENT

In order to understand more clearly what **project management** means, we can look at some definitions:

> **Project management is the application of the systems approach to the management of technologically complex tasks or projects whose objectives are explicitly stated in terms of the time, cost, and performance parameters.** Cleland and King. (1988)

> **The planning, organizing, directing, and controlling of company resources for a relatively short-term objective that has been established to complete specific goals and objectives. Furthermore, project management utilizes the systems approach to management by having functional personnel (the vertical hierarchy) assigned to a specific project (the horizontal hierarchy.)** Kerzner (1989)

> **Establishing a committee is not project management. Just about everything that characterizes committees is prejudicial to good project management...A committee is oriented toward recommendations; a project is oriented to results... Appointing a project manager is not, by itself, establishing a project.** Martin (1976)

The Decision Technologies Division of the Electronic Data Systems Corporation, a wholly-owned subsidiary of General Motors, defines project management as follows:

> **The process by which people seek to guide a project to achieve established goals within cost and schedule constraints. This process includes elements of planning, monitoring, analyzing, problem solving, and communicating.**

> **Automated project management systems help managers maintain the elements of control particularly for large, complex, data-intensive projects. With the aid of these systems and the support of project management services, the managers are better able to establish their plan, regularly assess the status of the project against the plan, and to assert possible alternative courses of action...**

Common ideas contained in these definitions include:

- Objectives
- Goals
- Resources
- Planning
- Costs
- Monitoring

- Performance
- Short term
- Systems
- Organization
- Schedule
- Controlling

Using some of these same words we can start to develop our own definition of project management.

Cleland, David I. and William R. King, *Project Management Handbook*, Van Nostrand Reinhold, New York, 1988. pp. 870

Kersner, Harold, *Project Management: A Systems Approach to Planning, Scheduling, and Controlling*, Third Edition, Van Nostrand Reinhold, New York, 1989, p.4

Martin, Charles C., *Project Management: How To Make It Work*, AMACOM, Division of the American Management Association, New York, 1976, p. 6.

APPLICATIONS FOR PROJECT MANAGEMENT

The project management approach of bringing a group of people together on a temporary basis to achieve specific goals has been used for centuries.

During the classical periods of Chinese, Egyptian, Greek, and Roman history, very impressive results were achieved and many of the fundamentals of this approach were employed. Of course it was not called *project management* at the time.

Only since the second half of the twentieth century have many of the tools of modern project management come into use. The sophisticated methods of planning, scheduling, budgeting, forecasting, and reporting have been developed only recently.

After the second world war, the concepts of logical sequencing of project activities in a graphical format, together with the subsequent use of the critical path methodology led to a prioritizing of the order of work. A greater emphasis on quality planning was the result.

At this same time projects were becoming extremely costly, and budget overruns were common. The costs of borrowing money for capital expenditures were burgeoning. Responding to a need to control costs, parallel efforts were made to develop better estimates and to better control changes.

Simultaneously, the drama associated with the computer was unfolding. This tool was quickly adapted to assist with the overwhelming task of processing the data necessary for scheduling and monitoring both the progress and the costs of the jobs.

The use of project management has been increasing rapidly in recent years. New applications are being discovered each year. Perhaps two of the more exciting uses are to be found in the management of personal projects and in its use in mending interpersonal relationships by diagnosing conflicts and setting goals and target dates.

Project management is very broad in its concept. It may be used in a wide variety of cases. Ideal situations for using project management exist where some of the following conditions are present.

- A high-priority undertaking
- Requirement for a multidisciplinary effort

- A non-repetitive situation
- A limitation on some of the required resources

Diverse areas using project management in recent years, most of which were suggested by Brunies (1989) include:

- Aerospace
- Defense Industries
- Engineering and Construction
- Manufacturing
- Electrical Generation and Distribution
- Process Plants
- Crude Oil and Natural Gas Exploration, Development, and Production
- Infrastructure for the Various Levels of Government
- Research and Development
- Data/Information Processing
- Health Care and Biomedicine
- Computer Hardware and Software
- Educational Institutions
- *Ad Hoc* Management Undertakings

Small projects of all types, although not requiring the more advanced technology of project management, benefit from the discipline and structured approach afforded by use of the techniques.

Brunies, Regula A., "Suitable Applications of Project Management", *Project Management: A Reference for Professionals*, Robert L. Kimmons and James H. Loweree (Eds.), Marcel Dekker Inc., New York, 1989, pp 5-12.

THE LIFE CYCLE OF A PROJECT

Few project managers are ever involved through the entire life cycle of a project. Information necessary to the project manager for making important decisions may involve an understanding of preceding phases of the project or what is expected in subsequent stages. The life cycle of the project consists of four stages.

1. **The Conceptual Stage**
2. **The Implementation Stage**
3. **The Operational Stage**
4. **The Abandonment Stage**

CONCEPTUAL STAGE: The project is conceived during this period. A need is identified, and a potential solution is developed. A feasibility may be made to determine whether the concept is technically possible. Very rough economic data are examined to justify pursuing the project.

Assuming that the project is feasible, a preliminary definition is made and very preliminary planning is done. A closer look is taken at costs and a viability study is prepared. The viability study determines the commercial feasibility of the project. Profitability and payout for the project are calculated. The financing source for the project is established. Capital may come from the owner, from outside financing, from the sale of bonds or elsewhere.

Once the source of money has been resolved, formal submission of the proposal or request for funding is made and approval is given if the project is to proceed.

The project manager should remember no matter at what stage of the project he becomes involved, that the reasons for proceeding with the work and the objectives for the project remain paramount. They do not change with the progression of the life cycle unless this decision is made by the owner. Faultless engineering design may seem to be the most important consideration to the project team of the moment; but it is seldom the true objective for the work.

IMPLEMENTATION STAGE: It is during this phase that the steps generally thought of as project management occur.

The chain starts with the detailed planning, followed by basic engineering, detailed engineering, procurement, construction and turnover of the facility to the owner. All of these steps are monitored using the performance assurance program established for the project.

OPERATIONAL STAGE: Even prior to the turnover, the owner has started marketing product and training operating personnel. Once the owner has assumed responsibility for the facility, production builds up to the design level. The installation is maintained to assure a continuous level of output. The operation of the facility is optimized and major or minor changes made to increase production, modernize or take advantage of technical improvements. The facilities may be expanded.

ABANDONMENT STAGE: The market matures, competition increases, and the market share may drop. Ultimately, the facility wears out, becomes uneconomical to operate, or becomes obsolete. The installation is then written off the books and the life cycle is complete.

A TYPICAL LIFE CYCLE CHART

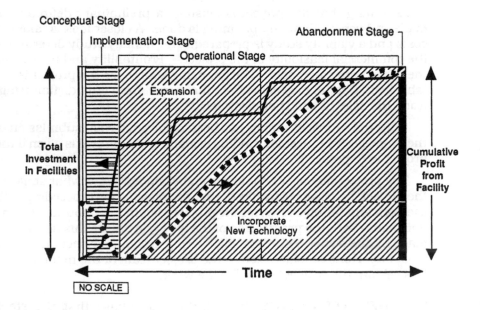

LONG RANGE PROJECT PLANNING

Projects may initially originate from work done by the R&D sector or from a marketing study. The idea for a project may come from the operating division. For an engineering construction firm, the projects are usually the result of receiving a request for a proposal. Some projects may be the result of changes in law or regulatory conditions. Others may result from the efforts of entrepreneurs.

INITIAL EFFORTS: Once an idea for a project is conceived, efforts to justify it start. The proposed project is evaluated and critiqued. Project definition begins. Obvious flows are eliminated. Enthusiasm must be generated in the management of the owner company as the process for justification is started.

After initial definition, a preliminary project feasibility determination should be made. Feasibility shows that the project, as conceived, is technically possible. Sometimes there are several alternative approaches to consider. If the project is considered to be feasible, an initial viability determination will be made. For this, a very rough cost estimate must be developed based upon information which can be rapidly obtained. Viability means that the project can be profitable or necessary to the company's operations and available at a reasonable cost.

Sometimes these initial efforts on behalf of a future project are covered by budgets of the functional group who will also sponsor the project. They may also be done by a corporate planning or corporate engineering group. Generally, once the initial feasibility and viability determinations have been made, the project is either approved, discarded or perhaps funding for further definition and justification is allocated. If approved, the project starts to have real identity.

The importance of keeping good records from the beginning of a project cannot be over emphasized. The scope of the project must be kept current and good communication maintained with all of the team who may be involved in the various studies and financial analyses. As more people become involved in the work, they must have access to the latest project information in a form to keep the familiarization process as efficient as possible.

STRATEGIC PLANNING: Corporate positions on future planning will vary widely. Some companies produce a comprehensive projection of future work on an annual basis. Others find this practice restrictive, and plan individual projects with approval of funding dependent upon the individual project justification. If the project manager is employed by a company which uses a sophisticated planning system, he should be sure to be aware of how his project fits into the strategic plan. This will assist him to make some of the decisions he will be called upon to make and help him to evaluate tradeoffs.

PRELIMINARY EFFORTS: Once placed on the calendar as a project, the definition of the work included continues. Until more definitive information is available, only minimum resources should be expended. Confirmation of the feasibility of the project is required, and a more exact estimate of costs stemming from additional definition follows. All of this information is consolidated and put into the form of a request for funding approval.

The natural tendency for those deeply involved in project development is to understate the costs during the preliminary phases of a project. Initial lower cost estimates improve apparent project viability. However, ideally, the **first estimate** of the investment cost expressed should be the **highest number** heard through the life cycle of the project.

PARTIES INVOLVED IN A PROJECT

There are **two principal parties** on nearly all projects:

1. The **owner** or **owner company**, sometimes referred to as the **client**. The project is being performed for this entity.
2. The **contracted party**, the **contractor**, or the **contracted organization**. This party does all or a major portion of the work not done by the owner.

The number of parties involved in a project, referred to by Cleland and King (1988) as **stakeholders,** is substantially larger than one might suspect at first.

The parties may belong to the same corporate structure or they may be employed by completely separate companies. The **contract** joining the two principal parties may be a formal written document, a simple letter, or even just an oral agreement.

The two principal parties will each have a project manager who represents that party on the project, together with a team actively working on project work. Other personnel from both entities may be involved in an advisory or consultant role.

There are also those who are involved in the project financing, either directly or by making guarantees. These would include banks and other lending institutions, investors, and all of the shareholders in the "owner company" and the "contracted company."

Those who supply goods and services to the project are also stakeholders. Examples of these would include licensors, vendors, suppliers, fabricators and subcontractors of various types.

Regulatory bodies are involved in many projects. A partial listing would include the Food and Drug Administration, the Environmental Protection Agency, the Nuclear Regulatory Commission, and all of the permitting and licensing arms of the local, state and federal government.

In addition to the direct stakeholders, the public, as individuals and as organizations, is involved. Examples of these public entities include labor organizations, environmental organizations, and civil organizations of many types as well as the neighbors residing in the area of the new facility. Some projects today attract the attention of the media, and the newspaper and television reporters become involved parties in these projects.

The extent of involvement may be substantial. The project manager must consider how to deal with each stakeholder to insure that the proper communication channels are established and maintained during the life of the project.

Cleland, David I. and William R. King, *Project Management Handbook*, Van Nostrand Reinhold, New York, 1988, pp. 274.

ALTERNATIVE FORMS OF ORGANIZATION

Project management is usually practiced in one of three different ways within the corporate structure.

A project, being of a short-term nature, is normally imposed upon an existing corporate organization. People may be assigned to the project for the duration of their involvement either on a full-time or on a part-time basis.

The permanent organization of a corporation is called the "functional" or the "departmental" organization. This organization is what is shown by the corporate organization charts and it shows reporting relationships of the divisions, departments, sections, and units where each company employee is assigned on a permanent or long term basis. Organizationally, the least disruptive solution to execute a project might be to assign the project to the department most involved. In fact, this is how projects were done in many companies. This type of a project organization is referred to as a **departmentalized** organization. Problems arise through confusion with priorities. Everyone worries about the departmental concerns and no one is really responsible for the project work itself.

At the opposite end of the spectrum is the **projectized** organization. In this environment, the project manager is given fairly broad, but by no means absolute, authority over the conduct of project personnel. While this approach may encourage effective performance for the project, it can be very disruptive to the conduct of non-project business in the departments. The benefit of a close on-going departmental relationship to provide continuity may also be lost.

In order to try to capture the advantages of each of these, a third type of organization, or the **matrix** organization emerged. Here the departmental managers assume authority for certain aspects of the project, while the project manager exercises authority over other aspects. It is extremely important that these areas of authority be carefully defined. The matrix has been termed "management by conflict" due to the system design calling for the escalation of unresolved disagreement upwards to higher management.

There are variations of the matrix organization which may be differentiated by the relative authority of the departmental management and the project manager.

In organizations where the project manager has more authority, a characterization of **strong matrix** is applied. Where the project manager's authority is less, the organization functions as a **weak matrix**.

PROJECT-DRIVEN ORGANIZATION: A relatively new type of organization has started to evolve, stemming from the economic pressures and the need to correct some of thé shortcomings and inefficiencies of the above organizations. This is called the **project-driven** organization. Here the project manager has a much broader authority, extending even to hiring and firing employees based only on project considerations. Most of the employees in this type of an organization are employed only for the duration of a specific project, which allows a corporation to minimize its full time staff.

THE MATRIX ORGANIZATION

The difficulties involved introducing matrix management into an organization should not be underestimated. Comprehension of the process is essential for success.

The matrix calls for adding a temporary parallel organization with a short term specific purpose. This temporary organization draws upon those resources of the permanent functional organizations until its identified purpose has been achieved and all of the work has been completed or terminated.

Some responsibilities are assigned to functional management and the others to the project manager. Certain of the personnel, such as the leaders of each discipline on the project assignment, have a dual reporting relationship, responsible not only to their discipline supervisor but also to the project manager.

Definition of responsibilities is important. Typically, **project management controls** what work is to be done (the **scope**), when it will be done (the **overall schedule**) and what resources will be required (the **overall budget**); while the **discipline management controls** who will do the work (**staffing assignments**), how it will be done (what **methods and procedures** will be used), and the **quality** of the discipline's work product. Functional management also has the responsibility for maintaining the technical position of the discipline and for administration and professional development of personnel. There are many variations of this assignment of responsibilities.

The most important advantages of the matrix organization are:

- Project objectives and the responsibility for achieving them are made clear.

- Employee morale is encouraged through visible achievement as a part of the project team while obtaining a continuity in career opportunities within the functional organization.

- Efficient use of specialists, part-time, on each of several projects. Integration of project personnel into a team with improved disciplinary coordination and communication.

A matrix organization creates problems. Any person who has worked within a matrix knows this and knows that the orderly flow of work may be affected if role definitions are not made clear.

- The protocol of a matrix system is complex; definition of responsibilities and authority must be made and followed.

- Conflicting priorities cause problems especially when the available resources are tight. Conflicts tend to be disruptive.

- Discipline leaders may receive different instructions from their two supervisors (functional and project).

- Management at all levels has difficulty in balancing the objectives of the projects vs. the considerations of the functional elements.

THE MATRIX ORGANIZATION:

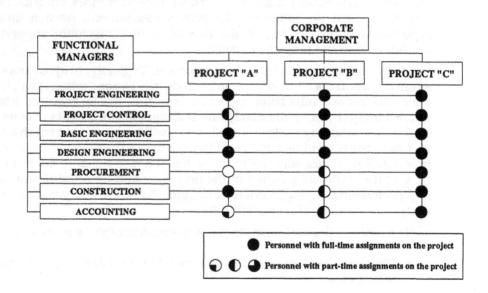

THE PROJECT TASK FORCE

The **project task force, in** effect, consists of all of those individuals assigned to produce a service or a product *for the project*. However, it is not usually considered to include those functional managers with employees assigned to the project from their organization.

The project task force may be a **grouped task force** where the majority of the members are located together in a geographical sense or in a common area; or it may be a **dispersed task force** where the members remain in their own departmental areas.

For a **grouped task force,** a common rule of thumb is that all members who will be involved in the project for 35-40 hours/week for a period of three months or longer will be relocated to the task force area. This principle may be modified depending upon the availability of space in the task force area, demands of the specific project, considerations for the demands on resources within the office, or the stipulations by the client and agreed to in the contract.

PROJECT MANAGER PREFERENCES: Most project managers want the members of their task force to be located in a single area. The primary reason for this is that the project manager can exercise a greater degree of control over the work. Improved communication, particularly with changes, is another very important reason to have all of the team members together. There is also evidence that a greater *esprit de corps* can be engendered with a grouped task force.

A grouped task force benefits those members who want to progress in their careers by assuming more responsibility for multidisciplinary efforts. It may hamper those who are interested in becoming more technically specialized in their own discipline by removing them from the day-to-day intimate association with those in their functional organization who may be more experienced technically.

DISADVANTAGES OF THE GROUPED TASK FORCE: It is very difficult to assure a steady workload for all team members all of the time. Where the team members are dispersed and under the direct supervision of functional management, overloads from all projects may be distributed where resources are available. On any one project, standby time is going to occur.

The layout of many offices does not allow for geographically separate areas for several task forces. It takes a truly flexible system and laborious planning to provide adequate facilities for the growth and reduction of several task forces simultaneously while not subjecting the members to inefficient moves. Generally speaking, using a grouped task force approach will require more total company office space.

QUALITY OF THE WORK OUTPUT: In an organization where fundamental responsibility for the output of a discipline is assigned to the functional organization, a grouped task force would logically result in somewhat lower quality. In actual practice where this responsibility for quality is delegated anyway, the output is not seriously affected.

The quality of the total combined work output which is usually the responsibility of project management, however, is generally materially improved by centralizing the efforts. This is probably due to improvement in communications by having the disciplines working in close proximity.

EFFECT OF USE OF A MODEL: A grouped task force is usually indicated where a plastic model is used for design. The model becomes a communication tool and must be easily accessed by all of the design groups to fully utilize it.

EFFECTS OF THE USE OF PERSONAL COMPUTERS: From the standpoint of quality and design communication, the personal computer tends to reduce the importance of having a grouped task force.

THE FUTURE: Increased use of networked personal computers will help to overcome some of the problems with the grouped task force concept, by allowing team members to remain at their own desks while providing them with the "model" and an even more accurate and rapid communication than has been previously possible.

THE AUTHORITY OF THE PROJECT MANAGER

The level of authority to be exercised by the project manager is delegated by senior management. It varies considerably from company to company. The authority of the project manager must be commensurate with the accountability to which he is held.

An organization where departmental management has a decidedly stronger voice in running a project has what is known as a **functional organizational structure**.

An organization where project management has undeniably more influence has a **projectized organizational structure.**

Senior management of a company must make a decision as to the desired relative authority on this compendium that they want the project manager to exercise.

SPECTRUM OF ORGANIZATIONAL ALTERNATIVES

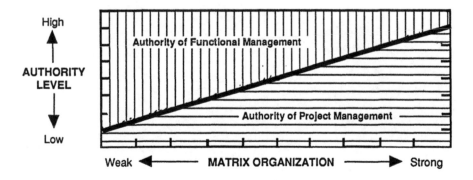

In a typical matrix organization where responsibilities are shared, the functional manager has authority to assign personnel to the various projects. The functions manager also has been the guardian of quality of the work output. This is accomplished partially by developing work methods, standards and procedures which are used in each discipline. The functional manager also established the level of checking to be used for the various operations. The functional manager is responsible for training, development and career progression as well as for salary administration.

The project manager in a matrix organization might well have authority over defining the scope of work to be covered by the contract as well as for the overall planning of the work. The project manager sets the overall project schedule and budget. The project manager directs the integration of schedule and budget, sets the performance baselines, monitors progress, and periodically issues the project progress reports.

The authority given to the project manager is dependent upon the corporate policies which have been formulated for this purpose. Accurate communication of this delegation of authority to all involved is very necessary in order to eliminate ambiguity and conflicts.

Even after the delegation of authority has been made and communicated, there are still opportunities for this authority to be misused or abdicated. The position of project manager can be weakened because he may not participate in salary administration, nominations for promotions, or career development. He generally does not hire and fire. In some organizations where the project manager has little actual authority, he may have a great deal of "perceived" authority in the eyes of the members of the project. The project manager gains in perceived authority by establishing a good track record for successful projects.

ROLES OF THE PROJECT MANAGER

Corporate management will formulate, define and communicate its expectations to functional managers and to project managers very carefully. This may be done best by preparing a written description of the project manager's role and the functional manager's role in each of these areas. In any given situation or company, there will be other areas that need role definition.

- **Project Planning**: It is usually the project manager's responsibility to prepare the project plan. The role of the functional managers in assisting the project manager must be clearly defined. They should also usually bear the burden of the detailed discipline planning to conform to the overall project plan.

- **Project Organization:** The project manager usually adapts the standard project chart to the specific requirements of the project at hand. The role that functional management plays in concurring or modifying the project chart must be determined by senior management.

- **Project Staffing:** For each position shown on the chart, the functional manager will supply candidates. The project manager's role in selection/approval of the project team requires clarification by senior management.

- **Personnel Administration:** Normally, this is the responsibility of the functional manager. The project manager is responsible for maintaining discipline within the task force area.

- **Contract Administration:** The involvement of the project manager vis a vis the legal department in interpreting and administering the contract should be clearly defined so that each is aware of the split of responsibilities.

- **Technical Management:** The exact expectations as to the responsibility for management of engineering and other technical personnel need to be defined. Management responsibilities are frequently split and the interfaces need to be clarified.

- **Project Administration:** A function of project management. Any exceptions should be identified and made clear.

- **Final Administration:** A function of the project manager with each of the specific exceptions and limitations noted.

- **Communication**: Communication requires dedication from both project and functional management. Senior management expectations should be noted.

- **Materials Management:** In organizations with strong procurement involvement, it will be necessary to specifically define those responsibilities which are assigned to project management.

- **Construction:** The project manager's involvement during the construction phase and at the jobsite requires careful definition to distinguish his responsibilities from those of the construction manager.

- **Turnover of Facilities to Owner:** The split of responsibilities among the owner, initial operations department, and the project should be carefully identified, preferably by means of a checklist assigning each anticipated activity to one specific party.

- **Performance Assurance:** This should be the responsibility of each individual for his own work, of functional management for the work done by each discipline, and the project manager for the overall project work.

- **Client Relations**: The basic responsibility must remain with the project manager. He must have help from senior management and from discipline specialists.

- **Job Closeout:** A complete listing of project responsibilities and departmental responsibilities is required. Instructions for charging of time are needed.

The clearcut assignment of responsibility to functional and project management in each of these areas will reduce unnecessary conflict and confusion during the execution of the project.

EFFECTIVE MANAGEMENT IN A PROJECT ENVIRONMENT

The managerial demands in a project environment differ from those in the functional organization because of the very nature of a project assignment.The project manager must face certain handicaps that arise from these differences. The three most important are:

- The duration of the relationship between the project manager and those working on the project is relatively short.

- The authority of the project manager is divided and frequently is not well defined nor understood by those working on the project assignment.

- The project manager may be perceived as having little influence on the careers of those on the project, e.g. pay increases, promotions, and selection for development training.

Offsetting these handicaps, the project manager counts on benefits accruing because of other differences in the nature of the project assignments.

- Intensive planning efforts lead to a clearcut definition of responsibilities. People have a sense of knowing exactly what they are supposed to do.

- The large number of short-term goals appeals to **results-oriented** people.

- Project performance is continuously monitored and can easily provide timely feedback to the project staff.

The prudent project manager will analyze the presence of these handicaps and benefits in the particular environment in which the project is executed. He should attempt to offset the effect of the handicaps and maximize the potential of the benefits available to him.

Authority on a project is divided between the project manager and the functional managers. Split authority is often more equitable in theory than in actuality. The perception of authority in the minds of the people working on the project may be very different from the division of authority set down by policy. This major discrepancy may be due to the force of the personality of one of the managers involved or the system of rewards/punishments administered by the manager.

Departmental managers may try to play on their long range relationships with their own employees because of the career influences that they can exert. The project manager who does little to offset the perception of this power inequity will cause his own authority to erode.

The project manager can counter these inequities by substituting his personal leadership when sufficient assigned authority is lacking. He depends upon the willingness and desire of the people on his project to follow him, not because of what he is organizationally, but because of who he is personally.

MANAGEMENT OF SMALL PROJECTS

Numerically most projects fall into the small project category. The criteria for classifying a small project defies exact quantification. Some projects are expensive, but are relatively simple to execute. They are, nevertheless, small projects. Some of the characteristics of a small project would certainly include:

- Actual monetary limits for a project to be termed "small" are very arbitrary. Perhaps no limitation should be set on the lower end. The upper end should be flexible and dependent upon the project type.

- The project manager of a small project will also be an active contributor to the work.

- Personnel working on small projects will tend to be generalists rather than specialists. They may handle work from more than one discipline.

- Project management concepts of planning, monitoring and control are fine for a small project; however, the more sophisticated tools and programs may be counterproductive and wasteful.

- On most small projects there will not be a complete spectrum of disciplines required.

- The flexibility of the project teams to adjust the operation to the real requirements of the individual projects is a key to small project success.

- The project manager may personally monitor the progress and costs on the job. He may also do some of the project accounting.

Personal computer programs are ideal for small project control because of their simplicity and the immediacy of response.

A few examples of types of small projects are research investigations, equipment-intensive projects; phased development studies; ad hoc assignments for management; pilot plants; small production units; plant turnarounds; revamps of existing plants; software development; and facilities consolidation planning.

Managing a small project is not like managing a large project, and the manager of small projects should realize the differences. On of the most significant of these is the limited reaction time. On a small project there are only very limited resources available for recouping schedule or improving productivity to meet the budget. Managing small turnkey projects is an ideal training ground for project engineers. It offers an opportunity to see the entire picture not just a small piece of it.

2 PROJECT MANAGEMENT TECHNOLOGY

ELEMENTS OF PROJECT MANAGEMENT TECHNOLOGY

In the past few decades projects have become increasingly multi-disciplinary in nature, technically more sophisticated and subject to severe schedule and cost pressures. Project managers began to look for help in the areas of discipline coordination and project controls support. The development of the computer together with the quantum leap in project magnitude/complexity at the beginning of the second half of the twentieth century led to the development of a new structured approach to project management. These aspects of project management may be termed **project management technology**.

Project management technology is comprised of seven elements:

- **Planning:** Establishing objectives, defining work, selecting strategies, sequencing the work and writing the overall plans for project execution.

- **Work organization**: Organizing the work using a method such as the **work breakdown structure (WBS)**, so that the most realistic baselines may be set for tracking performance.

- **Scheduling**: The plan is put on a calendar basis. Critical activities are identified. Resource requirements are optimized. The baselines for monitoring the physical progress on the project are established.

- **Estimating/cost management:** A cost estimate is made from the definition of work scope. The work plans, the schedule, the project budget and spending schedules are set. The budget is integrated with the schedule and the cost baselines are set.

- **Monitoring**: The physical progress/earned value of the work actually completed and the costs actually committed are compared against the planned figures at regular intervals. Variances are pinpointed.

- **Controlling**: By forecasting future performance and by use of trending techniques, potential variances are identified. Actual and potential performance variances are analyzed. Corrective action plans are implemented to bring performance back to the planned status.

- **Reporting**: Communicating results and progress in the appropriate detail to the proper people is important to project success.

The project manager should have a comprehensive understanding of the details of this technology and the many tools that are available to assist him with its use.

3 PLANNING THE PROJECT

PLANNING THE WORK

The cornerstone of the project management approach is the **project plan**. Management of projects requires that planning be done on a very detailed and professional level.

Scheduling is often confused with **planning**. These are two separate and distinct functions. The plan must logically precede the schedule.

The planning process must be simple and practical. Planning is hard work and the rewards are not immediate. **The planning process has to show a payoff for those who plan**. The success of any major undertaking is dependent upon a large number of people and the results are directly proportional to their understanding of the roles that they are to play.

The project manager will always have extraordinary demands on his time at the start of a project. The pressures are toward action and not toward planning. Therefore, the system calls for the plan to be **documented, distributed, understood, and kept current**. The written plan is used to communicate the project manager's strategy for achieving the project objectives. The plan itself is not rigid nor fixed. The results and expectations should not change. Fine tuning is a continuous process. Every time there is an adverse occurrence or a variance from the plan, corrective action must be devised and implemented to regain the planned position.

It has been suggested that the best project managers perpetually live about two months in the future, mentally testing their project plans. Certainly those who successfully anticipate problems and resolve them in advance end up ahead of the game.

This technique also illustrates the flexible nature of the project plan. Continuous minor adjustments to the fine tuning of the plan will ensure that the results conform to the expectations on which the plan was originally based.

The planning process follows a commonsense approach by telling what is to be done, why it is to be done, who is to do it, how it is to be done, and in what order. The following listing shows the steps in preparing an execution plan.

ELEMENTS OF THE PROJECT PLAN

- **Define the work to be done**
- **Determine project objectives**
- **Identify unique problems/constraints/assumptions**
- **Select strategy**
- **Sequence the work activities**
- **Review constructability**
- **Fine tune sequencing/organize plan**
- **Develop detailed execution plans**
- **Develop performance assurance plans**

SCOPE DEFINITION

The logical first step in starting a complex project is to completely define the work included. This is done by means of a written document called the **scope of work** document, which is prepared by or under the direction of the project manager. It is initially used by members of the project team for planning purposes.

If there is a formal contract, especially if the work is to be done on a lump sum price basis, the scope of work is usually well defined. The scope may not be in a format that is most convenient for project personnel to use in their activities.

More often than not there is a split in responsibilities. The owner, the contractor, and other third parties will each have designated parts for which they are responsible. Ideally, the scope definition will consider all of the work to be done, assigning each part to the proper organization. Potential omissions may thus be discovered and misunderstandings eliminated.

The scope of work cannot conflict with the contract. It supplements and provides additional details for the provisions contained in the contract. It does not call for more work than the contract covers. It may contain work that is not specifically mentioned, but is implicit under the terms of the contract.

The work to be done may be thought of as being of two types:

- **Services** to be performed
- **Documents** to be produced

All of the work items may be expressed as one of these two categories.

An outline of a typical **scope definition** is as follows:

- Official identification of the project
- A brief description of the project
- Pertinent contract data affecting the work to be done
- Licensing information/conditions/constraints

- Responsibilities (Services, Documents) by

  Contractor, broken down by discipline
  Owner
  Third Parties: licensors, subcontractors, etc.

- **Available Descriptive Material Defining the Work,** such as flow diagrams, general arrangement drawings, and equipment lists

- **Decisions that have already been made,** which affect the amount of work required or the way in which it will be done, such as pre-selected equipment items or owner-designated procedures, systems, and methods

PROJECT OBJECTIVES

Projects are approved in order to realize some potential advantage for the owner. If the project is executed so that this advantage is negated, then the project cannot be successful.

Project execution must be directed to achieve the project objectives. The objectives must be known to those who plan the project as well as those who do the subsequent work. The platitudes "on time" and "under budget" are sometimes given as project objectives. No project can ever be wholly successful if, at completion, it does not meet these two criteria. This, however, represents an oversimplification of the real intent of *project objectives*.

During planning, the project manager should make sure that the project objectives have been set and approved by the owner. Some owners are open about their real objectives; others may be reluctant to share the project objectives.

The project manager has to be certain that he knows what the true project objectives are. This may require restating and presenting them to the owner for confirmation.

A project may have many objectives, so prioritizing the objectives is necessary. Objectives should be assigned priorities with #1 being the principal objective and identifying others in order of descending priority until all of the owner's objectives have been covered.

Some of the typical priorities, not listed in any particular order, include:

- Avoiding unproven equipment
- Safety during construction
- Final costs within budget
- Designing for specific project life
- Enhanced public image
- Facility appearance
- Fastest completion time
- High level of automation
- Lowest capital investment
- Lowest operational costs
- Maintaining low owner profile
- Safety for maintenance
- Minimizing startup time
- On-time completion
- Reliability of operations
- Safety during operations
- Quality of product
- Security of information
- Use of local subcontractors
- Use of local suppliers

By establishing a priority listing of pertinent objectives, project decisions can be made consistent with the owner's expressed desires. Trade-offs that may be required can be evaluated based on the priorities set. Any decisions which are not consistent with the owner's objectives, must be reviewed carefully. The order of the selected objectives will be instrumental in determining the strategy to be used in project execution.

The people assigned to the project should have a good understanding of the project objectives. People tend to remember what was insisted upon for the previous project. The tendency will be to continue to work accordingly unless new directions have been given.

IDENTIFYING UNIQUE PROBLEMS

Every major undertaking has its associated problems. Project managers are supposed to guide their projects through these problems.

If a problem can be anticipated, in many cases it ceases to be a problem. When problems are considered early, the best of various alternatives identified and resolved in advance, they cease to be problems and tend to disappear.

In the project planning process, it is the intention that unique problems that can be anticipated on the project will be identified. It is not the purpose of the plan to solve these problems, **only to identify them**.

Consider the following categories when trying to identify potential problems on projects:

- **New Technology:** Unproven processes where the objectives of the project are not open to accepting this risk

- **Prototype Equipment:** Scaled-up or newly developed equipment presents an area of risk not compatible with projects demanding reliability of operation and maintenance.

- **Site Conditions:** Unusual climates such as arctic or desert conditions as well as challenges presented by outer space and the bottoms of the oceans.

- **Limited Resources:** A shortage of skilled technicians or laborers at a jobsite, the possibility of owner imposed restrictions on spending, limited space for the facilities with accompanying design and erection complications.

- **Delays in Obtaining Permits:** Start of construction or start of operations is dependent upon receiving the corresponding permits.

- **Process Control Systems:** Complications with the design, procurement, installation, and startup of very complex systems.

- **Difficult Access:** No conventional transportation means to site.

- **Labor:** Some areas have a history of labor turmoil threatening a prolonged construction period and poor productivity. Where labor contracts are expiring, renegotiation may cause delays.

- **Economic Conditions:** High rates of escalation, the threat of supplier business failures, and uncertain markets all may create create problems.

Each project will have certain problems which are obvious, and others which may not be so apparent. The project team should walk through the project during the planning phase to identify potential problems including those which are initially hidden. The possibility of developing adversarial relations between the owner and contractor project teams can also be a source of serious problems. This should not be neglected during problem identification.

SELECTING A STRATEGY

In the project management approach, **strategy** is that system of logic which will give the highest probability of achieving the defined project objectives while overcoming the identified problems.

If the **project objectives** are the ultimate destination, times of arrival, and overall cost of the journey, then **strategy** is selecting the general direction to follow and the mode of travel. **Planning** is the implementation of strategy to reach the destination by the choice of vehicle, specific routes, and speed of travel.

In beginning a project, the manager is very busy. It is easier to do things the usual way, but because each project is special and differs from others, he must resist taking the easy way. This is the time for freewheeling thinking in developing the best strategy. He must not allow himself to get caught up in the narrow limits of conventional thought to solve unconventional problems.

The project manager, in developing a strategy for his project, analyzes his resources and decides how best to deploy them. In executing the project, resources might include specific strengths in the capability of his people, the depth of related experience in his company, or the flexibility in the method of operating that he has been given.

Likewise, he should examine weaknesses. Where these are present in areas vital to project success, he should immediately conceive the means to compensate. He must be aware of any vulnerabilities and be prepared to reinforce them.

Project strategy depends to a large extent on what happens in the future. Alternate scenarios should be considered, and "*what-to-do-ifs*" looked at. Project management must then put the possible alternatives into the proper perspective.

A well thought out project strategy will devise ways to do things differently and better for the specific project at hand.

Always an important consideration in selecting the project strategy is the overall sequencing of the operations at the jobsite. This, in turn will set the pattern of the engineering, procurement, and all of the intervening work. Frequently strategy will be set by long-lead equipment items. Shortage of skilled labor at the jobsite may also set strategy. Strategy may be dictated by the need to minimize the risk of failing to meet primary objectives.

The major problems anticipated on the project have to be identified, so that the strategy may be developed to avoid or eliminate the problems or reduce them to a tolerable level.

A difficult obstacle for the project manager is the complaint that a change from the norm is "*going to require us to do something differently.*" Productivity on the job will suffer if this feeling is allowed to prevail. When changes are introduced, it is necessary to make sure that everyone understands why the changes are being made.

The development of project execution strategy is an intergral part of the planning process. Planning should not take place until the strategy has been selected, and then should be done following following the selected strategy.

CONSTRUCTABILITY

Constructability is that necessary examination throughout the project which asks: **"Is what we are doing the very best, the very fastest and the least expensive way to achieve the expected results?"** Constructability reviews ideally start very early in the project. It is during this initial period that maximum benefits can be gained from this technique.

The project specifications should be minimal, only sufficient to make sure that the proper results are obtained. Over time, specifications get to be confusing compilations of decades of "improvements," containing the "preferences" of a succession of previous clients. When establishing a constructability program, reviewing the standard specifications of the firm is an excellent way to begin.

The plant layout is critically reviewed to determine the best arrangement. Layout mistakes may easily be compounded from project to project. A block model is used to develop the optimum layout. Layout has a major impact on the cost and operability of the plant.

When a suitable standard piece of equipment is available from the manufacturer, it should be specified rather than to attempt to customize each piece of equiment.

Mat foundations may be used in place of multiple independent ones; structures may be combined.

The construction activities are considered in the design. The sequence of construction activities and the construction techniques to be employed are keys to operational efficiency in the field.

Unnecessarily complex procurement procedures should be carefully streamlined. Requirements for vendor drawings and the number of types of drawings requiring certification should be minimized.

Although these comments have been directed primarily toward a project involving design and construction of a processing plant, the approach expressed and the methodology indicated can be applied to a wide range of project types.

The ten rules of constructability on the overleaf were suggested by Walter J. Boyce. They summarize succinctly the constructability approach to a better project.

THE KISS APPROACH

- **KEEP IT SIMPLE AND STRAIGHT**
- **KEEP IT SAME SIZE**
- **KEEP IT SHOP STANDARD**
- **KEEP IT SQUARE AND SQUATTY**
- **KEEP IT SPECIFICATION SIMPLE**
- **KEEP IT STANDARD SIZE**
- **KEEP IT SUPPORT SIMPLE**
- **KEEP IT STANDARDS SIMPLE**
- **KEEP IT SCHEDULE SACRED**
- **KEEP IT SITE STANDARD**

– Walter J. Boyce

Boyce, Walter J., President of Boyce Consultants, International Constructability, Houston Texas.

CONSTRUCTABILITY CONCEPTS

The Construction Industry Institute, (CII) located at the University of Texas in Austin, has defined constructability as follows:

> **Constructability is the optimum use of construction knowledge and experience in planning, design, procurement and field operations to achieve overall project objectives. Maximum benefits occur when people with construction knowledge and experience become involved at the very beginning of a project. This is illustrated by the chart.**

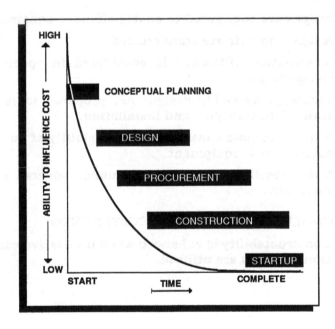

The CII has identified fourteen **Constructability Concepts** which serve to enhance the constructability, and hence the cost effectiveness, of a project:

CONSTRUCTABILITY CONCEPTS DURING CONCEPTUAL PLANNING

I-1. Constructability programs are made an integral part of the project execution plans.

1-2. Project planning actively involves construction knowledge and experience.

I-3. Early construction involvement is considered in development of contracting strategy.

I-4. Overall project schedules are construction sensitive.

I-5. Basic design approaches consider major construction methods.

I-6. Site layouts promote efficient construction.

CONSTRUCTABILITY CONCEPTS DURING DESIGN AND PROCUREMENT

II-1. Design and procurement schedules are construction sensitive.

II-2. Designs are configured to enable efficient construction.

II-3. Design elements are standardized.

II-4. Construction efficiency is considered in specification development.

II-5. Module/preassembly designs are prepared to facilitate fabrication, transport and installation.

II-6. Designs promote construction accessibility of personnel, material, and equipment.

II-7. Designs facilitate construction under adverse weather conditions.

CONSTRUCTABILITY CONCEPTS DURING CONSTRUCTION

III-1. Constructability is enhanced when innovative construction methods are utilized.

Constructability Task Force, *Constructability Concepts File,* The Construction Industry Institute, Austin, Texas (1988).

SEQUENCING THE WORK:
THE PROJECT LOGIC

After the definition of scope containing a list of all work items has been prepared and the project strategy has been formulated, the work must be properly sequenced. The project strategy must respond directly to accomplishing the specific project objectives while avoiding or resolving the anticipated problems. Following through with the selected strategy may lead to sequencing work in an unconventional manner.

Project managers must resist any artificial boundaries in their thinking patterns during this planning phase. Although similiar projects may have been done in a certain order, it does not automatically follow that a new project has to use that same sequencing if there are valid reasons to do it differently. For a project in a locale where skilled construction labor is scarce, modularization may be a solution. The first decision to modularize, or to do the work *differently* represented a risk; yet now this technique is an accepted, even preferred, mode. Modularization also works well where the unique problem is the short construction season. If you have limited resources at the site, you should consider doing some of the work elsewhere.

The project manager must think about those adverse conditions which will be unavoidable on the job. When planning access, long equipment deliveries may present a challenge in setting the delayed items. Site erection of large vessels may exclude the most convenient timing of underground and foundation work in the vicinity. Dense equipment layout will cause intolerable congestion among construction personnel unless the work is scheduled bearing this in mind.

Sequencing may be started by thinking **"initial operations,"** **"construction,"** and **"priorities."** Carefully analyze the order in which the field work can be best organized to ultimately accommodate startup. Divide the work into areas, and decide where the work can be started most efficiently remembering that the testing and startup will be by systems.

Once the construction sequencing, based upon startup needs and deliveries, has been decided upon, then all of the engineering and procurement activities must be scheduled to support the field schedule. All detailed design, subcontracts, equipment, and commodity materials must be available at the time they are required for the field work. The hallmarks of the successful project manger are (1) continually thinking about what is going to be happening later on in the job and (2) anticipating and resolving problems. During the planning process this anticipation is especially beneficial.

TYPICAL QUESTIONS TO ASK IN SEQUENCING THE PROJECT WORK

- What is the needed **date for plant turnover** to the client?
- What is the proper **order of system start ups** for the plant?
- Where will all of the **equipment and materials be available first**?
- Where will **deliveries cause delays**? How can an **overall schedule delay be avoided** by working around incomplete areas?
- Where can **early construction** benefit the remainder of the work?
- How can **construction labor be utilized more effectively** by sequential scheduling of the crews on like work in various areas?
- How will the **turnover sequence be benefited** by early completion of particular system?

THE EXECUTION PLAN

The **execution plan** is a formal document which serves as a communication tool to explain the project manager's work plan. It is developed in such a way to make it easy to gain the positive support of all of those individuals who will be working on the project.

PLAN CHARACTERISTICS: The plan must be documented, distributed, understood, and kept current. It must be specific, concise and clear. It should be written in simple terms and structured to follow the chronological development of the work. It should not detail standard practices and procedures, but should clearly explain all planned departures from the standard methods.

PLAN COMPONENTS

- **Definition of Scope:** A listing of all services to be performed and the documents which must be produced in accordance with the contract terms.

- **Objectives:** Clearly stated in order to be used for setting priorities and making tradeoffs during execution.

- **Plan Assumptions:** Where concrete data is not available, any assumptions made to allow work to start should be listed.

- **Constraints:** A list of any known impediments to orderly progression of the work. A problem with cash flow or limited resources, for example.

- **Pending Decisions:** Decisions which cannot be made or should not be made at the beginning of the job should be itemized. Responsibility must be assigned for making these decisions and a time should be set for them to be made.

- **Alternatives:** On nearly every project, there are certain areas where there are choices. Additional studies may be involved. A plan of action and responsibility should be assigned for each identified alternative.

- **Unique Problems:** Serious problems which can be identified should be listed. A course of action as to how to resolve them needs to be presented.

- **Execution Strategy:** This portion of the plan outlines the project manager's concepts of how the project will be executed in order to achieve the objectives and avoid the identified problems. The work plan will follow this suggested course of action.

- **Project Organization and Staffing:** The organization structure necessary for executing the project together with the planned staffing requirements is presented here.

- **The Work Breakdown Structure (WBS):** The project work is presented in hierarchical form as set by the control requirements for the work.

- **The Overall Project Plan:** The outline of how the project is to be executed.

- **The Project Schedule:** The project plan put on a calendar basis. The master project schedule should be included initially in the execution plan.

- **The Project Budget:** The control budget is developed from the most current estimate available. Cost information must be coordinated with the plan and the schedule.

- **Job Closeout Plan:** This plan should be formulated at an early date so that the information required for closeout can be collected in the form required by the closeout plan.

    Issuing a complete execution plan is an ambitious undertaking. Content should be very carefully tailored to the needs of the project. Regardless of how small the project is, the discipline of going through each one of these steps is important. What is actually included in the plan will depend upon the need to communicate the thoughts to those with project involvement.

THE PERFORMANCE ASSURANCE PLAN

Project expectations are clearly defined in the project plan, the specifications, the project budget and the schedule. The object of the performance assurance program is to make sure that these expectations are realized and that this is done in a cost effective manner.

Productivity is important to the project manager. The project personnel should be made aware of that fact by consistent, factual feedback. High productivity from each person for all time charged to the project is a requirement for achieving project success.

Project management cannot depend that a clear definition of the work will guarantee satisfactory final results. Production must be followed step by step through the project. This can be done if realistic baselines are established and comparisons made regularly against these baselines in the four principal areas of concern.

1. **The Schedule:** Once the work has been scheduled and all activities have been placed on a time scale, the planned efforts project for each of these activities can be weighted. The summation of daily, weekly or monthly efforts in terms of percent of the total job requirements may be plotted against time. Regularly, actual progress, sometimes stated as earned value may be plotted against the plan. Additionally, all critical milestones must be tracked to assure that these are being completed on time.

2. **The Budget:** The forecasts of costs may be plotted on a time scale following the schedule of activities. Periodically, the costs as of a specific date are determined and added to the projected costs of the work remaining from that date.

3. **Productivity:** If actual costs and physical progress have been kept so that they are synchronized, then a comparison with the planned productivity is possible. This gives an indication of actual versus planned productivity current project technology encourages this comparison.

4. **Quality:** Specifications set the baseline for quality. Regular inspection verifies the acceptability of the work done. Quality is of interest not only during any fabrication and construction efforts during the project, but also in the engineering, procurement, and the controls area itself.

The **performance assurance plan** details:

- how **baselines** for each area will be developed
- the **detail** for which baselines are necessary
- the **frequency** of verification
- the **feedback** mechanisms are to be used

The project manager must **keep performance assurance in perspective**. It should never cost more to get acceptable performance than the differential is worth. In the past, some of the control programs have cost much more than could be justified by the results. The **minimum effort to produce acceptable results** is what should be specified and used.

WORK BREAKDOWN STRUCTURE

For the most effective control of a complex project, integration of schedule and budget is imperative.

In the past, the percent of physical progress on a job was tracked independently using the schedule as a baseline. The cost of a project was based on tracking and making *"to complete"* predictions against the baseline of the budget. As there was no real relationship between the two after the work had started, it was difficult to relate cost and progress.

A concept called the **work breakdown structure** or the **WBS**, has been introduced and is gaining rapid acceptance in project management. This concept allows integration of the schedule and the budget into a single system so that meaningful tracking can be done. The WBS also allows organization of the work so that accounting requirements of the job are more easily met and job charges are arranged for proper coding.

The WBS consists of showing successive subdivisions of the work on a chart similar to that used for conventional organization charts. This hierarchical representation of the project makes it possible to show task relationship at all levels. For example, the total project is represented by a single block at the top of the chart. The project is subdivided into logical divisions as determined by the project scope, the plan of execution, and the accounting requirements for coding the costs. These subdivisions are then further divided into logical groupings following the same reasoning.

This same procedure is followed consistently until the packages of work become the reasonable division of the project at that level. A **work package** may be defined as an identifiable grouping of related work from one or more disciplines. It represents a *"manageable"* segment of the work. Continued subdivision of the work packages into discipline activities follows. These consist of activities of about two hundred hours as a minimum. Even individual work assignment could be shown, but this is seldom practical.

A WBS dictionary is prepared for each job. It defines in some detail all of the elements of the work breakdown structure..

The work breakdown structure may be matrixed in with the project organization chart. The account coding can be developed so that each discrete part of the work and each part of the project organization assigned responsibility for that work can be clearly identified. The hours charged during each time period are also coded to this level of detail making performance statistics immediately available.

The project schedules and budgets are prepared using the work packages as a basis. Each package is separately costed over the time period indicated by the schedule. The rate of resource usage on the project can be determined. This information then serves as a set of baselines for project monitoring using the **cost/schedule control system (C/SCS)**.

WORK BREAKDOWN STRUCTURE

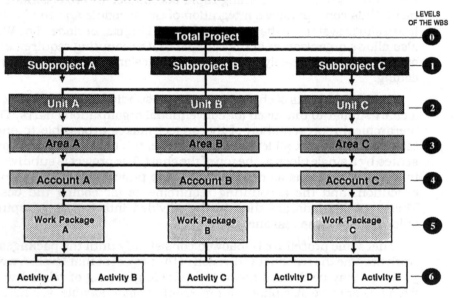

WORK ASSIGNMENT SHEET

Work assignments should be made in such a way as to eliminate doubts as to expectations from the standpoint of content, schedule, or resources required. **Work assignment sheets** are a tool to make sure that the supervisor and the individual worker are in agreement as to what is expected on work assignments for the immediate future.

Typically the worksheets are prepared and reviewed every two weeks and they cover a period of three weeks. Overall, the preparation and review of the assignment forms do not require any additional time on the part of either the individual or the supervisor. There is a time saving because of the imposed requirement for understanding the task assignments more fully. A few of the reasons for using work assignment forms are listed below.

- Work assignment sheets provide a method for identifying and clarifying the work expectations of the supervisor.

- Work assignment sheets involve every engineer in planning his work, budgeting his time, and providing a better perspective of his contributions to the overall project.

- The work assignment sheets provide a mechanism for performance feedback from management to individuals as well as feedback from each individual to management.

- Worksheet monitoring provides timely warnings for trouble spots and triggers remedial action.

WORK SHEET FORMAT: A typical format for a worksheet might look like this:

TASK	ESTIMATED HOURS	WEEK ENDING DATE 11/06	11/13	11/20	11/27	12/04	ACTUAL HOURS
#1 - Review Design, EW-33	60	■ ■ ■ ■ ■ ■ ■ (PLANNED WORK TIME) ▬▬▬▬▬ (ACTUAL WORK TIME) 40 / 15 / 10 (ACTUAL HOURS WORKED)					65
#2 - Size Utility Lines, Area 42	20		■ ■ ■ 15				15
#3 - Requisition Control Valves, EW-33	70		■ ■ ■ ■ 10	■ ■ ■ ■ 30	■ ■ ■		40
#4 - Review Bids for Pneumatic Instruments	10					■ ■ ■	

PROCEDURES FOR USE

- Every two weeks the supervisor and the individual worker review the tasks that are to be worked on over the following three weeks. These tasks are taken from those that are required by the discipline's schedule of work. The tasks are listed on the work assignment sheet.

- The supervisor and the worker will agree upon an estimate of the jobhours required for each of the tasks. The tasks listed will include all of the work items for the next three-week period only. The estimated number of hours to complete each of the tasks is entered on the work assignment sheet.

- Bar charts showing when the tasks are to be worked on are shown on the work assignment sheet

- Each week the worker will enter the number of hours spent working on each of the tasks. The total number of hours spent to complete each task is recorded when the task has been completed on the work assignment sheet.

- At the end of the two-week period, the status of work on each task is reviewed and a new three week projection is made. Completed tasks are analyzed. New tasks are added.

Special Considerations: Any situation which may affect the work and any assumptions are noted as such on the work assignment sheet.

THE PROJECT ORGANIZATION

The **project organization** should be developed starting with a corporate standard, if this is available. The standard chart should be modified to accommodate the requirements of each project. It should also be consistent with the final work breakdown structure.

Most project organizations are structured as follows with modifications when required.

1. The project organization is headed up by the **project manager**. The chart should also indicate the reporting relationship of the project manager to his senior manager.

2. In addition to his **secretary**, individuals responsible for the major production efforts will report to the project manager. These typically include the **project engineering manager**, the **procurement** or **materials manager**, the **construction manager**, and the **controls manager**. On a very large project, an **administrative manager** or a **deputy project manager** may be required.

3. Reporting to the **project engineering manager** will be leaders from each discipline involved. Project staff specialists (engineering consultants) will also report to the engineering manager.

4. The supervisors of purchasing, expediting, and traffic report to the **procurement manager**.

5. Reporting to the **construction manager** or the **general superintendent** will be the area superintendents, field engineer, field control superintendent, materials superintendent, and the field office supervisor.

6. Reporting to the **project controls manager** will be the lead scheduler and the lead cost engineer.

7. There are different philosophies about the assignment of responsibility for **material management**. One sector advocates single responsibility from requisitioning from bills of material through ordering, expediting, traffic, and receipt of material at the jobsite. Others believe that each discipline should be responsible for its own part in the flow of materials for the job.

8. In some organizations quality control is under the **quality control manager**, who reports to the project manager. Elsewhere

this function is a part of the procurement organization or the engineering organizations.

9. Where size and responsibilities justify, there may be an **administrative manager** who has personnel reporting to him with the responsibility for the project account, the details of contract administration, change order control, project communications, the project computers/terminals, etc., and the project secretarial and clerical staff.

The project organization structure must respond to the project's needs. With computerized management information systems, the managerial/supervisory span of control is greater now than when many of the standard charts were developed. For each position, a job description should clearly outline the performance expectations.

TYPICAL PROJECT ORGANIZATION CHART

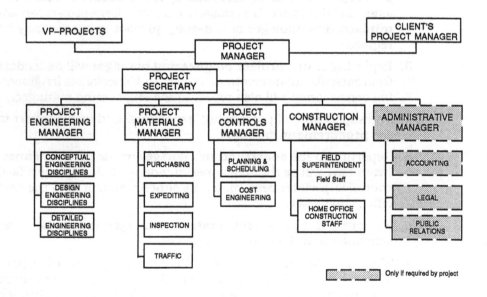

COORDINATION PROCEDURES

The **coordination procedures** or **job instructions** give administrative direction for the project work. This document is issued by the project manager early in the project and contains the following type of information.

1.   Proper project title and number references
2.   Pertinent contract data on project administration
3.   Project representatives/project organization charts
4.   Approvals required
5.   Correspondence protocol

6.   Administrative and procedural constraints
7.   Security provisions
8.   Work breakdown structure chart and dictionary
9.   Issue of specifications/approval requirements
10. Issue of drawings/approval requirements

11. Engineering administrative procedures
12. Purchasing administrative procedures
13. Inspection administrative procedures
14. Field construction procedures

16. Subcontracting procedures
17. Accounting procedures
18. Changes to the contract
19. Field changes
20. Progress reports

21. Job status photographs
22. Operating manual requirements
23. Startup administrative procedures
24. Job closeout
25. Distribution of documents by type

APPENDIX - Equipment Schedules, Drawing Control Indices, Typical Letter Format, Change Notice Format...

The coordination procedures require frequent updating responding to any modifications as the job progresses. It is helpful to date the pages of the various revisions as they are issued. The revised index should contain the dates of the current issue of each section so that everyone is made aware of all revisions to the document.

found to be useful. Those portions which are needed immediately are sent out early, while those which requre more time to prepare are issued at a later date. The experienced project manager will stress the importance of the document by insisting on strict compliance from the very start.

BASIS FOR DESIGN/PROJECT CRITERIA

Projects have voracious appetites for data. Basic information is used repeatedly for calculations and detailed design. The project manager makes the basic design data or project criteria available in an accurate form so that all personnel are working from the same data base. The efficient way to do this is to publish all basic design information in one place. Doing this will also make the information readily available for project-wide perusal and feedback in the case of mistakes.

CATEGORIES OF DATA WHICH SHOULD BE INCLUDED

- **Plant Characteristics:** Location, type and capacity of facility; on stream time; design production rate; provisions for expansion; safety and insurance requirements.

- **Site Characteristics:** Site elevation; atmospheric, wind, soil and seismic conditions; rainfall and snow data; ground water elevation, and depth to frost line.

- **Access to Site:** Existing access by road, rail, water and air; requirements for new access routes by roads, railroad, water, and air.

- **Buildings:** Description of existing buildings; new buildings/additions required; type of buildings desired; characteristics of building mechanical elements, and exterior and interior finishes.

- **Utilities:** Characteristics of existing utilities and cost information; requirements of new utilities for the following: water, process water, demineralized water, plant air, instrument air, fuel gas, other gases, steam, electricity, heating, ventilating, and air conditioning.

- **Waste Disposal:** Characteristics of existing systems and requirement for new process, sanitary and storm drainage systems, and any special requirements for hazardous waste handling and disposal.

- **Feedstocks/Raw Materials:** Feedstock specifications, battery limit conditions and feed rate; feedstock storage requirements; feed stock costs; and the same information where applicable for other raw materials/catalysts required for plant operation.

- **Mechanical Equipment:** Governing codes; material specifications and corrosion allowances for vessels, heat exchangers, pumps etc.

- **Electrical/Electronic Equipment:** Governing codes and material specifications for substations, motors, instrumentation, and communications and computer systems.

- **Products:** Product specifications; applicable industry standards; battery limit conditions; production rates; product storage requirements; and value in $/unit.

- **Waste Products/By-Products:** Characteristics; codes governing waste treatment; storage requirements; and shipping/disposal method as these are determined.

With all of this information located and maintained in one place, many jobhours will be saved during the course of the project. A **basic design book** that is kept current will prevent errors introduced by the use of incorrect or superceded data.

4 THE PROJECT SCHEDULE

SCHEDULING THE WORK

From the beginning, the project manager has certain tasks that have to be started even while planning of the entire job is underway. In order to keep control of this work, he relies upon the **early work schedule.** This schedule is merely a listing of all of these initial activities together with the assignment of responsibility to a specific individual and an assigned date for completion.

The planning of the work is done by experienced people, preferably the leaders who will be in charge of the efforts. Scheduling is done by people experienced in scheduling techniques. The mechanics and arithmetic may be done by less experienced personnel manually or by computer programs designed for this use. With the advent of simple scheduling programs for the personal computer, even the smaller jobs can be efficiently entered and processed by the computer.

Following is the sequence in which the various scheduling activities should be done:

1. **Task Identification:** The discrete activities of the proper size for control are chosen. They are selected based upon the system defined by the work breakdown structure. These activities may be entered on an individual input sheet or directly into the computer data bank.

2. **Sequencing:** The work packages and the activities within each package are sequenced following the provisions of the project plan.

3. **Logic Diagram:** A logic diagram of the work packages/major activities is made. Activity restraints are entered in the computer or on input sheets.

4. **Staffing Analysis:** Estimates are made for the normal jobhours required for each of the activities based upon (1) the scope of the activity, (2) historical data input, and (3) best judgement for the job. These may be entered in the data bank or on the activity input sheets.

5. **Activity Durations:**   Based upon the activity, its staffing level, and best judgement, the normal activity duration is determined. This is entered in the computer or on the input sheet.

6. **The Critical Path:** Using all of the data entered into the computer, a run is made to determine the critical path or the chain of activities which have zero float. This sequential linked group of activities determine the earliest completion date based on the logic diagram, the staffing level and the activity durations set. All activities on this chain are critical activities in that any delay in completing any one will delay the project completion.

7. **Resource Profile:** This program or manual determination and the subsequent graphical representation shows each discipline staff level throughout the project. There will probably be conflicting demands for people on the initial runs.

8. **Resource Leveling:** By adjusting non-critical activities, periods of high staffing demand for the individual disciplined may be reduced.

9. **Scheduled Plan:** Once the system has been optimized with respect to calendar time, activity duration and staffing level, the results can be approved, and it becomes the schedule for the project.

10. **Bar Charts:** The schedule is usually communicated to management and to others having a general need to know this information by means of bar charts. These are less cumbersome and more easily understood than the detailed scheduling information developed during the prior step.

THE EARLY WORK SCHEDULE

A project that gets off to a good start has a better than average chance of being a successful project. On most projects work has to start immediately on some of the activities. These probably are or will become obvious to the project manager. The value of planning is lost if the project ends up in trouble because too much attention is put on formal planning during the first weeks to the exclusion of starting work in some critical areas.

The **early work schedule, EWS,** defines those tasks which require action prior to the issue of formal schedules. It provides an easily developed monitoring document at the very early stages of the project.

The early work schedule gives the project manager freedom of mind to know that all of these various activities, once identified, are being taken care of. He can then dedicate more of his efforts toward the immediate task of planning the project.

An early work schedule is a simple technique for relieving the project manager's concerns for those activities that need to start rapidly. As he recognizes non-postponable activities, the project manager adds them to a list of those tasks included on the EWS. He assigns the responsibility for getting the work done and sets target dates for starting and completing each activity. He always specifies the expected deliverable.

The format of the EWS is very simple. It might be only a skeleton as in the example shown below:

ACTIVITY/TASK	ASSIGNED TO	TARGET DATES Scheduled/Actual
Plan layout of task force area in Building C, 2nd. floor. Prepare sketches suitable for partitions, furniture, and equipment location.	Henry Pillips Architect	Immediately November 14,1990
Visit state EPA office to develop guide to environmental permitting requirements.	Emily Posten Sanitary Engr	August 18, 1990 attend meeting. ——— October 1, 1990 issue draft of guide for comments.

The EWS may also be put into a bar ·chart format if the project manager prefers. The project EWS is really a tool for the project manager; however, the technique may be used by any of the discipline leaders or the project engineers for early work assignments in their own areas.

On a small project with a short schedule, the early work schedule assumes a great deal of importance as it may be used to control the project for a relatively greater proportion of the total time. On small projects with tight schedules, the importance of the EWS is even greater.

The project manager monitors the early work schedule. If he uses a personal computer for the listing, he can easily generate an exception alarm triggered when a target date is not met. The PC will also let him make hard copies of the schedule for distribution to help improve early communication with the project staff.

THE MASTER PROJECT SCHEDULE

The **master project schedule (MPS)** is the schedule that identifies the major milestones for the project. It is usually presented in a bar chart format with restraints for some of the milestone activities also identified.

Scheduling for a project sets the project plan to calendar dates. Planning activities always precede scheduling theoretically, but in actual practice the two are developed in concert.

The **master project schedule** shows all of the critical dates important to achieving the objectives for the project. For projects where the completion date is of paramount importance, the project planning and the master project schedule start with the completion date, working backwards with the preceding activities.

Areas may be selected for construction scheduling as entities and priorities assigned based upon the anticipated arrival date of all of the equipment and materials to be installed in that area and its relationship in the commissioning and startup process. For the initial pass, normal delivery periods are used, but for long leadtime equipment and material in priority areas, the deliveries may be accelerated by special expediting or delivery incentives.

At this point in time, any limitations of resources needed to execute the project must be taken into account. If the objectives of the project are jeopardized by these resource limitations, then alternatives must be found to alleviate the problem.

Where there is a limitation on the flow of the project funding, the master project schedule must be developed taking into account the availability of working capital. It is difficult to optimize project execution while tailoring progress to the released funds. Compromises will be necessary to achieve good performance under fiscal restraints.

During planning it is generally advisable to try to optimize field construction as project expenditures are greatest during this period. There may be a tendency to allot disproportionate amounts of time during the definition and conceptual stages of a project. Adequate time must be given to provide for a well-thought-out design concept, but precautions should be taken against wasting time at this stage of the project. It is well to target a "freeze" on the design concept at a date compatible with providing sufficient time to do detailed design work efficiently and to issue purchase orders for critical equipment and material.

The master project schedule is used as a communication medium in dealing with the upper management of each of the parties involved in the project. There is sometimes a temptation to make it more detailed than it needs to be; this should be avoided. Only those major milestones should be shown. Often bars are shown for engineering, procurement, and construction for the milestones. These bars indicate dates on which critical events should occur. Some organizations will superimpose "S" curves for engineering, procurement, material deliveries, and construction to show the indicated rate of resource expenditure inferred by the MPS.

Once the MPS has been approved, it becomes the basis for all of the derivative schedules used on the project. **The MPS is never changed** unless there has been a radical change of scope for the project or a major uncontrollable postponement of the work. The derivative schedules are changed as necessary to adapt to new conditions and to assure that the milestones set in the MPS are attained.

As change requests are received, there must be a careful analysis of their effect on the master project schedule and the milestone dates included. Every effort must be made to accommodate the changes that are needed without disrupting the MPS. If there is absolutely no way that the change can be accepted without modifying the master schedule, then the project manager must seek approval for the needed change or the decision must be made to forego the change.

TASK IDENTIFICATION

Selecting the level of activities, tasks or work items to be monitored during the project should be given careful consideration during the development of the work breakdown structure.

There is leeway in selection of what will be termed an "activity" or the lowest level of monitoring in the control of the project. On a very large project, design of all of the pump foundations in an area might be considered one single activity. Conversely, design of a single pump foundation on a small project might constitute one activity.

The total number of activities is of importance. If a project is monitored manually, the activities should be carefully chosen as not to exceed the total number that can be reasonably followed. This limitation is becoming of less importance as the use of project control programs with personal computers gains acceptance.

Computer programs can handle projects with from 250 activities on the low end to in excess of 100,000 activities on the high end when using mainframe computer software. These limits are very approximate as capacities are increasing monthly with new developments in software and hardware being announced that frequently. With different approaches in handling *subnets* and *fragnets*, the top figure is further flexible.

The project manager needs to break away from considering the capabilities available from the various programs. He needs to ask: ***"What is the level of control required to provide assurance of a successful project with the least amount of monitoring?"***

For a very large project there will be successive levels of control. A macro view of the project with a minimum of detail is best for top management use. It is also possible to bring the level of microcontrol down to show where the efforts of each person working on the project should be focused for each hour that he is scheduled to work. This may be particularly important for a turn-around on an operating plant where every hour of loss of production is extremely costly; but it is certainly not cost effective for most project schedules.

A project involving 50,000 engineering jobhours might consider activities of 200 jobhours or more as individual activities. Items requiring less that 200 jobhours but critical to the work would also be separately identified and controlled. Such a project might have a range of 200 to 300 activities.

For tightly scheduled work such as maintenance (turn-arounds) in an operating plant, repairs to fire damage, or projects where life is threatened, the proper level of activity monitored might be much smaller. Any potential threat of delay in completing the work as early as possible on such a schedule might be represented by a separate activity.

An activity, regardless of its size, that is critical to achieving the objectives of the project must be carefully monitored and controlled. Efforts which are not individually critical to project success may be lumped together in a logical combination for control purposes.

The activities selected as the basis for control, should be given an identification code as dictated by the work breakdown structure. The codes will be used to input these activities into the computer programs.

The project manager's ability to select activities judiciously will improve with experience. At first the tendency is almost always to over-fragment, making control too costly and cumbersome.

SEQUENCING ACTIVITIES: THE NETWORK LOGIC

Sequencing of major segments of the work is developed during the planning phase by careful consideration of the objectives, the unique problems and the particular project strategy. The scheduling phase calls for detailed sequencing of the work activities and is dependent upon an extension of the strategic thinking used earlier.

DIAGRAMING TECHNIQUES: By their nature, some activities will precede others. These activities must be completed before the following activity can be started. In other cases, the earlier activity must have been started and have progressed to a certain point before a subsequent, dependent activity may start. The start of some activities depends upon the start of another. Some activities have an end-to-end relationship.

These interdependencies may be graphically shown by means of a **logic** or **arrow diagram**. These diagrams chart all of the activities on a project depicting how each precedes, follows, or is restrained by others. There are many variations in these charting techniques.

The first use of network diagramming was by duPont in the mid-1950's. Later developments resulted in the **critical path method (CPM)** which is very closely related to the work done by duPont earlier and in the **program evaluation and review technique (PERT)** used first in the U.S. Navy Polaris program. The precedence diagram is similar to a CPM diagram, and represents a subsequent development, probably initiated by the U.S. Navy Bureau of Yards and Docks. Today, variations of these techniques form the basis for the computerized project control programs. The activity interrelationships may now be portrayed very realistically on many of these programs.

Because of the number of activities on extremely large jobs, it may be expedient to develop *subnets* or *fragnets*. These are just more detailed diagrams of separate segments of the project. On any project care should be taken to avoid **over-controlling** by having an excessive number of activities. Maintenance of the computerized program in these instances will require more time than it is worth.

STRATEGIC THINKING: Altogether distinct from the obvious emphasis on the mechanics of these various computerized control programs, a most important value lies in the information that can be generated to evaluate alternative sequencing early in the project.

These network programs allow the strategy to be checked in detail. Inoperable execution sequences may be eliminated or modified. Alternatives may be suggested by the results of the trial runs.

Use of **standard networks** may save home office control hours as the logic does not have to be reinvented for each job. Every project offers the possibility of saving a lot of schedule time and a lot of money by innovative thinking in sequencing the project activities. Where there can be a beneficial change in the logic or sequencing of these activities, the project manager should be eager to take advantage of the possible improvements. Standard networks may help; but each project is different. The planning, strategy, and scheduling must be individually thought out.

FACTORS WHICH DRIVE THE SCHEDULE

In developing a schedule, stepping back from all of the details is occasionally important to the project manager in determining whether that schedule is going to respond to what is actually required by the project.

The example used for this topic relates to a typical plant construction project, but the methodology is certainly applicable elsewhere where schedules are being developed. The example is taken from work done by the Construction Industry Institute.

The premise is that the schedule is driven by *different factors* during the various phases of the project. When you are just starting out a project, the conceptual design, the process engineering, and basic engineering concentrate completely on the **systems** to be included in the plant. All of the drawings, sketches and other data are produced by system. This is true also for the chemical, mechanical, and process control engineers.

When the basic engineering information has been completed and the project moves into the detailed design, then the driving factor shifts and becomes the **area**. The plot plan is divided into areas, and the design of foundations, structures, piping, electrical, and instrument control wiring proceeds around the different areas of the site.

When it comes time to requisition equipment and material, the driving force changes from area to what has been called the **procurement train**. Like items are grouped, regardless of their system or their area, so that they can be readily handled by the requisitioning, bidding, ordering, manufacturing, expediting, inspection, and delivery activities involved in management of materials.

The driving force during the initial construction efforts reverts to the **area**. Working from the detailed drawings promotes this approach. As construction nears completion, the work has to be completed based on **systems** as the driving force. This is the way the project must be finished as the job is testing out, commissioned, and later started up by **system**.

The graphic immediately following illustrates the process described in the paragraphs above. Unless the scheduler understands the driving forces in play during the different phases of the project and, particularly where the driving force changes, the wrong activities may be scheduled and much time wasted prior to starting the following phase. This is very noticeable in the interface between construction, testing, and startup. There has to be a concerted effort made to integrate the initial work done by area and completion by system in order to optimize efforts.

FACTORS WHICH DRIVE THE SCHEDULE

PHASES \ FACTORS	SYSTEM	AREA	PROCUREMENT TRAIN
BASIC ENGINEERING	●		
DETAILED DESIGN		● →	●
PROCUREMENT			●
CONSTRUCTION	● ←	●	
START UP	●		

STAFFING ANALYSIS

THE SELECTION PROCESS: Staffing must be approached from the viewpoint of the numbers of people required as well as the capabilities and experience of the individuals themselves. It is particularly important that the project manager be satisfied that his key managers and the discipline leaders are competent and capable of the work they are scheduled to direct.

Initially, the positions shown on the project organization chart are filled. Timing of the assignments is approximated by the project manager and communicated to each of the functional managers involved. The individuals assigned to the project in a matrix organization are usually selected by their functional managers. The project manager may or may not have a voice in the selection process. Unfortunately for the project manager, one of the prime qualifications in making assignments turns out to be the availability of the individual rather than the ability, related experience, or track record on other projects.

The project manager should have an intense interest in the senior staffing on his project as this one factor will have a definite influence on the success of the endeavor.

STAFFING LEVELS: The project activities have been identified, classified, and defined in the **work breakdown structure dictionary.** It is necessary to evaluate these activities to determine the number of people required to do the work and how these will be organized for the effort.

The project discipline leader (if assigned at the time or otherwise the functional manager of each discipline) must analyze the activities to determine jobhours necessary to accomplish the work. Simultaneously, the leader must consider the optimum length of calendar time required to complete the activity. Total jobhours and duration will give an indication as to staffing levels. For monitoring and control purposes, the estimates must conform to the WBS descriptions. Activity estimates are reviewed by the appropriate project discipline leader and are approved by the project manager. A functional or departmental review is a requirement in many organizations.

The discipline leader relies on his experience to estimate jobhour requirements for each activity. During the estimating process, he necessarily will have to think through in more detail exactly how the work covered by the activity will be done. Relying on past statistics may be somewhat dangerous. Return cost figures will probably include hours spent in recycling, redoing and correcting together with job changes and other inefficiencies. Statistical figures may include not only necessary jobhours for the work, but also hours which were added to cover all of these other items. The project manager should encourage the discipline leader to estimate the work based on the best judgment of what it really should take to do the work. Any allowances or provisions for changed conditions should be expressed separately and clearly as such. Unfortunately there sometimes appears to be a reward for those who are able to include a lot of "generosity" in jobhour estimates. Invariably, hours included in these high estimates are spent on the job except when workloads are high. Project managers should never bypass checking the validity of the discipline jobhour estimates.

The staffing analysis should provide input for the discipline job-hours required for each activity. This input should be made to the computer or manually recorded for later use in resource leveling and optimizing the critical path schedule.

At this time the staffing levels are reviewed in conjunction with the discipline workload for other projects to confirm availability of the number of people required. Staffing plans are formulated and any conflicts are resolved by consultation with all of the project managers involved.

ACTIVITY DURATION

Establishing the proper duration of each activity is critical to the development of a realistic project schedule.

There has always been some controversy about what criteria to use in determining activity duration. The duration of an activity may be defined as being **that period of time from when the work is started until the work included in that scope has been completed to the point where a subsequent and completely dependent activity may start**. Activities may involve follow up work or cleaning up details which would not exclude the start of other work. This time would not be included in the planned activity duration. All activities should be as described in the work breakdown structure dictionary.

The duration of an activity should be established in concert with the estimate of the work effort required. The duration will be determined by each discipline's project job leader (or the discipline manager if the project leader has yet to be named). The initial duration should be a realistic view of the optimal duration for work efficiency.

The selected durations should be based on times which can be met under normal conditions. After the durations have been established for all activities, they are used in conjunction with the logic diagram to establish the total project duration. The initial run to determine the critical path will indicate those activities that must be improved to reduce total project length. If very optimistic activity times are used through the exercise, a distorted picture will result. The project length will be too short and improvements will be difficult to achieve. On the other hand, assigning very pessimistic durations encumbered with provisions for possible adversities during execution will create an overly long project schedule. The modification to reduce the project length will be tedious because of the number of activities involved.

The effect of known conditions should be reflected in the estimating of the duration of activities. The environment which favors or which handicaps work will have an effect. Rain, snow, or adverse weather may affect progress. These factors are known or have an historical basis for affecting duration and should be taken into account.

Involvement of the functional management, through the discipline job leader has been stressed. There are two reasons for this:

- **The best experience and historical background available in this organization is brought to bear**

- **Commitment of the project discipline personnel to the schedule is enhanced by involving them in the process.**

The project manager should be involved if there are problems in establishing a realistic duration for a critical activity in order to be assured that there are no overly pessimistic nor optimistic projections which could influence the end date. Usually the project manager will assure himself that there have been intermediate spot checks run on the setting of activity durations. The project manager's principal involvement will come later during the intensive analysis of the critical path activities.

THE CRITICAL PATH

The **critical path method (CPM)** uses, as a basis, the logic diagram prepared earlier. The logic diagram charts a series of activities or events using **blocks** or **nodes** interconnected by **lines** or **arrows**. Either the **blocks** or the **lines** may represent **activities** depending upon the system selected. **Events** are the start or completion or some other identifiable point during the activity. In some systems, the **nodes** represent the **events**, and the connecting **arrows** represent the **activities** or work required to reach the events.

For our purposes we will assume that the blocks represent the activities. The precedence method of CPM is typical of this system of diagramming. The lines connecting the blocks show interdependence and have no time value in the **precedence diagram.**

Calendar time for the schedule may be expressed as days, weeks or months. Any unit of scheduling time may be used in CPM, but the same unit of time should be used throughout. The level of control desired sets the unit of time to be used. For very large, lengthy projects, jobweeks may be used. Jobdays are used on other projects that call for closer monitoring. On a normal engineering/construction project, use of jobhours as the unit of time is common. Because durations are expressed for a large number of individual activities, the accuracy of the figures is usually good as the errors tend to be compensating when developed by experienced individuals.

The critical path method, using either manual calculations or a computer program, establishes the earliest date that each activity may start and the earliest that it can finish. The earliest completion date of each activity is calculated by progressively taking the earliest completion date of the preceding constraining activities and adding the duration of the activity in question. By following this procedure repeatedly, the duration of the entire project is determined.

The process is then reversed. Taking the completion date of the last activity to finish, the activity durations are successively subtracted from the latest completion date of the activity which follows it. The latest completion and start dates are thus determined for each activity. These chains of calculations are referred to as a "**forward pass**" and a "**backward pass**" respectively.

The early start and the late start dates for each activity are compared. If these are identical, then the activity lies on the critical path. If they differ, then the time between early start and late start is known as free time or **float**. Project completion will not be delayed as long as the activity starts on or before the late start date.

Analysis of the results demands the project manager's attention. The initial project schedule invariably needs to be shortened to fall within the date established by the project objectives. This can be done only by improving those activities on the critical path. The duration of these activities must be cut, possibly by assigning more people. If this is not possible, the logic of the diagram has to be rethought. The critical path method concentrates project thinking on that small percentage of the activities where the payout will be found.

The critical path method is *not* a panacea for project managers. **It can tell us what work we should concentrate on at a given time during the project and where resources can be used most effectively**. It is not a substitute for know-how or experience and it certainly is not a substitute for individual thinking. It is a tool for organizing thought, and, when used with a computer, it is a method of making many calculations rapidly. It is a good communication tool and particiularly valuable in playing "what-if" games in evaluating the effect of changing conditions during execution of the work.

RESOURCE LEVELING

Resource leveling is the **process of scheduling work on noncritical activities within their float so that resource requirements on peak days will be reduced**. This technique may also be used to protect the resource requirements for critical path activities in order to increase the probability of on-time completion of these activities.

The adjusted computer run or manual solution which comes up with an acceptable project duration generally assumes unlimited availability of resources and that the people from the proper disciplines and with the proper skills to do the work will be forthcoming as needed. Most modern programs now provide for a method to identify resource limitations and to restrict assignment of "nonavailable" personnel.

When the consolidated requirements are produced, the critical path activities are considered first as they present the more serious problem. If a critical path activity requires people who are not available, an adjustment to the duration may be the most ready solution. The effect of the corresponding lengthening of the schedule must be weighed against the possibility of somehow increasing staff for that activity by bringing temporary or contract people onto the staff for short periods. Each resource problem on critical path activities is considered separately and an acceptable solution to each resource problem is reached.

Next, the requirements for the whole project are looked at using the early starts for each activity. The numbers of people required for the activities scheduled for each day for each discipline are plotted to give a **skyline** or the resource demand. There will be peaks and valleys which may be attenuated by delaying noncritical activities within their own float times.

Scheduling of people over the duration of the activity is normally averaged. An activity which required 480 jobhours over the period of 20 eight-hour days would have an average of 3 people assigned. Reflecting the realization that activities don't start off at full speed nor finish abruptly, many computer programs have additional flexibility to use other than straight line distribution for assigning people to the activity by using a bell curve or an "S" curve as selected by the scheduler.

There may be cases in which an absolutely rigid limitation is placed on resources and no acceptable alternative is open. Computer programs can place this limit as a restraint. The duration of the activities so affected is extended and the overall schedule is correspondingly lengthened.

Resource leveling may be used both as a scheduling tool and as a planning tool for personnel assignment. Crews may be formed to do a specific series of like noncritical activities consecutively rather than two or more crews doing them in parallel.

Planning for project assignments can be done by the functional managers using the same tools. Multiproject requirements from each discipline can be leveled within the constraints presented by the float and after consultation with the respective project managers. Effective functional management in a matrix organization depends upon the ability of the functional manager to use his people effectively, to minimize total staff requirements, and to eliminate the non-productive time of his personnel between assignments.

THE SCHEDULED PLAN

The **scheduled plan** is the final result of six planning steps:

SIX STEPS TO A SCHEDULED PLAN

1. Establishing the **objectives**, anticipating **problems** and developing **strategy** for doing the project

2. Developing the **work breakdown structure** to be used on the project. Using the WBS, identify individual project work packages and those activities which make up each work package.

3. **Planning the project**, preferably on a participative basis, then sequencing all activities on a network diagram.

4. Assigning **durations** to the activities on the network diagram. Using this information to determine the **critical path**. Fine tuning by an iterative process to determine the **best schedule**.

5. Assigning **resource requirements** to each of the activities. Making sure that critical activities have adequate resources. Reconcile resource requirements by changing the timing of non critical activities. Incorporate this fine tuning into the program.

6. Fixing the schedule in accordance with **optimized sequencing, critical path determination**, and **resource requirements**.

CONTENTS OF THE SCHEDULED PLAN

1. All **work packages** and **activities** required by the project are completely described, scoped, and costed. An early start date and the duration for doing the work are both given.

2. All **critical work packages and critical activities** are identified.

3. The resource utilization requirements for the project are established both in terms of personnel and cost.

This information will be used to communicate expectations to all of the project participants in sufficient detail so that the work can be efficiently and effectively done. In addition, the **scheduled plan** will provide a basis for continuous monitoring of the status of the on-going project work so that variances can be identified and corrected in a timely manner. ***Once approved, the schedule is fixed.*** It is not to be extended arbitrarily. It can only be changed if there are substantial changes of scope or approved changes to the contract which incorporate additional work, and which require corresponding schedule extensions. Internal changes to portions of the schedule may be adopted as a part of the corrective action to get work which has fallen behind back on the original schedule.

BAR CHARTS

The bulk of computer output from the scheduling process will not be well understood by many of the people who will be working on or associated with the project. This will become less of a consideration as the project staffs become increasingly exposed to working with the computer. Many of the computerized scheduling programs can produce easily-understood bar charts from the data base.

The bar chart is never the plan, but it is always based on what the plan is at the time the chart is prepared. It is convenient to present the project schedule in bar chart form for certain purposes, some of which are described below.

- **Corporate Planning:** Corporate Planning may utilize the bar chart to show future project plans graphically. The corporate plan may show the project as a single line with only the start and completion dates indicated on the bar chart. The time scale on these charts is generally by quarters, and sometimes only by years. Other major projects under consideration during the same period would be similarly shown on the chart to give an indication of relative timing for the proposed major projects.

- **Preliminary Project Scheduling:** When future planning has progressed, the next step might involve breaking each project into its major phases such as **project definition, detailed engineering, procurement**, and **construction**. During this phase and the subsequent two, a great deal of reliance has to be placed in the hands of those knowledgeable individuals who have the experience and access to historical performance on similar projects to come up with the initial scheduling efforts.

- **Master Project Schedule:** Once the project has been defined and the project planning is underway, a preliminary master schedule showing the start and completion dates for major milestones is developed. This schedule reflects milestones in engineering, procurement, and construction.

- **Detailed Master Schedule:** A detailed master project schedule in modified bar chart form would incorporate additional important project milestones. Many of these bar charts also use special symbology to indicate constraints.

- **Work Package Scheduling:** The bar chart is also a convenient manner of expressing the time relationships of the activities on

individual work packages. In this context, it is frequently used
on the most detailed level of schedule when dealing with design
or construction activities. The bar chart is an excellent tool for
communication with small groups of people who would benefit
form a better understanding about how the work activities fit
together timewise.

• **Status Reporting:** Bar charts are also convenient to use for status
reports. These charts will have means of showing planned
progress, as well as that of indicating the actual status of work.

5 THE PROJECT BUDGET

COST MANAGEMENT

The project manager actively participates in the three elements of **cost management**. These are **cost forecasting, cost reporting,** and **cost containment**, frequently referred to as **cost control.**

Initial decisions are important. On a process facility, once the type of facility, the process, the capacity, the location, the general arrangement of the equipment, and the specification philosophy have been selected, the theoretical minimum cost of the proposed facility is set. This cost probably will remain unknown as it is only rarely calculated. The goal of all of those involved with the project should be to complete the work at a figure close to this minimum cost. For non-process facility projects, a similar analogy may be used.

After only a very few basic parameters are established, the **theoretical minimum cost** of the project is fixed.

COST FORECASTING: At any stage during the project, the total predicted cost consists of four components: (1) the **defined elements**, (2) the **contingency**, (3) the **escalation**, and (4) the **job growth**. If the forecast is made early in the project, the defined elements will be less precise, the contingency on that number must be higher as must the escalation. Job growth is very difficult to fix. Probably, past corporate experience is the best basis for setting this number. As the project develops, all of these number become progressively more precise until they merge as defined elements to form the total job cost at completion.

COST REPORTING: Cost reports are statements of funds that have been expended as of a designated date. They may cover funds committed and funds billed. Two important requirements of the reporting function are: (1) the need for **timeliness**, and (2) the importance of **accuracy.** Cost management and accounting accuracy are different. For the former only that accuracy essential for subsequent analytical use is needed. The project manager cannot wait for *accounting accuracy* in order to produce meaningful forecasts or to order corrective action.

COST CONTAINMENT: Cost containment is, by far, the **most important component of cost management**. Cost containment works hand in hand with constructability throughout the project.

The true minimum cost of a facility is established early with acceptance of a few basic definitions. It follows that there are the areas where the results of cost containment can be most fruitful.

A project should be programmed to conduct **cost containment reviews (CCRs)** on each of the documents that set the true minimum cost. Each should be examined to ascertain that all of the stipulated provisions and conditions are really needed. Those that are superfluous should be discarded before production engineering is started.

Throughout the project, CCRs should be held to review the work that is underway to make sure that the minimum cost definitions are being followed. As the project develops, the detailed project execution plans should be reviewed from the cost containment standpoint. If substantial amounts of money can be save by making modifications to the plan, the project manager should order the changes made.

ESTIMATING AND ESTIMATES

An estimate, very simply, is a prediction of the final cost. Very early in the project, the scope definition, component pricing and quantity takeoffs will be very approximate and other cost information will be sparse. It follows that an early estimate will be much less accurate because of these limitations. We try to compensate for this by adding a contingency to account for costs that are a part of the intended work scope, but which have not yet been completely defined. We also try to adjust for anticipated changes in present day costs by adding escalation.

The project manager should not spend money to develop estimates that are any more accurate than are required for the intended purpose. Initial estimates, especially, are made with very little firm data. These estimates are used for early project screening to determine the viability of the project.

Although estimates may be classified in many ways, classifications generally follow those listed below. Each estimate type lists the estimating methods, the type of backup information required and the expected accuracy. Accuracies are given by percentage limits that the final costs will not underrun or exceed. The four usual estimate types are listed in chronological order.

COMMON TYPES OF ESTIMATES

Viability Estimate: This type of estimate is made from a preliminary scope definition from historical cost curves for the type of facility, or by scaling up or down from the return costs for another similar plant. Accuracy is from -25 to +40 percent.

Appropriation Estimate: An appropriation estimate is prepared from a more developed scope definition using a multiplier on estimated major equipment costs and is sometimes referred to as a *factored* estimate. It has an accuracy of from -15 to +25 percent.

Approximate Estimate: Approximate estimates also make use of the factoring method. The difference is that the final scope definition is available and the equipment costs will normally have been quoted by suppliers and are fairly firm. The range of accuracy goes from -10 to +15 percent.

Definitive Estimate: This estimate is prepared using material takeoffs, quoted equipment and material prices. About forty percent of the engineering for the project will have been completed to do a definitive estimate. The accuracy is considered to be from -5 to +5 percent. This type of estimate is required for a lump sum bid.

COMPUTERIZED ESTIMATES: Computer programs for developing cost estimates are being used for making appropriation and approximate estimates. Some of these programs generate some of the costs from an historical data base. Computer software programs are also being introduced that will progressively refine estimates up to the final cost report.

RELATIONSHIP WITH WORK BREAKDOWN: In order to provide an orderly progression through each of these types, the early estimate should be prepared based on the appropriate level of the work breakdown structure. The earlier estimate will be tied only to the upper levels of the WBS, while the definitive estimate will be tied into work packages and activities. The latest and most accurate estimate is used as a source for the project budget development or as a basis for variance analysis.

ACCURACY RANGE OF COST ESTIMATES VS PROJECT DEFINITION

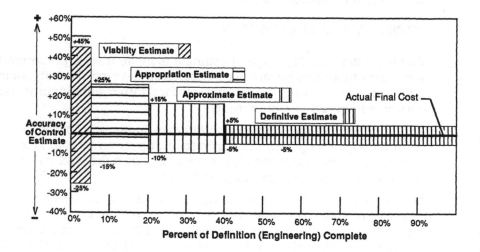

VALUE ENGINEERING

Value engineering on a project is a **critical analysis for improvement which involves each step of the project and breaks down the entire project into easily analyzed pieces.** The discipline demonstrated by value engineering, or value analysis, may be very beneficial in making sure that the most cost effective decisions are made on the project.

Value engineering was first used in the manufacturing industries and then in the Department of Defense and the Army Corps of Engineers in the 1960s. Later it found support in other areas of project management. Value engineering was a precursor to quality circles which to some extent supplanted value engineering in manufacturing firms during the late 1970s. It has also found application on project work.

Currently, constructability, which has some very similar concepts, is finding a great deal of acceptability with project managers worldwide.

Value engineering consists of a number of steps conducted by a nominated value engineering team:

- Gathering information
- Development of alternatives
- Comparison of alternatives
- Selection of a firm proposal for change
- Selling management the selected alternative

Information for each particular item under consideration is gathered, reviewed, defined, and quantified.

- What is the item?
- What purpose does it actually serve?
- What should it really do?
- What is the cost of the item as planned?
- What is the real value of the item?

The Society of American Value Engineers headquartered in Northbrook, Illinois defines value engineering as **a function-oriented, systematic team approach to provide value in a product, system, or service. Often this improvement is focused on cost reduction; however, other improvements such as customer-perceived quality and performance are also paramount in the value equation.**

Creation of alternatives should be a free wheeling exercise. Preconceived limits should be discarded and a departure from the routine and ordinary should be encouraged. Each of the best alternatives should be compared and tested against the planned way as well as against other alternatives.

Recently Westney (1989) has stated the definition of value engineering as being **a creative, organized method for optimizing cost and performance.** He stresses the need to consider the optimum design for the *entire life cycle of the project* when applying value engineering.

Should the project manager decide to utilize a value engineering program on his project, he must be aware that value engineering has a payoff, but it doesn't come easily. Tradition and customary procedures are both difficult to change. Time is limited because a project is not an on-going operation for improvement. Training in optimum use of the value engineering techniques is beneficial. In using value engineering on projects, the "big ticket" items should be investigated first, along with those which appear to the project team to have elements of gross inefficiency. The process can be made to have a beneficial effect on project morale.

IMPROP is an acronym for **IMPR**ovement to **OP**erations. It is designed specifically to elicit the participation of all levels of a matrix organization in performance management and the identification and resolution of performance barriers. A full description of this technique is furnished by Kimmons (1981).

Westney, Richard E., "What is the value of quality?" *1989 Transactions of the AACE,* American Association of Cost Engineers, Morgantown, WV, July 1989, pp. E.3.1-E.3.5.

Kimmons, Robert L., "Improve operations with IMPROP." *Hydrocarbon Processing,* Gulf Publishing, Houston, TX, January 1981, pp. 232-237.

RISK ANALYSIS

Project estimates cannot be more accurate than the reliability of the information used. Early estimates suffer from a lack of firm data, and must be conditioned to compensate. A rigorous probability analysis would have questionable validity early in a project due to the poor definition that exists.

Risks in estimates may be looked upon as "a recognition of the probability that actual costs will be the same as estimated costs." The risk analysis is applied to all individual line items taking possible, minimum, probable and maximum costs into account.

Four steps are involved in adjusting the estimate to reflect the degree of risk:

- Identifying the risk
- Evaluating the risk
- Making the risk allowance
- Compiling the summation of the risk allowances to be added as estimate contingency

Dependent upon the stage of the estimate, each area, work package, or activity should be analyzed to determine that portion of the estimate obtained from elements having:

- **Very High Certainty:** The portion of the estimate for the component that is based upon firm numbers such as actual expenditures to date; quoted firm lump sum bids for equipment, materials or subcontracts; known pay rates; exact firm takeoffs from construction drawings for materials. The risk factor for these items is low, and little would have to be added to their estimate to cover risk.

- **Moderate Certainty:** Such items as preliminary material takeoffs and pricing from recent, similar plants adjusted for capacity differences and escalation; labor productivity from recent or current jobs in the same area; equipment pricing taken from current quotes for similar equipment on other projects, etc. The risk factor for these items would be higher than for the preceding category.

- **Moderate Uncertainty:** Estimating elements which are factored for a type of plant or for a site where there is a lack of current experience; or where many assumptions have been made which have not been fully checked out.

- **Undefined or Unknown:** This category has to be based upon the proportion of total information contained in the three preceding paragraphs. If there is a high percentage already identified, then there should be a relatively smaller number of undefined/unknown elements remaining. Lack of current similar plant experience and site experience will tend to make this category very risky in comparison.

Some risk can be appropriately applied to the entire project where the risk will affect entire segments of the work. This risk would include such things as possible delay in obtaining permits, delays due to regulatory difficulties, and the possibility of strikes.

SENSITIVITY

The project estimate has a high **sensitivity** to those items where **any change exerts a significant effect on the project cost**. Such items have a leverage influence on expenditures. Items may be considered as being sensitive for any one of several reasons.

1. **Pricing of Repetitive Items:** The estimated cost of repetitive items may be considered to be sensitive. A relatively small incremental error in pricing multiplied by many repitions results in a large error. Repetitive items would include such things as the estimated cost of piping each of a large number of identical pieces of equipment with similar hookups, or the estimated unit cost of work consisting of a large number of repetitive operations such as cutting, beveling, and welding a particular size and grade of pipe.

2. **Factors:** Factors applied to the cost of a large number of items, such as field labor hours, may be considered to be sensitive. Productivity factors are a prime example of this type of sensitivity.

3. **Nonstandard Items:** Preliminary estimates are low for covering the incremental costs of buying nonstandard equipment items or materials. If the owner insists on a large number of nonstandard purchases, the early estimates for the project cost will be sensitive to the factors applied in moving from the costs of standard items to the special items. In going from a standard item to something nonstandard, the extra costs of the changes are usually disproportionately high for the incremental work. These costs usually tend to be underestimated.

4. **Nonstandard Procedures:** The costs of the direct work, the supervision, and the inspection are increased where nonstandard procedures are specified for fabrication or construction. If repeated throughout the project, the tendency is to understate the cost of the work.

5. **Effects of Weather:** During the earliest stages, projects are usually planned to take advantage of the anticipated favorable cycle of weather conditions. Initial estimates are made on this basis. The project schedule may slip due to delays in approving the project, obtaining funding, or getting the necessary permits, causing the work to be done during the unfavorable period. Where climatic effects exert a strong influence on field productivity, the project

costs are sensitive to the additional costs of adverse working conditions and the costs of delays to project completion.

6. **Subproject Activities:** There is a tendency to give short shrift to some of the estimated costs of the subproject activities such as demolition, site preparation, offsites, cleanup, testing, and initial operations. Cumulatively, any shortfall in the estimated cost of these activities can cause a major problem with the total project costs.

These sensitive items are typical of those that should receive extra consideration in the estimate reviews.

CONTINGENCY

Contingency may be project management's least understood term. There is little agreement of what it is. Graf (1984) observes that **Contingency is a provision, usually cost, for unforeseen elements that experience has shown are likely to occur.**

The American Association of Cost Engineers considers contingency as a two-part allowance to be added in the estimate summary:

1. To cover **undefined costs**
2. For **unpredictable occurrences**

Contingency should not be looked to for covering "job growth". Contingency is applied to the current defined scope. Contingency should cover only those items included or implied by that scope.

Due to many past abuses, contingency has gotten a bad name. Large amounts of money, in the guise of contingency, have frequently been lumped into project estimates with little thought nor justification given. The layering of contingencies, evolved by adding cushions to individual line items, then area rollups and again at the end of the estimate, is bad. The concept of adding the cost of elements which are undefinable or uncertain is alien to some individuals in management.

Contingency is a legitimate cost element. It must be included in an estimate if the total cost prediction is to be realistic. Experience is probably the best basis for the contingency allowance, but can be assisted by careful analysis of the risks involved in the line items. The risk analysis may be intuitive for small projects, but still should have the conclusions documented. There are formal risk analysis programs available that may be of use in the later estimates; but an individual assessment of each line item to fix the possible extent of the "soft" areas may be more practical in setting the contingency buildup.

Examples of areas where contingency funds might be required are:

- Elements not fully defined when the estimate is made
- Items omitted because of lack of definition
- Items defined, but omitted by mistake
- Abnormal conditions/problems
- Bad estimates of price or quantity
- Unforeseen price changes/schedule delays

- Faulty assumptions made during project execution
- Lack of experience, corporate or personal, in any element
- Changes in regulations, codes, or owner's direction

The owner, the contractor's management, and the project staff should agree on the contingency amount and coverage for the specific project. The last of the contingency can be safely eliminated from the estimate at the end of the job only when all of the unknowns have become known.

To better quantify the amount of contingency to be added to an estimate, a sophisticated means of matching risk to probability is finding increasing use on projects. This technique is called **range estimating**. One of the initial proponents was Hertz (1979) who described a method of determining the most likely outcome of investments uncertainties. Recent literature, Curran (1989), tells of the combined use of Pareto's Law, Monte Carlo simulation, and heuristics to arrive at the most probable project cost. The tedious mathematical calculations involved in the process have been incorporated into computer programs.

Graf, M. W. "An Overview of Contingency Considerations." *Cost Engineering*, AACE Inc., Morgantown WV, February 1984, pp. 25-34.

Hertz, David B., "Risk Analysis in Capital Investment." *Harvard Business Journal*, Boston, MA, Sept.-Oct. 1979, pp. 169-182.

Curran, Michael W., "Range Estimating: User-Friendly Risk Analysis." *Proceedings*, Project Management Institute, Drexel Hill, PA, 1989, pp. 64-71.

JOB GROWTH

Job growth is that component of the project that falls outside of the defined scope of the project when the funding approval is given. It is a trap for the unwary project manager.

Only a very few companies provide money in their appropriation for job growth; and yet overrun after overrun on previous projects can be attributed to the fact that there was little or no control on the work that was outside the scope and in addition to the approved funds for the project. Some companies recognize that, based on historical data, job growth can be on the order of 20% even in a well run organization. They will insist that this money be included in any plant estimate, but it should never be put in the project budget until the items of job growth are identified, priced out, and approved.

Job growth is an insidious adversary for the project manager. It frequently comes in the guise of a "*better*" way to do something, often late in the job— something not required by the objectives, but something which cannot be objected to except for the attendant costs, schedule delays, and general disruption to the work. The project manager must hold firm with a policy of **"no changes"** for all work outside the approved scope unless the proper evaluations have been made, additional funds provided, and the work approved by the owner/ client prior to starting work on the change.

Of course, some companies want be able to make late changes on project work. Any project closely associated with current research and development, new technology, or state-of-the-art equipment design must expect late breaking changes even as the project reaches its final stages. These companies should understand when they approve such projects that there will be changes; and these will cost money over and above the estimated costs of the defined scope of work. They must also realize that this never represents a proper use of the contingency money approved for the project.

There are compelling arguments for providing, or at least realizing, that additional funds will be needed for the project to cover job growth.

- Historical records will indicate the extent of the company's record of overruning projects due to job growth. This is largely a result of the particular environment set by the management of the company.

- Many projects initially are marginally viable. Common sense dictates that you don't add extra money onto a project in this situation.

- Senior management is not accustomed to allocating and approving money that does not cover a specific benefit. Job growth, by its very definition, cannot be pinpointed in advance.

There are also persuasive arguments for not being concerned with this funding until it is actually required.

There is no universal solution to the dilema of providing funds for job growth. It is very much a matter for the management of each company to set guildelines as to how they want job growth handled. The project manager must be aware of these guidelines; or he should discuss how he should handle job growth on his project with his own manager.

THE PROJECT BUDGET

Even though the terms **project estimate** and **project budget** are sometimes used interchangeably, they are different. An **estimate** is made as a prediction of what each activity, work package or total project will cost. The **budget** is a tool used to *control* expenditures. The estimate and the budget may be the same for many activities or work packages, and differ for others. The total budget shown for the overall project may be different from the estimate for the total project.

Estimates are used to obtain the corporate appropriation of money for the project. The estimate may be adjusted upward or downward to set the approved level of funding for a project.

The practice of "*padding*" the estimate deserves mention. The project manager should insist on complete honesty in the preparation of the estimate. Individual activities and work package contingencies should be calculated based upon the risk analysis for each item. Then all of the contingencies should be lumped together as a separate line item at the end of the estimate. If everyone involved is honest, the result will be a proper basis for fixing the project budget. If senior management has a discernable pattern of arbitrarily cutting the appropriation requests, the project manager will have to protect himself accordingly.

The estimate thus serves as a basis for both the appropriation and the budget. The budget is a control tool. If the amount of money approved for the project is lower than the estimate, then the project budget will also have to be lower than the estimate. The approved budget should never exceed the approved appropriation, and it normally is lower.

The estimate *should* be broken down according to the work breakdown structure. The budget, however, *must* be expressed in these same WBS terms. Each activity and work package must have an identifiable budget. It will also have a definite schedule. Both cost and schedule parameters are needed in order to exercise proper project control. The criteria for broader controls at higher levels of the WBS are achieved through a rollup of the data for the activities and work packages.

Once the final project control budget has been approved, it cannot change unless the scope of work is changed by means of an approved change order. The budget can not be changed to exceed the funds approved for the project.

There are various other reasons for having a project budget that differs from the project estimate. One of the principal reasons is the desire to set more challenging performance goals for the project team. It might be imprudent to change the estimate itself because this act would represent a variance from the historical performance records.

Keeping the costs of each activity within its budget is the responsibility of a designated individual as indicated by the work breakdown structure assignments.

BUDGETING THE WORK

The initial control budget may be derived from the viability or the appropriation estimates. As the subsequent estimates are developed, the margin for error is reduced by better definition, quantities, and prices. The control budget is then adjusted as may be necessary to reflect the new information. This does not mean that the project manager has carte blanche to increase the budget, but he should be sure that the interim control budgets track the input from the latest estimate. When the final control budget is prepared , it is submitted for approval. After the final control budget has been adopted, it is never changed without an approved scope change. It can never exceed the appropriated funds.

If the system is working right, the estimate for the original scope will decrease slightly with each updated estimate. Unfortunately, this is not generally the case. The project manager should devote a great deal of his effort to making sure that there are no surprises for the client or for his management in the budgetary process.

The project manager assures that there is only one control budget in use on the project at any time. Everyone working on the project should be advised when a change to the budget has been approved. Fortunately, most of the staff buildup is done after the final control budget is in place. This helps minimize confusion.

If the project is being released by phases, the current control budget may cover only that portion of the total project that is active at the time. Only under very special circumstances should any substantial amount of work be undertaken without a control budget even though it may be difficult to subdivide the budget into corresponding segments.

The responsibility for doing the work on each activity within the budget for that activity is assigned according to the work breakdown structure to a specific individual. For example, budgetary responsibility for the design of a structure to be included in a heat exchanger work package would be given to the lead structural engineer working in that area unless otherwise indicated. The cost of doing the design work as well as the cost of the structure would be his responsibility. Similarly, the cost responsibility for the equipment specification, design, and the purchase cost of the exchangers would lie with the lead mechanical engineer.

The responsibility for the total cost of the elements of that particular work package belongs to the area project engineer who coordinates all of the area work being done by the various disciplines. In some organizations, this responsibility might be given to an area project design supervisor.

All of those individuals who have cost responsibilities should have a good understanding of the scope of the work and the budget for that work. They should have a detailed plan for doing the work included for the money allocated. As problems arise, they should be brought to the attention of the next level of supervision.

OPTIMIZING THE BUDGET

The project manager must give due consideration to the subject of optimizing the budget. He must carefully review the project scope, the plan, the schedule, and the estimate for mutual compatibility before submitting the project budget for approval. He must take a number of things into account when making his review.

Meeting the budget is probably the single most important factor used to judge the success of a project. As the cost of money has spiraled over the past decades, the project budget has assumed increasing significance as a determinant of project success.

A project manager looks at completing his job "under budget" and so he has a vested interest in keeping the budget sufficiently high to permit an underrun. He realizes that his performance will be judged on how successful he is in adhering to his cost target.

A project manager also must have a concern for performance on his job. Performance management involves setting ambitious cost goals in the form of a tight budget. A plan which provides for continuous monitoring and the prompt corrective action will provide the positive indication of his interest to the project staff.

At the beginning of a project there is always a temptation to be optimistic about costs and sometimes to understate projected costs in order to "sell" the project. When this occurs, the project starts out behind the eight ball and this generally continues throughout its life. As each new estimate is being developed, an overrun is indicated. The project manager faces a quandary of *"How much additional money can be requested without scuttling the project?"* Even on projects where completely honest estimates have been given, there may be pressure to cut costs if the company is going through a worsening economic cycle.

The project manager may be pressured by his own management to present a reduced or overly optimistic estimate. He is placed in a difficult position and each situation will call for a specific solution. Faced with this problem, one answer would be to go ahead and present the lower number as instructed. The project manager should document his own position in a confidential memorandum to his boss or to whomever issued the instructions.

It is not too unusual for a new project manager to be assigned after the project has already started. He may find himself running an underfunded project. At first, he cannot be held entirely responsible, but if he continues on the project without bringing the problem to the attention of his manager, he rapidly acquires that responsibility. He must decide very quickly what to do and be committed to that course of action. Many of the project staff may have worked on developing the low estimate. These individuals might be hesitant to support an effort to attack its validity. Again, each situation will present different pressures and circumstances.

There are few project decisions that are as vital to the project manager's career as optimizing the project control budget. Caution is merited as the implications may extend far beyond the project at hand.

CHANGE MANAGEMENT

Change, from a practical viewpoint is *inevitable.* When the contractor starts work there should be agreement on the scope of work; any deviation from that scope will constitute a change. Agreement on scope will be more certain on a lump sum contract. A reimbursable contract may have a vague scope initially. Changes are difficult to identify before the definitive scope has been produced.

CHANGE MANAGEMENT: Change management means that no change is made to the scope before the change has been reviewed and approved. No efforts are to be expended on the change until the corresponding approval and authorization has been given.

SOURCE OF CHANGE: Most changes come from the client organization. Other sources include changes necessitated by erroneous assumptions or misleading/conflicting specifications or stipulations, by changed conditions, or by *force majeure.* Everyone on the project has the responsibility for early identification of change. As soon as a potential change is seen, a project note should be written alerting the project manager and triggering the project change management process.

TIMING OF THE CHANGE: The earlier that a *necessary* change is identified and implemented, the fewer detrimental effects will be felt by the project. Even a small change late in the job may involve changing the work of several disciplines. This introduces more opportunities for error. Projects closely involved with research and development are destined to have frequent changes. On this type of project, the project manager must be prepared to accept change and to be able to implement it with a minimum of project disruption. **He must plan for change**, and incorporate it into an updated project plan with dispatch. Project team members who cannot tolerate change should not be assigned to this type of project.

THE CHANGE MANAGEMENT PROCESS: Any change will be requested by someone in either the client's organization or in the contractor's organization. From a practical standpoint, anyone associated with a project can and will request changes. Some projects fall victim to an abuse of change requests. Although changes, from a practical standpoint, may be requested by many they may be approved by very few. Every change must be defined, evaluated, and costed. Every change has the potential of affecting cost and schedule.

Proper assessment of its effect must be made. Based on this information, the proposed change is approved and authorized as stipulated by the provisions of the contract. A formal change order should be issued promptly. No work involved in the change should be started, other than the definition, evaluation and costing, until approval is certain.

CHANGE ORDER IMPLEMENTATION: As soon as the change order has been issued, the project budget, schedule and plan should be adjusted to reflect the corresponding modifications.The cost engineer is the key individual for change management on most projects. On a large project with many changes, change order administration must be specially planned and usually with a dedicated staff. One approach calls for having centralized change control where the status of each change is tracked and delinquent activities are expedited.

The **successful project manager sees a large part of his job as the control of changes**. He must resist change because of its effect on the project costs, the schedule, and the morale of his staff. For those changes which are inevitable, he must attempt to minimize the cost, schedule disruption, and any significant problems with the attitudes and perceptions of those working on the project.

SCHEDULING EXPENDITURES

When a project manager starts to schedule the expenditures for a project, he must immediately identify how that schedule is to be used by himself and also by others. From the project manger's standpoint, once an order is placed, the project has committed the corresponding funds. **Project cost management is concerned primarily with committed costs.**

In planning how to draw the cost curves for his project, the project manager will select those numbers that can be easily and meaningfully monitored. The numbers used for the curve should be comparable to those which will be used for the interim status reports. The planned project costs should be scheduled based upon the budgets and the schedules for the WBS work packages. Projected costs should be summarized over the project life and the cost curves developed accordingly.

Accounting on a project is based upon receipt of invoices from vendors, fabricators and subcontractors . The expense to the project is realized at that time. These "invoiced" or "billed" amounts represent another viewpoint of expenditures. These costs are the usual basis for project cost reporting and stress the importance of making commitments on time. The "invoiced" expenditures can trail the "committed" expenditures by as much as several months.

The point at which **cash must be paid** for equipment, material or services **is of primary importance to the owner's corporate financial organization**. Depending upon the contract arrangements, the engineering contractor may be deeply involved with these expenditures. The "cash disbursement" expenditures normal trail the "invoiced" expenditures by from one to two months.

Both the owner's and the contractor's project managers should be aware of the difference in these three types of expenditure forecasting: (1) committed, (2) invoiced, and (3) paid. Whenever information of this type is furnished, the basis should be clearly identified. Unfortunately, each department is firmly convinced that the other instinctively knows what is wanted.

Construction financing may be a very significant element of project cost. Even a seemingly short delay in payment of invoices may benefit the project financially. On the other hand, the payment conditions for some invoices may include early payment incentives which might be overriding. The project manager must be aware of the importance of financial schedules in his area of responsibility.

Where a contractor is called upon to make payments to his own employees, to vendors, fabricators, and subcontractors prior to receiving reimbursement from the owner, a serious financial burden may be posed. for the contractor. This must be anticipated, evaluated, and compensated for in some manner. Advance payments for anticipated expenses or project payments from a "zero balance" bank account are ways to reduce the need for the contractor to finance the work. Some contacts provide no alternative except for the contractor to include his estimated "cost of money" allowance in his commercial terms when bidding the work.

MONITORING THE WORK

THE COST PLAN: The **cost plan** for the work is set by the scope of work, the work breakdown structure, the work and performance assurance plans, and the schedule.

The cost plan can be portrayed graphically by a curve showing planned expenditures on a cost vs. time grid over the duration of the project. This curve is developed by tying the cost of specific groupings of work (work activities and work packages) to the time schedule of this same work. The cost of all the work scheduled for each period (week or month) is totaled for preparing the plot. Because of the way that is has been constructed, the curve also represents the rate at which the schedule work is planned to be completed. We can call this curve the **"budgeted cost of work scheduled."** This is the basis for *cost/schedule integration.*

IMPORTANCE OF SOUND INFORMATION: To make good decisions, the project manager constantly relies upon a comprehensive knowledge of the current project status. He needs to know where the project is and where it is heading. Gathering this information is called **project monitoring**. Producing the cost figures in organized and communicable form is **cost reporting**. Cost reports must be accurate and they must be timely for maximum benefit. Accuracy of costs for cost reports does not mean *to-the-cent* accuracy expected of an accounting report but rather meaningful figures for job analysis purposes.

MONITORING CRITERIA: The cost plan is monitored according to the provisions of the performance assurance plan. For a large project, monthly cost monitoring is probably sufficient assuming that interim performance monitoring is being carried on. For small projects, it may be necessary to monitor costs more frequently.

The project progress status is gathered and compiled by the person who has project scheduling responsibility. The cost status is done by the individual who has cost responsibility. On many projects one person will do both jobs.

Monitoring the work requires very specific techniques. The status must be reported in the same categories as it was planned. Monitoring must be done at regular intervals—weekly or twice a month for most jobs. It must be done consistently. On some jobs, the monitoring is done at meeting with the discipline, cost and scheduling personnel in attendance. Care must be taken that the cost of gathering the status information does not become greater than the potential savings. Other projects rely on information submitted by the discipline leader. The prudent project manager will arrange for spot checks to be made to verify status.

STATUS REPORTING: Cost forecasting consists of taking the project status as obtained by the monitoring process and adding the remaining predicted costs. Total forecasted costs are the actual costs to date plus the predicted costs to complete.

6 PROJECT CONTROL

CONTROLLING THE WORK

Control of the work can also be expressed as **those measures that are necessary to make sure that the expected happens.** We can never *control* the project time, but we can control what is done to achieve the schedule. We don't actually *control* costs, but we do *contain* the costs to complete the work within the budget.

To effectively control the work, there are several things that must be done:

- **Establish Baselines**: Baselines must be established representing expected or acceptable performance. These baselines come from the budget and the schedule, integrated by means of the work breakdown structure.

- **Monitor Status:** Performance must be measured regularly or monitored against these baselines. Current status is noted both for budget performance and for schedule performance.

- **Forecasts:** Projections must be made predicting future performance. These projections, when taken with the actual costs to date, result in ongoing predictions of the final job costs and the completion date.

- **Variances:** Current and predicted performance variances must be identified and quantified. The sooner a potential variance can be spotted, the easier the resolution will be.

- **Analysis:** The potential effects of variances on final cost and schedule must be analyzed. Priorities can be established based on this analysis. Reasons for variances are also investigated to head off other variances stemming from the same or similar sources.

- **Alternatives:** Alternative courses of corrective action must be conceived, evaluated, and compared. The best is selected to remedy the variance.

- **Implementation:** The chosen course of corrective action is implemented by modifying/supplementing the work plan.

111

- **Assessment of Remedy:** The work associated with the corrective action is carefully monitored to assure its success. The results of the corrective action are evaluated for effectiveness in recovering the planned project position.

Project control with respect to schedule, cost, and quality is so important to project success that **it must be supported by the entire project staff**. Project control may be achieved by fostering a consciousness of cost, schedule, and quality through the project, visibly emphasizing their importance at every opportunity. In this respect, project control is intimately tied in with performance management.

COST/SCHEDULE INTEGRATION

The basis for cost/schedule integration is the work breakdown structure. Budgeting and scheduling is done following the coding for the work packages and activities as designated by the project WBS. Both the budget and the schedule are optimized to come up with the approved project schedule and the approved project budget. In graphical format, these become the primary performance baselines for the project.

In past years the individual components of the schedule and the budget were not tied in to each other. In preparing the schedule and the budget, the two groups went off in different directions. One came up with a schedule for the project, and the other with a budget for the project. Basically there was no way to tie them together. This made control of the project extremely difficult. Erroneous interpretation of the status was readily possible.

RESOURCES UTILIZED: For each of the activities, the resources expressed in jobhours, material quantities, dollars or percentage of forecast totals are spread over the period of time called for by the schedule. A computer program calculates the rate of expenditure as selected from standard profiles in the data bank. The total of the planned resource utilization for each period for all of the activities is calculated over the life of the project. A curve is then constructed with the cumulative planned use of resources plotted as the ordinate and time as the abscissa. If the use of resources is plotted in dollars, then the resultant curve is known as the **budgeted cost of work scheduled (BCWS)**.

A second curve may be plotted using the above chart as a background and the information gathered during project monitoring for the period. This curve shows the cost of the work done to date. It is called the **actual cost of work performed (ACWP)**. This curve may be extended with a dotted line to show projected future expenditures to the end of the job.

PHYSICAL PROGRESS: Progress is measured in terms of **actual physical accomplishments**. For engineering activities, these are specifications, drawings, purchase requisitions, and the like actually issued or with partial credit taken by means of a preset standard percentage progress allowance. Expenditure of jobhours is not considered a valid measurement of progress except for some elements of management and supervision where no specific measurement is possible. These items are evaluated on the basis of calendar time or as a percent based on the progress for the rest of the project. For equipment and material deliveries and for construction work, actual quantities are used.

Physical progress is plotted against time. If the actual physical progress is converted to dollars at the budgeted amount for doing the corresponding work, a third curve is generated— the **budgeted cost of work performed (BCWP).** This may also be referred to as the **earned value.** Here, again, the predicted future performance may be plotted as a dotted line.

The relative position of the three curves gives the project manager an excellent appraisal as to the health of the project.

COST/SCHEDULE INTEGRATION BASELINE

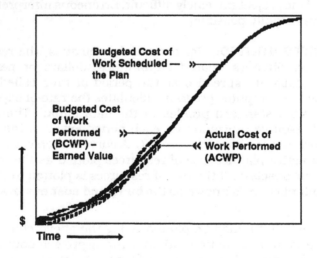

ANALYZING SCHEDULE VARIANCES

After monitoring has been completed and the status reports prepared for each reporting period, the actual earned value achieved is compared with the planned earned value. The differences are analyzed to ascertain what the affects have been on the project to date and predict what will be the possible effects in the future.

The work packages that are on the critical path and which are behind schedule are given the highest priority in the schedule analysis. Every effort should be made to devise plans for corrective action to return work on these packages to acceptable performance. The project may be on schedule based on the earned value compared with the plan. Nevertheless, if non-critical activities have been completed ahead of schedule and critical path work packages are behind schedule, the project may well be in serious trouble.

Once the critical path work packages have been studied, variances in actual earned values are compared to planned earned value and the results analyzed by looking at the **schedule variance** and the **schedule performance index** .

Schedule variance is defined as the planned earned value or the budgeted cost of the work scheduled (BCWS) less the actual earned value or the budgeted cost of work performed (BCWP). The result of this calculation will be in dollars.

$$\text{Schedule Variance (SV)} = \text{BCWS} - \text{BCWP}$$

The schedule variance in time units can be obtained from the same curve, by drawing a horizontal line from the actual earned value or the budgeted cost of work performed (BCWP) to the intersection with the planned earned value of the budgeted cost of the work scheduled (BCWS) . The length of this line will represent, to scale, the time that the work is ahead or behind schedule.

If we compare where we are at any point in time with where we are supposed to be, we have a measure of our schedule performance. The **schedule performance index (SPI)** is defined as the earned value or budgeted cost of work performed (BCWP) divided by the budgeted cost of work scheduled (BCWS).

$$\text{Schedule Performance Index} = \frac{\text{BCWP}}{\text{BCWS}}$$

If the value of the SPI is greater than 1.0, then the job is ahead of schedule. If it is less than 1.0, the job is behind schedule. The values for each period may be plotted to see the schedule trends more easily.

On a large project, the schedule performance may be viewed at different levels in the work breakdown structure. The analysis should be directed in successively greater levels of detail to pinpoint precisely where the trouble spots on the project are with respect to the plan. Once the real offenders, those that jeopardize the schedule, have been identified, they are analyzed to determine where the problems lie or what is holding back progress.

We don't spend time analyzing schedule variances which will not seriously affect the overall schedule.

ANALYZING COST VARIANCES

The costs are analyzed at the end of each reporting period based on the results of the monitoring information and the cost reports generated. The actual costs are compared to the planned cost.

If there is a cost variance as well as a schedule variance, the objectives of the project must be reviewed for guidance as to the possibility of tradeoffs. If cost is the primary objectives, then the schedule may have to slip. If on time job completion governs, then the cost variance may have to be sacrificed to reach that goal.

The project costs may apparently be below the plan; but, if the job is also behind schedule, the cost picture may be deceptive. This points out the real value of cost/schedule integration.

The cost variance is the apparent budget overrun to date or the difference between what it was supposed to cost for the work done to date versus what it actually did cost. The **cost variance (CV)** is equal to the budgeted cost of work performed (BCWP) less the actual costs of the work performed (ACWP). A positive number represents a budget overrun.

$$\text{Cost variance (CV)} = \text{ACWP} - \text{BCWP}$$

Comparing the budgeted costs for the work done to date with the actual costs, we have a measure of our cost performance on the project. The **cost performance index (CPI)** is the budgeted cost of work performed (BCWP) divided by the actual cost of work performed (ACWP)

$$\text{Cost Performance Index (CPI)} = \frac{\text{BCWP}}{\text{ACWP}}$$

- for CPI values of **1.0**, the project is **on budget**
- for CPI values **> 1.0**, the project is **under budget**
- for CPI values **< 1.0**, the project is **over budget**

A running plot of the CPI can be very helpful in spotting cost performance trends

This process of analysis enables the cost engineers and the project manager to spot specific areas within the project which are giving trouble. The elements of the work breakdown structure for which there are budgets and schedules can be studied individually.

Any element showing major cost variance should be reviewed to make sure that the allocated charges have been correctly applied. Mischarging should be looked upon as a prime suspect for variances. Here, correcting the mischarge may correct the variance.

If the charges are correct, then a review should be made for each element with an overrun sufficient to cause the project cost to overrun. The money to cover these additional costs will have to be provided from somewhere else within the budget. If the work on the elements which are overruning is well advanced, it will be necessary to devise different ways of doing some following activities in a more cost effective manner.

COST FORECASTS/PROJECTIONS

We have techniques to identify and analyze variances in project cost and schedule on an ongoing basis. Where we are and how we got there are both important, but they always need to be supplemented by asking, **"where are we going?"**

The project manager needs to know the **current forecast date for project completion** and the **current projected final cost.**

The most accurate and straight forward method of determining these two answers is simply to take the work still to be done and reassess the time requirements to complete it. If the project is currently on schedule and going well, there should be little reason for concern. If the project is behind schedule, those activities without float or with little float would be considered in an attempt to come up with a revised plan to recoup schedule time. If the project is currently ahead of schedule, the remaining work should be reviewed with the objective of moving the completion date forward or in reducing peak resource requirements by extending durations of selected activities. The project objectives would determine which option is selected.

The forecast for the final cost of the project is made by taking costs to date and adding the present estimate to complete all of the unfinished work. If the project is running on budget and performance has been good, final costs will probably be in line with the budget. If the project is running over budget, then a detailed analysis of the remaining costs should be made. The remaining items with the greatest cost sensitivity should receive the greatest attention in this review. If the project is under budget and the projection shows that the project will probably underrun, the project manager should investigate the desirability of accelerating the completion date, if possible, by spending some of the surplus funds. This option must be carefully studied and any move in that direction in accordance with the project objectives and approved by the proper authorities.

If a project is over forty percent complete, over budget, and behind schedule, there can be little optimism in continuing without a major effort to change the execution plan. At this point the project manager and his staff may tend to justify overruns by reference to the **"peculiar difficulties"** presented by **"this project"**. If very stringent and possibly unorthodox measures are not taken with a great deal of urgency, the project will not be successful. At the very least, this is the time to redouble efforts to improve productivity and reduce spending wherever possible without further eroding the chances of completing the project successfully.

A project that is consistently running behind schedule but does not concurrently evidence serious budget overruns will probably eventually overrun the budget. A number of the project costs are closely related to time rather than measurable work output. These activities include project management and project control time charges, supervision from most of the disciplines, and accounting and time keeping charges.

The project manager must develop his forecasts and projections realistically. He must present them to his management and to the client honestly, maintaining belief in the predictions that he makes. A project manager's credibility is on the line whenever he changes his completion projection or his final cost forecast. If this becomes a monthly ritual, he will end up with no credibility at all.

TRENDING

For certain of the the job's major sensitive activities, the prudent project manager and cost engineers will not want to wait for return cost information, but will want to do some on-line comparisons with the plan. Many of these techniques will fall under what is called **trending**. Trending uses a relatively small sample of work for extrapolating future performance.

Trending may be used for overall performance of the entire project or for the performance within special areas, systems or disciplines. It shows its greatest payoff for activities with a fairly long duration, a substantial amount of similar or like output, and which are sensitive elements of the estimate. Both cost performance and schedule performance may be trended.

An ideal example of trending would be an analysis of the design quantities specified for one of the initial concrete equipment foundations. Jobhours which were actually used in the design may be compared to those included in the budget for the same work. The design quantities of form work, reinforcing bar, and volume of concrete can be compared with the quantities approved in the control budget. If any of these accounts are significantly higher or lower than the estimate, the possibility of a trend exists. The cost engineer should alert the project manager and discus the problem with the civil/structural job leader.

The effect of changed design quantities will have an effect on both the procurement and the construction efforts. Advance knowledge will allow for adjustment of the work plan. Job forecasts and predictions will be necessary for the remaining foundations on the job; and, of course, alternative corrective actions should be examined, a selection made, and then introduced to alleviate the adverse trends. This work should be carefully followed to determine effectiveness of the improvement measures.

Trending, no matter how it is done, is not a science. It is a procedure for bringing the possibilities of overrun/underrun to management's attention while there is still time for corrective action. It is not a method for obtaining exact numbers. The process should always be kept in perspective. It makes absolutely no sense to trend every activity on the project. Only those few activities with sufficient significance to materially affect the project outcome should be selected for tracking.

Kerridge (1983) lists four of the methods of trending being used on projects:

- Future work will be performed at the budgeted rate.
- Future work will be performed at the actual rate to date.
- Future work will be performed at the budgeted rate to a specific point and afterward at the actual rate to date.
- Performance deviation for individual activities is determined. Future performance for the area, system, or discipline is based on a weighted deviation of included activities.

As with other scheduling and estimating techniques, the project manager should not abandon his common sense in the use of trending techniques. If the forecasts and projections determined by trending methods do not seem reasonable, they should be questioned. Trending is useful only when properly applied.

Kerridge, Arthur E., "Predict Project Results with Trending Methods." *Hydrocarbon Processing*, Gulf Publishing Company, Houston TX, July 1983, pp. 125-152.

NEED FOR TIMELY INFORMATION

The selection and proper use of an adequate management information system is sometimes difficult for the project manager. Within the limitations afforded him by the available systems, he must assure himself that he has the information at the time that he must make decisions.

Only a few years ago, one of the project manager's biggest headaches was the length of time it took to get good solid information on the status of his project. This has changed, and there is no longer any excuse for delay in getting current project information.

All but the smallest projects today can support computerized information systems. The best of these are comprehensive data base systems operated in an on-line mode. Even smaller projects can have access to networked personal computers with management information programs to assist the project staff in running the job.

Definite responsibility is assigned for inputting each type of data promptly into the data base. The data are then immediately available to all who have a need for it. Access to input and change data is restricted to those who have the responsibility for it. There are types and levels of information that have restricted access, particularly in the case of salary and profitability information. No restriction should be placed on obtaining the information needed for the work efforts.

On small projects, the need for timely information is critical. The status of the project can literally change completely from one day to the next.

People have two reactions when they don't get information when it is needed. Both are detrimental to the project manager in his effort to run an efficient project. Some people abdicate responsibility if they do not have all of the information needed to work. This causes schedules to slip. Others tend to "invent" the information they need, taking into account their prejudices, perceptions, and bits and pieces of half-truths available to them.

Computer programs have the capability, in effect, of producing information in advance. This is a tremendous advantage for the project manager. If he has a thorny decision to make, he may input **"what if"** data into the program and come up with nearly instantaneous results. Various alternatives may be compared very rapidly in this manner.

Graphics should be used whenever possible to summarize large quantities of raw data into a readily understandable form. The computer has made it possible to do this rapidly and at a very low cost once the information has been input into the data base.

Communications technology is changing almost from day to day. Many companies now use electronic mail or "E-Mail" for the project correspondence and reports. It is much easier to get information to the project staff using this system. Morale is improved because people feel more involved and there is less likelihood that someone will be forgotten in a distribution list.

NEED FOR THE RIGHT INFORMATION

The information collected during the project for control purposes serves as the basis for many of the most important project decisions. The information must be right, not only in the sense of being correct, but also that it is the proper information and that it is used properly.

The degree of accuracy required is dependent upon **what the information will be used for** and **the urgency for the data**. For project control purposes, knowing today that an item will cost about a half-million dollars rather than a quarter-million is more important than finding out six weeks from now that it will cost exactly $496,985.13.

During the planning stages of the project, the need for control information should be considered from the standpoint of payout. Large, complex computer programs are available, and it may be tempting to follow the easy way and use one of these even for a small project. The capability and complexity of the control program should always be appropriate for the project. This must be determined very early on, and the decision documented in the performance assurance plan. No more information should be collected than is necessary to make the decisions required for the work and to manage the project effectively.

On any project, there will be honest mistakes made in gathering, inputting and interpreting data. The project manager will realize this, and when an important decision is made, he will take pains to confirm the validity of the data used.

The project manager will also insist on honesty on the part of each one on the project staff. He will never tolerate instances of deliberate falsifying or furnishing intentionally misleading information. The project manager will see that procedures for data checking and verification are in place, and will occasionally do some spot checking himself.

The information used for control and management information purposes must come from people who are in the best position to know. It must not be filtered or distorted so that it appears more favorable that it is. Numbers must have a basis in fact. Entering data for control purposes into the computer has to be looked upon the same way as making a critical engineering calculation.

The data collected for control are used for feedback on performance. The project manager's credibility will suffer if the performance statistics are not accurate or are not properly used for that purpose.

Everyone tends to rely on information that is printed on a computer report. It is supposed to be accurate. Many times the figures are not right, either because of faulty input or due to a glitch in the software. Those who rely on computer reports should never abandon use of their common sense. If a particular number does not look right, you should follow your instincts and investigate rather than merely accept it.

Information should be received in the form that it can best be used for the purpose intended. Not so long ago the computer gave us the numbers configured so that it was easy for the computer or convenient for the programmer. Modern technology has left that concept far behind. There is no longer any excuse for not taking advantage of the computer's ability to collect, manipulate, screen, sort, and present information in the most usable format; and then to transmit it electronically via networks or to generate hard copies.

IDENTIFYING PROBLEM AREAS

A problem may be thought of as a situation that will create a disruption to project execution, produce an interruption to the project plan, or jeopardize the success of the project by causing one or more of the objectives to be missed.

The most successful project managers seem to live about two months in the future. They thrive on anticipating problems by living out what will be happening on the job a few weeks from now. A more natural course would be to avoid thinking about problems because they involve increased risk. Most people avoid getting entangled with problems because thinking about problems will transport you mentally into the future and the unknown. Dealing with problems is uncomfortable because we are vulnerable and we are concerned about being found wrong.

It is an almost unanimous belief that those problems which are anticipated and for which solutions are determined in advance seldom seem to be the ones that cause difficulties on a job.

Some of the project's unique problems will have been identified in the project plan, but identifying problems should be continuous throughout the project. Undoubtedly some of the most frustrating problems will occur toward the end of the job. The project manager will encourage his project staff to continue to undercover problems.

Problems have a nasty habit of repeating themselves. Project managers study the patterns of prior jobs to find out where the problems have been. The past is an excellent source of forecasting future problems. The project manager will talk to a wide range of people to get input from various points of view and backgrounds.

Establishing that a problem of the potential for a problem exists is sometimes not easy, but before a problem can be resolved it has to be recognized. Once a problem has been recognized, the project manager must determine if it is serious enough to warrant concern. He should analyze the potential effects on the project.

If the problem is deemed to be sufficiently serious, the next step involves defining the problem. A performance deficiency may be behind a problem. In collecting information about the problem, good communication skills will be required so that the problem is not be aggravated before a solution can be implemented. Quite often the *symptoms* of the problem are initially thought to be the problem itself. Only at the time the problem is being defined are the symptoms unmasked to reveal the true difficulty. While the problem is being defined, try to isolate the root cause of the problem.

It is necessary to determine who has responsibility for dealing with the problem. In a matrix organization the problem may be a project problem, but the responsibility for resolution may, by definition of responsibility, belong to someone else. If this is the case, the project manager's responsibility is to bring the problem to the proper authority and see that there is a timely response. If he gets no action, he must escalate the issue to higher levels of management. Even though he may not be responsibile for the actual resolution, he is answerable to assure that the problem is settled.

INVESTIGATION OF ALTERNATIVES

Once an identified problem has been defined and acknowledged to be detrimental or potentially detrimental to the project, a solution to the problem must be found. It is always desireable to be able to identify alternative solutions; occasionally there will be instances where finding even one plausible solution will be taxing.

The facts should be examined to determine the cause of the problem. There is always a possibility that removing the cause(s) will eliminate the problem. Most often, even if this is done, additional remedial work may be required.

The goals for problem resolution should be clearly expressed. What end result is sought in solving the problem? In the case of many problems, the end result sought is a return to the original project schedule and budget within a specified time period.

There may be premature attempts to resolve a problem, even before it has been defined. The project manager should insist that a sincere effort be made to definite the problem and to develop alternative options before attempting to make a decision as to the proper solution.

Sometimes clues to a possible solution will be given by the indicated path from the present situation to the desired situation. If this approach gives only one possible solution, the search should continue.

Alternatives may be developed by using a brainstorming technique which involves group generation of a large number of ideas. The results will depend very much upon the composition of the brainstorming group. The prime prerequisite of the participant should be a creative and innovative nature. Related technical experience may be very helpful, but it may also be a hindrance if it limits the thought process of the group. Every proposed idea should be accepted and investigated including the most far-fetched. One of the benefits of the free-wheeling sessions is the fallout of derivative ideas based upon previous suggestions or combinations of suggestions. If there are a number of alternatives produced, the chances of the optimum solution being among them is correspondingly greater.

Once the alternatives have been proposed, they must be evaluated. Each alternative should be ranked with regard to its contribution to resolving each of the results desired of the final solution. The alternative that has the highest ranking should then be "fine tuned."

Finally, the **selected course of action** is tested, "walked through", or simulated in order to prove its feasibility. There will always be some element of risk present in dealing with a problem area, and the project manager must keep this risk commensurate with the benefits to the project.

CORRECTIVE ACTION

The purpose of a continuous monitoring program is to provide opportunity for timely correction of real or anticipated adverse effects on the project schedule or budget.

As soon as there is a definite indication of such an effect, the supervisor should work with the individual assigned the responsibility to develop a program for getting back on track.

At times this can be done between the supervisor and the individual, but sometimes it will be necessary to broaden the focus and bring in other people to help resolve the problem.

PERFORMANCE PROBLEMS: Some problems occur repeatedly. Some of the different types of performance problems and ideas for resolution are given below:

- **Information Not Available:** A very handy excuse for not performing is that the necessary data had not been received. The first question the supervisor must ask is: *"What have you done to expedite getting it?"* The employee must not be let off the hook unless he has really tried to get the information. He should already have advised the supervisor of the problem before the date has been missed. If he has tried and been unsuccessful, the expediting effort must be escalated. Overtime may be a solution for recuperation after the data has been received.

- **Optimistic Target Date:** Often the amount of time required to do a specific job is underestimated. A new fix must be made, and its effect on the following project activities analyzed. There will be an effect on both schedule and cost stemming from a low estimate. Care should be taken that this does not create a cascading effect on subsequent work. For activities on the critical path, a delay in completion should be considered a serious matter in order to minimize the damage to downstream activities.

- **Adverse Quantity Trends:** Early material takeoffs may bring up evidence of an underestimated quantity estimate. The project budget may be sensitive to errors in quantity estimates. An overall evaluation is called for to determine the effect of the actual design on the budget. Redesign is one alternative that must be considered. An offsetting estimate is sometime possible, but this is not usually an option. Far more frequently, a general trend of underestimating may be discovered. At this time all of the available brain power must be brought to bear to reduce the potential budget variance.

- **Mistakes, Errors, and Omissions:** Even with many of the calculations computerized; and an aggressive checking procedure, errors are possible. If an individual has been directed to proceed with work based upon assumed data, there will be complications in completing the scheduled work on time and within budget if the data turns out to be erroneous. Where critical path activities are involved, serious consequences may arise. The supervisor should make sure that the performance of the innocent employee is not jeopardized because of something for which he is not responsible. They must work together to get the activity back on track with as little disruption to the project as possible.

7 STATUS REPORTING

PROJECT REPORTING

Project reports represent an excellent opportunity for the project manager to communicate on a routine basis with a broad spectrum of people who are interested in the project.

The reports will go to people with different interests in the project. They will probably not all be issued the same reports, nor will the reports be issued with the same frequency.

Reports are generally thought of as being written. More and more, certain reports are being given by means of oral presentations. Video-taped reports are finding increased application. The use of oral presentations for reports to the owner and to senior management are particularly valuable as they give a better opportunity for questions and for mutual feedback on job status and problems.

In order to be a meaningful communication tool, written reports have to be read. They will only be read if they are accurate, concise, interesting, and of benefit to the reader. These same criteria should apply to oral presentations and to video reports.

The project manager, in the absence of specific instructions as to report content and format, should always analyze what aspects of the job are of particular interest to his audience. Depending upon their level in the organization, their relationship with the project and their own particular personalities and agenda, interests will vary from summaries and rollups of the job schedule and cost status to very detailed reports by system, area, discipline or work package. The project manager should be sure to get agreement on the content of reports required by the owner and by his own management. Keeping these two groups abreast of the job progress in accordance with their own desires will be very beneficial to smooth relations throughout the project.

If a comprehensive, detailed progress report to the owner's management is required, the first item on the report should be an executive summary which condenses the most important information concisely right at the beginning. This summary should include overall project status information, significant milestones reached during the period, schedule and cost status, and any major problems. The individuals

133

receiving the report can then go deeper into the report proper to the extent they feel is necessary.

Status reports should provide an update showing progress made only during the period covered. Don't make the mistake of stating future performance as *factual*; but rather state it in terms in terms of *planned events*.

It is helpful to furnish as much of the information as possible in graphical form. Using the same format for the graphs in successive issues of the report helps the reader as he acquires familiarity and feels comfortable with the way the information is presented.

Collectively, the status reports should furnish an accurate history of the job from beginning to end. They become invaluable for reference in planning similar projects in the future.

WHAT REPORTS ARE REQUIRED

One way to categorize reports is by the individual or the individuals to whom they are addressed. A broad distinction may be made between reports that are issued internally to the project staff, and those which are issued outside the project.

INTERNAL PROJECT REPORTS: Internal reports are more detailed and are issued for day-to-day management of the project, as well as to disseminate information. Internal reports are issued more frequently. Internal reports issued on a weekly basis would include distribution of time charges which is a computer report showing individual charges to activities or work packages using the daily or weekly time sheets as input. Other weekly or monthly detailed reports would include such items as procurement status reports, quality assurance reports, reproduction charges, communication charges, postage charges, and charges and allocations from outside the project staff for support. Reports are also generated by the various project management programs which include comparisons of earned value with the plan and costs with the planned expenditures.

One of the most useful types of reports is the exception report that pinpoints all of those activities which were supposed to occur on a specific date but did not. Another important source of reports on a project are the written minutes of job meetings. Timely issue of these minutes is the responsibility of the individual chairing the meeting, even though he may have delegated the actual compiling of the minutes to someone else.

Reports distributed to functional management with respect to the project should be considered as internal project reports. Even though strictly speaking these managers are not part of the project staff, they are intimately involved with project matters.

Internal reports serve as a fundamental communication channel for the project. Good reporting enhances the effectiveness of the project staff.

EXTERNAL REPORTS FOR MANAGEMENT: The project manager's most important external reports are those which are prepared for the owner's management and for his own management. Expected support from those two sources is dependent upon their understanding of the project which is largely garnered form the status reports. These reports may be detailed or they may be in summary form. The project manager should make sure that the content and format of the reports conform to the expectations of these two management groups. This may mean preparing reports which differ in format, but never in the facts which are presented.

For government work as well as for some very sophisticated owners, very detailed and comprehensive reports are requested. The preparation of these reports is a major project effort and should be treated as such. Every effort must be made to eliminate extraneous material, but at the same time all of the information asked for should be presented in the requested format.

OTHER EXTERNAL REPORTS: Periodic or occasional special reports may be required by regulatory or other governmental agencies, by third party investors or financial backers for the project, or by licensors of technology. Here, again, the purpose of the report and the use to which it will be put have to be known in order to assure that the content will be appropriate. On some projects, reports are prepared by financial or performance auditors. Although the project manager does not have responsibility for preparing them, he must provide suitable project support for gathering the information.

WHAT MANAGEMENT EXPECTS FROM PROJECT REPORTING

A senior manager is interested in getting project status reports principally because of his ultimate responsibility for project performance. These managers are normally overloaded. They do not need additional piles of voluminous paperwork in the form of project reports. **The project manager should present the project status in an interesting, concise, yet comprehensive form.**

Frequently the company, either on the owner's or the contractor's side, will have a standard content and format for project status reports. If both companies have standards and differ only slightly, the project manager might try to obtain agreement so that he has to produce only one version of the report. If the formats are quite different and both managements are insistent on receiving their own standard report, then the project manager will have to prepare the report in both formats.

If no standards are furnished, then the project manager should use his own accustomed format, tailoring it to respond to the announced or perceived preferences of the two senior management groups.

Although portions of the status report may be prepared by various individuals within the project organization, **the project manager should be in agreement with all of the numbers and the analysis** of the status as presented in the report. He needs to be involved in the final compilation and editing process.

Most engineers are not especially noted for their writing skills. Their sentences are frequently complex, rambling, and convoluted. The project manager has the ultimate responsibility for seeing that the reports are easy to read and easy to understand. He should set guidelines as to what he expects, and should give liberal performance feedback to all of those involved in the preparation of the status reports.

The project manager needs to realize that senior management's attitude toward control is necessarily different from his own. Whereas he follows the project on an hour by hour basis, senior management has a much broader scope of responsibility. The senior manager cannot afford to spend a great deal of time on something that is running well and hence should not require much of his attention. **He needs to know**

promptly when there are matters that need his help. Most of his understanding will have come from the project reports.

The project manager serves as the eyes and ears of senior management. He sorts the information that needs to be passed on from that which is not significant in the greater perspective. A mutual confidence must be established, and the project reports are part of the foundation for this confidence. Management must feel that the project manager is on top of the project, that he knows what is going on at all times. He arranges this information into groupings, analyzes the data, and presents it so that it is easily understood.

The project manager should not use the project status report to avoid responsibility for future project difficulties. Running the project is his responsibility, and he cannot shift that responsibility to others via the status reports.

STATUS REPORT CONTENT

The content of a status report is dependent upon the type of project. Suggested content and format for a status report for an engineering/ construction facility is as follows:

EXECUTIVE SUMMARY: This section of the report should give a brief narrative covering the milestone accomplishments made during the period, give variances between the planned and actual earned value and the budget status for the overall project. Any significant problems that are foreseen should be highlighted along with what is being done to head them off. Status in graphic form is also helpful in showing trends or the status of any major corrective action programs underway. Overall job productivity can be compared with the target figures.

INTERMEDIATE SUMMARIES: An individual summary detailing the actual status of engineering, procurement, construction, and support services may be included along with comparisons with the planned status. This information should be presented using both narrative and graphical formats. Additional details of variances, trends, productivity, and achievements versus predicted performance are given. Corrective action programs underway should be given to back up the information in the executive summary.

DETAILED PROJECT STATUS

- **Engineering:** A detailed description covering the status of technical engineering and design along with additional performance details for each discipline follows. Actual versus planned progress should be reviewed, and schedule and cost variances highlighted. Further details should be given on the specifics of deficiencies in performance, trends, and corrective action programs. Both narrative and graphical material can be used.

- **Procurement:** The status of the procurement effort is broken down into details of requisitions received, items put out to bid, status of bid tabulations, purchase orders placed, detailed status of equipment being fabricated, status of items shipped from the vendor, and status of items received at the jobsite. This material lends itself to both chart and graphical presentation together with an overall analysis in narrative form.

- **Construction:** Construction status reporting may be broken down by area, by system or both and by craft, depending upon how the work breakdown structure is focused. Reporting will be in graphical form with a brief narrative summary. Field productivity measurements are of great interest and should be adequately covered by the status report. Progress photographs are invaluable in demonstrating progress at the jobsite as well as illustrating specific problems encountered at the site.

The report requirements will vary for each project. The project manager must take enough time to analyze the specific requirements for his project and to adjust to all its particularities so that meaningful information on project status will be adequately presented in the most readable form.

STAKEHOLDER COMMUNICATION

Many of the project stakeholders will not receive copies of progress reports or any other report on project status. On a small project, the intervention of other stakeholders will be nil or minimal. On a large project this may not be true. The project manager should have a strategy about how needed information will be communicated to the other stakeholders.

A clear understanding is needed between the owner and the client about how this nonroutine information will be handled. Generally, the owner will reserve the right to process project information to the public through his public relations department.

Specific points which should be considered for each of the common groups of stakeholders in a project are given below. Major differences are possible; and, for projects which are sensitive, the procedures for releasing information should be clearly spelled out.

- **Financial Stakeholders:** The responsibility for handling communications with investors, joint venture partners, and financial agencies participating in the project usually belongs to the owner. These communications can materially affect job relations, so they must be carefully handled.

- **Shareholders:** Shareholders only infrequently become personally involved in project matters. They generally make arrangements through corporate channels; some sort of an official request should come to the project manager along with any special instructions.

- **Vendors and Fabricators:** Some project managers of very large jobs have built an excellent esprit de corps by including the major vendors/fabricators on the distribution of a project newsletter, making sure it is received not only by the management of the firms doing the work, but also those actually doing the work

- **Subcontractors:** Jobsite bulletin boards can be very effective in posting home office and site news about the project. A jobsite newsletter can also transmit factual information rather than let the rumor mill provide information to the craftsmen.

- **Regulatory Bodies:** The most effective project managers try to establish and maintain a personal relationship with a member of the regulatory bodies involved. Because of the very formal way that the regulatory and permitting functions are handled, it can be very helpful to have some sort of an informal access or "sounding board."

- **Environmental and Civil Organizations, Site Neighbors, and the Media:** Care must be taken to avoid adversarial relations with each of these groups. Where good relations are difficult because of the nature of the project, the project manager must be guided accordingly. He must choose his words knowing that he will probably be quoted out of context. He must not unintentionally make the relationships more difficult.

8 ENGINEERING

CONCEPTUAL ENGINEERING

Conceptual engineering is that portion of the project in which the initial definition is undertaken. During this stage the "givens" are reviewed and the objectives set and taken into account on all subsequent work. Any constraints are set out. Preliminary planning of the project should be done concurrently with conceptual engineering.

During conceptual engineering **the minimum cost of the project is set**. It is imperative that careful consideration be used in establishing the guidelines and parameters to be followed during the later stages of engineering, procurement, and construction activities.

Decisions are made as to the source of the technology to be used. Initial definition of the various systems is established. The conceptual specifications and the philosophy to be followed in writing the subsequent detailed specifications are set. The amount of overdesign is decided, and provisions are made for future expansion. Sparing philosophy is defined. Suggestions for optimization of operation, utilities, and chemical usage are documented.

During this period the site is selected, and a provisional plant layout may be given by the licensor or developed in house. Consideration of alternate plant layouts is aided by use of a rough block model. Special attention is given to the arrangement of major equipment to avoid long runs of large diameter alloy piping. Assuming the site area is available and that there are no process requirements for elevation, equipment should generally be placed at ground level. Structures should be minimized, and, when required, they should be unitized to reduce their number. Common foundations should be considered for groups of adjacent equipment to reduce the need for costly hand excavation and small special sets of formwork. Wherever possible, piping runs should be placed at or near ground level.

How the field construction will be done should be determined at this stage of the project. Specifically what will be subcontracted and what will be handled directly by the construction manager or by direct hire. All subsequent engineering and procurement activities can then be more closely aligned and scheduled. Documents will be developed so that they comply with the planned requirements and are complete and self-explanatory.

When the overall master schedule is developed the field erection sequence should be set by consideration of the delivery times of the equipment, materials, and the engineering required for each of the various areas. Once these major field activities have been established, then priorities can be set for the home office work required to support them effectively.

With the process decisions made and the plant layout and specification philosophy decided, the constructability program is initiated. What has been learned before should be brought to bear on the proposed project. Many cost saving ideas do not fall clearly within one single discipline so there must be a combination of skills involved in the constructability studies. Not only are engineering design and construction people involved, but experts from plant maintenance and operations should be tapped for input to the study. Access requirements for operation and maintenance are identified and provisions made for them.

Safety should be high on everyone's priority list. Hazardous operations and materials should be identified and plans made to reduce and eliminate the potential for unsafe conditions.

The highest potential for saving money exists during the conceptual engineering stage. Large savings are possible by making adjustments or modifications to the basis for design, the plant layout, the specification philosophy and the field construction program. The early integration of plant operation and maintenance with engineering, procurement, and construction will pay great dividends in achieving a working plant at the least possible cost. Never again in the life of the project will a similar opportunity exist.

PLANT LAYOUT

The general arrangement of the plant equipment within the facility may have the largest single **effect on plant cost** after the (1) process design and (2) the plant site has been selected, and (3) the equipment design has been optimized.

FLOW CONSIDERATIONS: The layout of the plant starts with a study of the process or mechanical flow diagrams in the case of a processing plant, or with analogous documentation in the case of a commercial or public building or other structure. What comes onto the site, what operations are done with this and in what order, and what leaves the site are considered in the layout of the plant. It is also necessary to consider the utilities obtained from offsite and the transportation modes which are to be utilized .

A preliminary layout can be prepared from the flow diagrams. It is convenient to use paper cutouts, approximately to scale, of the major equipment items or subareas. These can be moved around in various configurations to quickly judge alternative arrangements. The flow considerations are only the first of many factors that must be studied in reaching the optimum layout.

PHYSICAL CHARACTERISTICS OF SITE: The next aspect that must be viewed in developing the plant layout are the attributes of the property where the plant will be sited. The topography will influence the general arrangement of the equipment. The subsoil conditions may set the location of heavy loads. Drainage is certainly a factor and wind direction may well be. Access to the site needs to be studied with respect to highways, railroads, and navigable waters. Ground subsidence may be a factor in some locales.

SAFETY CONSIDERATIONS: Developing the plot plan should take into account the various levels of risk afforded by the different areas of the plan. Where possible like items with like risks should be located together.

Areas where workers are likely to congregate should be located away from the hazardous spots to the extent possible or else they should be specially designed to avert damage. These areas would normally include control rooms, offices, warehouses, cafeterias, and laboratories.

INSURANCE CONSIDERATIONS: Insurance rates are based upon the type of protection accorded both with regard to the layout and to the emergency provisions in place at the plant. In addition, the rates will vary with the potential cost of the loss and the deductible. Plant layout will materially affect the first two of these three factors. A review of the plant layout with representative of the insurer should be scheduled at an early date to avoid surprises

CONSIDERATIONS FOR CONSTRUCTION SEQUENCING: Sometimes there is a need to establish the order in which the equipment will be installed in order to completely finalize the plant layout. Late equipment delivery may be a determining factor in setting plant layout.

OPERABILITY CONSIDERATIONS: Plant operating personnel should be given an opportunity to comment prior to the finalization of the plant layout plans.

MAINTENANCE CONSIDERATIONS: A plant layout may be chosen which will give minimum capital investment, and be extremely difficult to maintain. The prudent project manager will insist that all of those ultimately responsible for the maintenance of the facility review the layout early and periodically review throughout the period of design development. If such review is not possible, then people familiar with maintenance should be involved in reviews to make sure that proper consideration is given.

SPECIAL CAUTION: The proper role of safety is very difficult for the project manager to achieve. There is no one who will fight safety; but many may not be willing to pay extra for it. There needs to be a very careful balance maintained between the prudent and those items that should only be on someone's wish list. The project manager must consistently weigh the costs of improving safety provisions against the risks. Scheduling of a preliminary "Haz-Ops" review is indicated to bring safety into its proper role before the plant layout is finalized. Certainly this is the period during which **constructability** recommendations must be incorporated into the plant design.

Further Reading:

Kern, Robert, "How to Manage Plant Design to Obtain Minimum Cost." *Chemical Engineering*, May 23, 1977 to August 14, 1978, a series in 12 parts.

MODULAR DESIGN

When used in the proper circumstances, **modularization, skid-mounting, preassembly** and **prefabricaton** are techniques that can result in significant overall savings in time and money. Some level of **offsite construction** is probably beneficial to any project; and the project manager and his team should establish very early to what degree it should be used.

Many factors influence the use of offsite construction. Among these are:

- **Plant Location**
  - Climatic conditions,
    weather is less a factor
  - Hostile environment
  - Fragile ecology
  - Accessibility
  - Physical conditions
  - Political considerations
  - Congested, metropolitan sites
  - Shortage of skilled craftsmen

- **Plant Characteristics**
  - Process design is done with modularization in mind
  - Easily separable systems
  - Flexibility with plant layout
  - Layout and establishing module interfaces are critical
  - Unit is temporary at the location

- **Labor Considerations**
  - Differential cost of labor
  - Availability of labor
  - Productivity differences
  - Reduction of site social problems
  - Less construction supervision required
  - Labor relations more certain in shop environment
  - Added shifts easier in a shop than in the field
  - Can take advantage of existing facilities in other areas

- **Infrastructure Requirements**
  - Less site construction equipjment/transport vehicles
  - Reduced size/number of temporary facilities

- Reduced requirements for housing workers
- Less site construction equipment/transport vehicles
- Reduced size/number of temporary facilities
- Reduced requirements for housing workers
- Site facilities required for a shorter period
- Field indirects reduced due to shorter field schedule
- Quality enhanced due to shop fabrication and testing

• **Risk**

- May result in higher risk because of more exacting demands which require a higher level of planning and scheduling
- May result in a reduced risk because of higher degree of control over costs/schedule/quality possible in a more controlled environment
- Modular design appears more sensitive to late material deliveries than conventional construction

There are definite limitations on the size and weight of the modules or preassembled packages. These will differ with the site and the mode of transport to be used. Where the heavy lift capability of the offshore construction industry is available, module weights may exceed 7000 tons. This limit is greatly reduced for landlocked sites where transport and lifting capacity may be limited to a tenth of that weight.

ARCTIC ENGINEERING

About 20% of the land surface of the world may be viewed as being in regions where extreme cold is a factor in engineering design. Populated countries most affected are the USSR, China, and Canada, and the state of Alaska. The entire continent of Antarctica must also be included. These areas are becoming more important in the world economy and therefore to the engineer/designer.

Arctic areas are covered with tundra, an organic material from 6 to 18 inches thick. The tundra acts as an insulator for the underlying ice and soil. Permafrost, or permanently frozen material, underlies the tundra and may extend to depths of 2000 feet or more. Melting of permafrost creates the majority of problems for the arctic designer.

Two considerations are important in dealing with design where permafrost is a factor:

- **The effect of a foundation or buried pipe** on the permafrost which commonly causes thawing and the resulting loss of integrity of the permafrost as a support

- **The effect of the permafrost** on the foundation or buried pipe

Insulation is required to prevent these deleterious effects. Foam insulation has been found to be effective onshore. Foam has not been found to be practical offshore where gravel is commonly used. Gravel is not an effective insulator.

Large buildings might be set on permafrost directly provided they are equipped with a refrigeration system that would circulate refrigerant into the permafrost to keep it frozen.

In offshore installations, ice shifting poses a significant problem for designers. These high forces imposed on a structure have to be transmitted to the soil below.

PIPELINES: When pipelines are placed above ground in the arctic, engineers must guard against fatigue failures due to wind-induced vibration. Over-stressing at support points is also a consideration. Offshore lines are buried in trenches which must be deep enough to prevent ice scouring. The phenomena occurs in shallow waters during the freeze cycle when water begins to freeze underneath the surface ice and expands, creating tremendous forces.

Many materials which are used in temperate climates are not suitable for use in subzero temperatures. Common structural steel, polyethylene, and some forms of glass are typical materials which must be carefully reviewed before use. Anticipated temperature conditions must be included in all equipment and material requisitions.

WINTERIZING: Winterizing plants is common even in more temperate climates. However, the proper "winterization" of an arctic plant is imperative. There should be a thorough and detailed design review of all systems to be sure that all potential conditions have been predicted. Failure to do this can create problems in the piping, instrumentation, many of the equipment items, and the utility systems, and cause interruptions to the plant operation.

Maintenance workers in very cold climates will have low productivity. Design of the facilities should take this into account.

SCHEDULING: The arctic ice pack across the northern coast of Alaska allows passage of marine transportation for only about one month each year during the month of August and the early part of September. In this brief period, barges must be towed to the site, off-loaded, and towed out prior to the closing of the passage. This "window" in the ice pack is the controlling factor in most North Slope scheduling.

PROCESS ENGINEERING

SPECIALTIES TYPICALLY INCLUDED: Fluid flow; heat transfer; chemical reaction; mass transfer operations including distillation, absorption and stripping, extraction, humidification, adsorption, drying, crystallization; waste disposal: energy and material balances; plant testing and commissioning.

SERVICES PROVIDED: Supervise all process engineering efforts on project including scope clarification, staffing, discipline schedules. Indicate additional work and schedule time required by change orders.

Conceive process design or work from licensor data, maintain contact with licensor and obtain approvals for all process documents as required; develop information for process flow diagrams, develop information for process control, develop material balances, calculate catalyst and chemical requirements; define and calculate utility requirements, rate and size all critical equipment, reviews process data to make sure that all operating conditions have been met, design relief valves and relief and blowdown systems, review material selection criteria, make process guarantee checks, perform optimization studies, scope pilot plant tests, design data development, define pollution test frequency, and witness performance tests.

DOCUMENTS PRODUCED: All documents required for supervising the process engineering discipline including finalization of the details of discipline work scopes, discipline work plan, staffing projections, discipline work schedules, change requests, and individual work assignments.

Furnish basic process design data including process description, stream physical properties, liquid specific gravity curves, viscosity curves, enthalpy curves, vaporization curves, condensation curves, process flow diagrams, material balances, utility P&IDs, utility requirements summary, line lists, plan showing hazardous area designations, special vessel sketches, column tray traffic data, equipment data sheets showing all process information, catalyst and chemical requirements listing, and performance test reports.

INTERFACES — INFORMATION COMES FROM:

Project • Specific information about the project

Licensor	• All licensing information and data
Piping	• Plot plan
	• General arrangement sketches
	• Skirt heights (with process involvement/ concurrence)
	• Nozzle orientation data
	• Fabrication requirements (platform/ladder requirements,clip locations)
	• Model or orthographic drawings
Purchasing	• May be called upon to consult on special equipment offerings

INTERFACES — INFORMATION GOES TO: Project, process control, mechanical, process control, piping, civil, electrical, instrumentation, purchasing, construction.

PROJECT MANAGEMENT CONCERNS: Some areas may be short-changed during safety reviews. These include drains and vents, piping and equipment pockets, small piping systems, piping and equipment pressure rating specification breaks, emergency isolation of equipment, backflow protection and heat tracing. Good project management assures that these areas have been adequately reviewed to eliminate hazards.

PROCESS CONTROL ENGINEERING

SPECIALTIES TYPICALLY INCLUDED: Continuous type process control systems, sequencing and interlocking-digital devices, analog control loops, computer control, supervisory control systems, unit/regulatory control systems, field instruments and sensors, feedback and feedforward systems, microprocessor systems.

SERVICES PROVIDED: Supervise all process control engineering efforts on project including scope clarification, staffing, discipline schedules. Indicate additional work and schedule time required by change orders.

Develop process control philosophy and conceptual design working from process or from licensor data as appropriate, add process control information to process P&IDs, provide guidance to the instrumentation discipline depending upon the type of system chosen, review vendor drawings, and review model.

DOCUMENTS PRODUCED: All documents required for supervising the process control engineering discipline including finalizing the details of discipline work scopes, discipline work plan, staffing projections, discipline work schedules, change requests and individual work assignments.

Written description of control philosophy, control information on P&IDs, list of documentation to be provided by instrumentation discipline depending upon type of system chosen.

INTERFACES — INFORMATION COMES FROM:

> **Project** • Specific information about the project
>
> **Process** ◦ Process description
> • Process flow diagrams (PFDs)
> • Specific guidance about control requirements from a processing standpoint
> • Operating requirements
> • Piping flow diagrams (P&IDs) to which controls must be added
> • Equipment data sheets with process information

Licensor	• Licensing information pertaining to control
Piping	• Plot plan
	• General arrangement sketches
	• Model or orthographic drawings
Purchasing	• May be called upon to consult on special equipment offering

INTERFACES — INFORMATION GOES TO: Project, process, mechanical, piping, civil, electrical, instrumentation, purchasing, and construction.

PROJECT MANAGEMENT CONCERNS: The project manager must assure that the system, equipment and individual instruments conform to the client's philosophy and operating procedures. Process control engineers identify the requirements for control and the proper application of instruments to achieve the desired results.

The project manager must take precautions against an unproven and complex system being selected without a through evaluation of the risks involved. Process control technology is new and even newer technology is being developed rapidly. Many project managers do not have direct experience with process control. They must learn to proceed with caution when dealing with the complex decisions that have to be made in selecting a system.

DESIGN ENGINEERING

The information developed by process defines the plant. The project manager, in setting the schedule, needs to provide the necessary time for the process engineers to accomplish their work. This work approaches a plateau with regard to value earned vs. time spent. The project manager must cut off process work after the rate of useful progress has diminished. While process work is underway other disciplines are defining their areas in order to be ready for the detailed engineering phase which is the big user of resources in the home office.

PROJECT MANAGEMENT CONCERNS: Of primary concern is the early requirement for information needed for the design of structural support or foundations for all items of equipment, pipeways and cable trays. This information must be developed by the other disciplines; but the civil discipline is dependent upon receipt of this information to develop the support and foundation designs and drawings. These documents are among the first required by the field. Flow of the necessary information for civil design is extremely important in order to permit proper document flow as scheduled. The prudent project manager will monitor these activities carefully.

PROCESS CONTROL: Project management should be concerned about reaching an early decision on the type of process control that will be used. This should be decided in the conceptual phase, but frequently is not until the design phase. This creates problems for other disciplines and for the project.

MECHANICAL: Early development of the specifications and requisitions for all critical equipment is the leading concern of the project manager in the mechanical engineering area. These activities affect the orderly receipt of vendor drawings that are required by the downstream design disciplines.

CIVIL: The civil discipline must establish topographic control for the project. The system should be simple and clearly understood by both the home office design personnel and the field. In order to avoid confusion, a plant north is frequently established. which differs from true north. The variance of plant north from true north must be definitely established and documented. A plant elevation is also used to simplify calculations and field location. This elevation must be tied down relative to the true elevation, definitely established, and documented. Complications may be introduced into the process by the client who may be bridging two different units constructed under different topographic control parameters. Common sense must prevail in introducing a new or different basis for topographic control because of the potential for misunderstandings and serious errors in plant survey control.

Many firms have chosen to let civil be responsible for all the design of underground facilities because of the difficulty in routing conflicts with foundations. With the normal restrictions governing gravity flow of sewer lines, routing can present difficulties. Some companies choose to model the underground portions of the construction in much the same way the above ground is done. Of course as computer generated design becomes more prevalent, these checks for interference will become easier for the designers.

ELECTRICAL: The electrical discipline most often starts the job late and then tries to play "catch-up." This is a handicap for the rest of the project team. Areas particularly hurt may be the underground routing of cables and location of major electrical equipment.

INSTRUMENTATION: Because of delays in making the system selection, instrumentation gets off to a slow start. Even if these decisions have been made, instrumentation lags on many projects because of a failure to assign people early enough.

DISCIPLINE INTERFACES

Coordination of interdiscipline work is a challenging task in a matrix environment. Understanding **why** there are problems, **what** the effects are, **who** is responsible for maintaining coordination and **how** better coordination can be achieve will make the manager's job easier.

SOURCES OF COORDINATION PROBLEMS: In project work there are many opportunities for coordination problems. Some causes would include:

- Multitude of interfaces between disciplines
- Chance for contradictory instructions from functional and project management
- Confusion over scope or basic design specification
- Lack of sound planning in order to start the project rapidly
- Continual change found on many projects
- Poor interpersonal relationships
- Territorial protectionism
- Weak leadership from project or functional management
- Poor communication/communication channels

EFFECTS OF FAULTY COORDINATION: The **quality** of the work suffers as a result of any lack of coordination between disciplines. The **cost** of the work is higher and the **schedule** may be extended because of the need for rework where erroneous or superseded information has been used as a basis for design. The **morale** of the workers is adversely affected. Unless interrupted, all of these combine to form a cycle of increasing proportions.

WHO IS RESPONSIBLE FOR COORDINATION? Each individual in the organization has a specific responsibility for coordination of the work.

- On the highest level, **senior management** of the firm must establish an environment which fosters close work between disciplines. This is a most necessary requirement.

- Next, **the project managers and the functional managers** must operate confidently in this environment to make sure the expectations for cooperation are made clear to the project and departmental staffs.

- **The job leaders** at the supervisory level are key to assuring that effective interdisciplinary coordination is being implemented.

- Finally, each **worker** on the job has an obligation to seek out accurate information and to make sure that the information is conveyed to others promptly and correctly.

HOW TO ACHIEVE BETTER COORDINATION:

- Reduce interdisciplinary interfaces and clarify those interfaces that remain.

- Reduce chances for contradictory instructions from functional and project management by upper level coordination.

- Don't release production work until a firm design basis is established.

- Produce an adequate project plan early and communicate it to everyone.

- Control changes and improve communication regarding change status.

- Pay attention to interpersonal relationships which cause difficulties. Resolve these problems rapidly or change people as a last resort.

- Clarification of job roles will reduce the need for territorial protectionism.

- Make decisions promptly and let people know what these decisions are.

- Use all means available to improve communications . The use of on-line computer programs with networked terminals affords an excellent opportunity for enhancing communications.

- Use of a model will make it easier for all design personnel to become aware of current status in other disciplines.

MECHANICAL ENGINEERING

SPECIALTIES TYPICALLY INCLUDED: Heaters and boilers; rotating equipment; heat transfer equipment; towers; reactors; pressure vessels; tanks; material handling and transfer; packaged units for water treatment, chemical injection, and pollution control; materials selection; metallurgy; corrosion; coatings; acoustics and noise control.

SERVICES PROVIDED: Supervise all mechanical engineering efforts on project including scope clarification, staffing, discipline schedules. Indicate additional work and schedule time required by change orders.

Review all equipment items for applicable code applications; incorporate project specific and client requirements into standard specifications; select materials of construction; make all design calculations required for included equipment items; work with process control to assure proper elements are present for control of the process; add mechanical requirements to equipment data sheets prepared by process engineers; perform technical bid analysis on all equipment offerings; review vendor drawings and vendor data for compliance with purchase order technical requirements; review model; review welding procedures; participate in "what-if" or "haz-op" reviews as called for by the work plan.

DOCUMENTS PRODUCED: All documents required for supervising the mechanical discipline including finalizing the details of the discipline work scopes, discipline work plan, staffing projections, discipline work schedules, change requests and individual work assignments.

Mechanical equipment list, specifications for all included equipment items, mechanical design drawings for mechanical equipment as required by the contract, completed equipment data sheets, purchase requisitions for all equipment items, mechanical subcontract specifications; bid tabulations for equipment, initiate motor list with all services indicated.

INTERFACES — INFORMATION COMES FROM:

Project	• Specific information about the project
Process	• Process flow diagrams (PFDs)
	• Piping and instrument flow diagrams (P&IDs)

	• Equipment data sheets with process information
	• Thermal ratings for exchangers (shell and tube)
Process Control	• Process control philosophy
Piping	• Plot plan
	• General arrangement sketches
	• Skirt heights
	• Nozzle orientation data
	• Fabrication requirements (platform and ladder requirements, clip locations)
	• Model or orthographic drawings
Electrical	• Grounding clip requirements
Purchasing	• Purchasing plan
	• Vendor quotes
	• Commercial bid tabulations

INTERFACES — INFORMATION GOES TO: Project, process, process control, piping, civil, electrical, instrumentation, purchasing, and construction.

PROJECT MANAGEMENT CONCERNS: Experience has shown that the most successful projects are those in which major equipment items are placed on order promptly. Late process information causes the mechanical disciplines to fall behind schedule early in the project and prevents early purchasing activities from proceeding.

CIVIL, STRUCTURAL, AND ARCHITECTURAL ENGINEERING

SPECIALTIES TYPICALLY INCLUDED: Civil engineering, structural engineering and architecture, and topographic control.

SERVICES PROVIDED: Supervise all civil engineering and related discipline efforts on project including scope clarification, staffing, discipline schedules. Indicate additional work and schedule time required by change orders.

Site topography for drainage, streets and earth moving requirements, structural design, routing of underground piping and cables, fire protection system, liquid waste treatment facility design, railroad layout, assist in obtaining permits, review vendor drawings, and review model.

DOCUMENTS PRODUCED: All documents required for supervising the civil engineering and related disciplines including finalizing the details of discipline work scopes, discipline work plan, staffing projections, discipline work schedules, change requests, and individual work assignments.

Civil, structural and architectural specifications; site investigation report; soil investigation/report requisition specification; design drawings for site and site development, drainage, roads, railroads, walks and fences, structural steel drawings and ladder and platform designs, piling layout; foundation drawings; all architectural drawings including plot plans for indoor plants and finishing schedules; civil, structural and architectural subcontract specifications; and material takeoffs.

INTERFACES — INFORMATION COMES FROM:

Project	• Specific information about the project
Process	• Process description, PFDs and P&IDs
Licensor	• All licensing information and data
Piping	• Plot plan
	• General arrangement sketches
	• Skirt heights (with process involvement)
	• Nozzle orientation data

Piping	• Fabrication requirements (platform/ladder requirements, clip locations) • Model or orthographic drawings
Mechanical	• Equipment weights and other characteristics
Electrical	• Location, weights and other characteristics of electrical equipment, cable routing
Instrumentation	• Location, weights and other characteristics of control room equipment and other instrumentation requiring structural support, cable routing
Purchasing	• May be called upon to consult on special materials and equipment orders

INTERFACES — INFORMATION GOES TO: Project, process, mechanical, process control, piping, mechanical, electrical, instrumentation, purchasing, and construction.

PROJECT MANAGEMENT CONCERNS: Areas where project management involvement is indicated include:

1. Information flow to civil from other disciplines to allow critical site, underground and foundation designs/drawings to be developed.
2. Confusion resulting from working with more than one set of topographic controls.
3. Lack of clarity of requirements in early permitting activities.

SITE SELECTION

The selection of a new plant site is frequently a part of a project manager's responsibility, either in his role for the owner or in a consulting role. The first decision that has to be made is whether a new site is preferable or whether an expansion of an existing facility would be better. If the decision is made to look for a new site, the following process is recommended:

- **Establish Criteria:** What are the essential characteristics of the new plant site? What other features would be desirable?

- **Pinpoint Geographical Possibilities:** A selection of all of those areas which should be considered in the site selection process. This initial list should be screened using the criteria available or readily obtainable. Only those areas with the highest potential are retained for further consideration.

- **Select Specific Properties/Sites:** Visit each of the potential areas and investigate specific pieces of property. Each of these should be evaluated from a multitude of criteria which are included in the checklist below.

- **Get Options on Properties:** At this stage it is probably helpful to get options on each of the properties under consideration to eliminate disappointment in the future or price escalation as information leaks out.

- **Make Comparisons of Selected Sites:** Each of the sites should be ranked on all of the specific items which relate to three categories: (1) **operating costs**, (2) **capital costs**, and (3) **subjective factors**. This may be done in the form of a matrix with each of the areas of comparison weighted as to its importance.

- **Make Preliminary Choice:** Based on this evaluation, the preliminary choice of plant site should be made. Many times a subjective conviction will be controlling. This may well lead to doubts as to the validity of the selection process unless each factor has been well researched and documented.

- **Additional Investigation:** Once the preliminary decision has been reached, that site should be further studied to make sure that there are no "fatal flaws" which would preclude its use. If an unknown situation is uncovered during this process, the previous step should be iterated.

• **Make Final Recommendation:** As soon as the preliminary choice of site has been found to withstand the further scrutiny successfully, final recommendations may be made.

FACTORS WHICH INFLUENCE SITE SELECTION:

Natural

Climate
Seismic classification
Topography
Water availability/reliability
Waste disposal alternatives

Operating Costs

Feedstock availability/cost
Power availability/costs
Water cost
Labor costs
Productivity

Financial

Financial aid available
Construction costs
Land availability/cost
Tax incentives

Regulatory

Environmental permitting
Special labor laws

Demographic:

Community acceptance
Business climate
Quality of life
Labor supply

Market proximity
Transportation availability
Support services available
Labor relations history

Further Reading:

Granger, James E., "Plantsite Selection." *Chemical Engineering*, Vol. 88, No. 12, June 15,1981, pp. 88-115.

Wright, Paul B., "Selecting the Site." *Project Management: A Reference for Professionals*, Robert L. Kimmons and James H. Loweree (Eds.), Marcel Dekker, Inc., New York, 1989, pp. 151-166.

PIPING ENGINEERING

SPECIALTIES TYPICALLY INCLUDED: Plant layout and design, pipe sizing, pipe stress, model building, insulation, heat tracing, computer aided design/drafting (CADD).

SERVICES PROVIDED: Supervise all piping efforts on project including scope clarification, staffing, discipline schedules. Indicate additional work and schedule time required by change orders. Do plant layout for ouside plants, pipe routing, stress analysis; write piping specifications; draft and check all piping drawings; develop insulation schedules; design heat tracing; do vendor drawing review; make preliminary and final piping material takeoffs; build and check model,

DOCUMENTS PRODUCED: All documents required for supervising the process control engineering discipline including finalizing the details of discipline work scopes, discipline work plan, staffing projections, discipline work schedules, and individual work assignments. Plot plan (for outdoor plants); general arrangement sketches; skirt heights (with process involvement/concurrence); nozzle orientation data; insulation schedules; heat tracing installation drawings; fabrication requirements (platform/ladder requirements, clip locations); model or orthographic drawings.

INTERFACES — INFORMATION COMES FROM:

Project	• Specific information about the project
Process	• Process flow diagrams/material balances
	• Utility P&IDs/utility requirements
	• Line lists
	• Special vessel sketches
	• Plan showing hazardous area designations
Licensor	• All licensing information and data
Civil	• Site investigation report
	• Design drawings for site development, drainage, roads, railroads, walks, and fences
	• Ladder and platform design drawings
	• Foundation drawings
	• Structural steel drawings

Civil	• Architectural drawings
Process Control	• Written description of control philosophy • Control information on P&IDs
Electrical	• Single line diagrams • Equipment space requirements • Cable routing
Instrumentation	• Control room equipment requirements • Other control equipment requirements • Cable routing
Purchasing	• May be called upon to consult on special equipment or materials offerings

INTERFACES — INFORMATION GOES TO: Project, process, mechanical, process control, civil, electrical, instrumentation, purchasing, and construction.

PROJECT MANAGEMENT CONCERNS: Areas where project management involvement is indicated include:

1. Information flow to piping from process and mechanical to allow designs required by civil for foundations and structures to proceed
2. Changes to piping systems after the basic information has been frozen
3. Piping communicates changes to the affected discipline in a timely fashion
4. Interface problems between piping and architectural for indoor plants where the office is used to working on outdoor plants
5. Too much effort by pipe stress in analyzing non-critical lines
6. Multiplicity of piping material types

ELECTRICAL ENGINEERING

SPECIALTIES TYPICALLY INCLUDED: Electrical and electronic engineering, electronic communications systems.

SERVICES PROVIDED: Supervise all electrical engineering and related discipline efforts on project including scope clarification, staffing, discipline schedules. Indicate additional work and schedule time required by change orders.

Calculate voltage drops; make load studies; make short circuit calculations; calculate pulling tensions, duct bank heating, sag, and tension; specify temporary field power; coordinate with electric utility and with telephone company; make lighting calculations; review vendor drawings; and review model.

DOCUMENTS PRODUCED: All documents required for supervising the electrical engineering and related disciplines including finalizing the details of discipline work scopes, discipline work plan, staffing projections, discipline work schedules, change requests, and individual work assignments.

Electrical specifications; area classification drawings; single line electrical drawings; underground electrical drawings; grounding drawings; above ground power, lighting and instrument drawings; electrical subcontract specifications; requisitions for electrical equipment and materials; technical bid comparisons; communication drawings; connection wiring diagrams; alarm drawings (fire and security); cathodic protection drawings.

INTERFACES — INFORMATION COMES FROM:

Project	• Specific information about the project
Process	• Process description, PFDs and P&IDs
Licensor	• All licensing information and data
Process Control	• Written description of control philosophy
	• Control information on P&IDs
	• List of documentation to be provided by instrumentation discipline depending upon type of system
Piping	• Plot plan

Piping	• General arrangement sketches
	• Model or orthographic drawings
	• Electric heat tracing requirements

Piping
- General arrangement sketches
- Model or orthographic drawings
- Electric heat tracing requirements

Mechanical
- Equipment weights/other characteristics
- Motor lists

Civil
- Design drawings for site and site development, drainage, roads, railroads, walks and fences
- Platform designs
- Architectural drawings

Instrumentation
- Control room electrical/lighting requirements

Purchasing
- May be called upon to consult on special materials and equipment orders

INTERFACES — INFORMATION GOES TO: Project, process, mechanical, process control, civil, piping, mechanical, instrumentation, purchasing, and construction.

PROJECT MANAGEMENT CONCERNS: Areas where project management involvement is indicated include:

1. Issue purchase orders early for long lead time electrical switchgear, transformers and U/G cable
2. Projected use of existing substation facilities which prove to be inadequate
3. Delayed information from other disciplines affecting ordering major electrical equipment.
4. Difficulty of accelerating electrical field work and corresponding overall delayed job completion.

INSTRUMENTATION ENGINEERING

SPECIALTIES TYPICALLY INCLUDED: Instrumentation engineering, computer control, and electronic engineering.

SERVICES PROVIDED: Supervise all instrumentation engineering and related discipline efforts on project including scope clarification, staffing, and discipline schedules. Indicate additional work and schedule time required by change orders.

Make design calculations for control valves, relief valves, and rupture discs; specify materials of construction for instrument items; review vessel data sheets and drawings for proper instrument connections; review vendor drawings; review model; inspect panel boards, programmable controllers, and relay cabinets; make field instrument check.

DOCUMENTS PRODUCED: All documents required for supervising the instrument engineering and related disciplines including finalizing the details of discipline work scopes, discipline work plan, staffing projections, discipline work schedules, change requests and individual work assignments.

Instrument specifications; computer specification and software description; analyzer and sample conditioning specifications; logic diagrams and details; loop diagrams; connection wiring diagrams for instruments; instrument installation drawings; instrumentation subcontract specifications; requisitions for instruments and control equipment and materials; technical bid comparisons.

INTERFACES — INFORMATION COMES FROM:

Project	• Specific information about the project
Process	• Process description, PFDs and P&IDs
Process Control	• Written description of control philosophy
	• Control information on P&IDs
	• List of documentation to be provided by instrumentation discipline depending upon type of system
Licensor	• All licensing information and data
Piping	• Plot plan
	• General arrangement sketches

| **Piping** | • Model or orthographic drawings |

| **Mechanical** | • Equipment characteristics
• Motor lists |

| **Civil** | • Platform designs
• Architectural drawings |

| **Purchasing** | • May be called upon to consult on special materials and equipment orders |

INTERFACES — INFORMATION GOES TO: Project, process, mechanical, process control, electrical, civil, piping, mechanical, purchasing, and construction.

PROJECT MANAGEMENT CONCERNS: Areas where project management involvement is indicated include:

1. Issue purchase orders early for long lead time computer control equipment
2. Risk of component incompatibility with chosen system
3. If selected system is "first of a kind," a "prototype," or a "scale up" version, there may be many problems with pioneering detailed design
4. Difficulty of accelerating instrumentation work and corresponding overall delayed job completion

DETAILED ENGINEERING

The **process design should be frozen before production work/ detailed engineering starts.** The only changes that should be made after detailed engineering starts are those that mean that (1) the facility **will not operate** or will not meet guarantees unless the change is made; (2) the facility **will not operate safely** unless the change is made or (3) the change will mean a **substantial improvement in project schedule** or a **substantial reduction in the plant cost.**

PROJECT MANAGEMENT CONCERNS: During the detailed engineering phase of the project, the project manager must be concerned that there is no interruption to the rhythm of the work. The home office resources are being used at the maximum rate and productivity should be at its peak. Project engineers and scheduling personnel responsible for engineering discipline conformance to plan must follow the progress of the work with the discipline supervisors, realizing that any variance in performance will be difficult to recoup. During this phase the **process** and **process control** disciplines should be acting in advisory roles.

CLIENT RELATIONS: The project manager must communicate continuously with the client to make sure that there is an understanding about the status of the work. Problems must be dealt with in a timely manner. Decisions must be made promptly because of the effect a lagging decision will have on the work progress. The client should be discouraged from making changes because of the effect on schedule, cost, and morale.

MECHANICAL: There must be an effort to review and return all vendor drawings that have been forwarded for approval. Mechanical questions must be quickly resolved.

CIVIL: Considerable effort is necessary to produce the initial site development plans, the foundation and the underground drawings with all the information needed by the field in accordance with the schedule. Drawing completion should follow the priorities set in the project plan of execution. Expediting of missing vendor information or data required from other disciplines will be necessary. Bills of material for commodity materials must be kept current in accordance with the material control plan to assure a steady flow of these items to the field as they are needed.

ELECTRICAL: Information for underground installations should receive high priority as well as expediting vendor information for electrical equipment that is needed by electrical and the other involved disciplines. Frequently electrical staffing becomes a problem during the middle phases of production or detailed engineering.

INSTRUMENTATION: The vendor information should be expedited to permit production engineering/design/drafting to proceed according to the schedule.

CONSTRUCTION: Very close liaison must be maintained with the field forces. The home office engineers should be ready to interpret plans and specifications rapidly. Any problems encountered by field with errors, mismatches, or misfits must be addressed promptly to assist them in rectifying the mistakes with a minimum of lost effort.

JOB CLOSEOUT: On most projects the last ten percent of engineering is a very inefficient operation. There is an effort made to "gild the lily" as work on the production drawings comes to a close. For many engineers/designers/drafters there is a fear of the future at this time. They become concerned about the next assignment. Special attention must be given to individual supervision and work planning during the closeout of the detailing engineering effort.

On some projects, however, the opposite problem exists. In an effort to maintain budgets, people are taken off the job prematurely, before the cleanup work has been completed. Drawings have not been completely checked, calculations have not been readied for the project files, and material for operating and maintenance manuals has not been obtained. These situations create problems that make the project manager's life difficult; and proper provision has to be made in the work assignments to assure that these work items are finished.

VENDOR DRAWINGS

Vendor drawings may include general arrangement drawings, outlines, details, welding procedures, calculations, data sheets (including noise data sheets), and other documents specified in the purchase order. All of these may require approval prior to starting manufacture or fabricating of the material. In addition, performance curves, complete parts lists, list of recommended spare parts, instruction manuals, and certified data books should be submitted prior to shipping the item to the jobsite and certainly prior to submitting the final invoice for the order.

Within the engineering organization, there are **two primary considerations** involved in the vendor print process. These are (1) that the **project schedule is supported** by the approved or certified drawings and that they are available to use for the detailed structural, piping, electrical and instrument designs, and (2) to provide assurance that the vendor drawings **comply with the terms and conditions** of the purchase order.

TRACKING THE VENDOR DRAWING SCHEDULE: Issue dates for vendor prints required for approval and/or for downstream design should be issued with the purchase order. When the prints are received by the engineering office, they are distributed to the proper disciplines for review/ comments. For a larger project, a specified individual within the engineering office can be named to receive, track, expedite, and return the vendor drawings. In doing this he uses a schedule showing promised and actual dates of issue by the vendor, the date of return by the engineer of the approved (or approved with comments) drawings to the vendor, and the date of issue of the approved (or certified) vendor drawings for the downstream design. Tracking can be done manually for a small project or with a computerized program for a more complex project. Progress payments may be conditioned on satisfactory performance by the supplier. Final payment should not be made until all material for the manuals have been received as stipulated.

For critical path activities, it may be necessary to take extraordinary measure to expedite information from the vendors including sending engineers to the manufacturer's plant to obtain the information rapidly. Sometimes, the needed data is being held up pending completion of the entire package.

CHECKING THE VENDOR PRINTS: Some of the important points that must be checked are itemized in the following list. This list should not be considered complete, and the disciplines should add other items from experience. Based on his own knowledge the project manager should make sure that other trouble spots are adequately covered.

- **The Design Specifications for Rotating Equipment, Heat Transfer Equipment and Vessels and Tanks:** Check the the capacity, the applicable code requirements, the type of service, the operating conditions, the physical size, the materials of construction, linings and coatings, and accessories to be supplied with the order.

- **Structural Steel:** Check that connections are adequately dimensioned and identified as to size and type, and that the materials coatings are properly specified. Depending upon the understanding of the dimensioning responsibility, check or spot check member dimensions for compliance with information furnished in the purchase order.

- **The Mechanical Requirements for Piping:** Check that all piping connections are adequately dimensioned and identified as to size and type, and that the service is indicated as well as the design and operating pressures and temperatures.

- **The System Requirements for Piping:** Check that spools are designed in accordance with recommended piping details in the purchase order. Check that the item can be installed in the area provided. Will operation be possible with the item as designed?

- **The Electrical Requirements:** Check to see that the design is in accord with the applicable codes and with the provisions of the area classifications given in the purchase order. Make sure that the sizes, types and motor speeds are all in conformance with the specifications. Has the proper cooling been provided for the motors?

- **The Erection Requirements:** Check for any extraordinary measures required for lifting and/or erection of the equipment.

- **Maintenance Review:** Verify that the supplier will provide checkout and startup services if called for by the purchase order. Are warranties in accordance with those stipulated by the purchase order? Are the drawings necessary for maintenance, such as wiring diagrams and instrument wiring connection diagrams, included?

Once all of the disciplines have reviewed the drawings and any conflicts have been resolved, the final comments must be consolidated.

DOCUMENT CONTROL

The project manager has three principal interests in establishing and maintaining good document control and handling on his projects.

(1) **Effective communication** on the job. It is important that the project team knows the exact status of all of the activities on the project and that the summary of this information is available to the senior managements of the owner and the project management organization. This information is contained in the project documents.

(2) The ever-increasing need to be able to **reconstruct why certain decisions were made** as they were. Nowhere is this more important than in prudency audits being conducted in many of the larger projects completed in recent years. Each major decision may have to be justified by careful reconstruction based upon the documentation available long after the decisions were made.

(3) **Historical value** that the documentation may have in running and organizing future like jobs.

Effective document control assures that all of the contractual and procedural requirements are met during project execution while providing a ready answer as to the status of any of the myriad documents required.

There is a cost for maintaining good document control. This is an obvious cost. More subtle costs are those involved if good document control is not maintained. The cost of not having current information readily available can be very high in a rapidly moving project setting. A well-organized document control and retrieval system may save many times its original cost in the preparation necessary to defend or to initiate a legal action.

It is almost axiomatic that a well organized manner of handling the project documentation will reflect a job itself that is organized and well-run.

The first step in good document control must be that of optimizing the flow of the paperwork. An analysis must be made of the purpose of each major type of document and the people or organizations who are involved in producing, processing, expediting, reviewing, approving, acting upon, monitoring, current filing, retention filing, and disposing of all of this paper. The analysis is then translated into optimized **document control procedures** for the project.

SOME TYPICAL CANDIDATES FOR DOCUMENT CONTROL

- Incoming and outgoing correspondence
- Minutes of meetings where significant decisions were announced
- Licensor information and data
- Significant design calculations
- Specifications (various issues)
- Documentation relating to permitting
- Purchasing documentation
- Vendor prints (various issues)
- Design drawings (various issues) with particular attention to computer generated drawings where there may be many originals of the same drawing.
- Change order documentation
- Documents relating to possible claims from vendors/subcontractors
- Printed material for plant operating manuals, maintenance manuals, and the plant design manuals

SECURITY: Some of the documentation on a project may need to receive careful consideration with respect to control because of its confidential nature. For any such material, special procedures should be implemented so that each document is under the personal control of a specific individual. These procedures should be understood by all of those individuals entrusted with their care and custody.

PERMITS

The few project managers who have a knowledge of permitting requirements have learned by experience on other projects. There is little
academic training in permitting, although some general programs are
being presented. The project manager has the responsibility to see that
permitting on his project starts out right and continues to a successful
conclusion.

Federal, state, regional, and local requirements may be numerous
and not readily identifiable—which authorities are responsible, the
maze of legislation and regulations which may or may not be applicable,
and their sometimes complex interrelationships, all of which make a
plan for permitting necessary. Requirements for many of these permits
are very dynamic in nature. The basis for the permit may change before
the permit application can be filed, while the application is under consideration, or even after the permit has been granted but before the
facility is put into operation.

PERMITTING: A general discussion of permitting does not allow for too
many specific statements. The conditions are very different depending
upon type of facility, project location, and the number of jurisdictions
that may be involved.

In the United States, federal laws set certain standards with regard
to air and water quality. Some of these include the Clean Air Act, which
is administered and policed by the Environmental Protection Agency
(EPA). The Bureau of Land Management has jurisdiction over federally
owned land. The Army Corps of Engineers regulates the navigable
waters of the United States and the Fish and Wildlife Service protects
plants and animal life. Before construction of most facilities can be
started, an environmental impact statement must be filed before a
permit application will be considered.

State laws supplement the federal regulations and, in some cases,
provide even more stringent conditions on issuing permits for new
facilities.

Additionally there are regional and local regulations which may set
further conditions or impose further restrictions on new plant construction. Local interpretation of the regulations is subject to considerable variation. These differences can have a measurable effect on
project schedule and costs.

There are a multitude of minor permits including construction permits for demolition, grading, building, electrical, and use of public highways for transporting heavy or oversized loads. The need for this type of permit is frequently more obvious. These permits are usually obtained with less difficulty.

THE PERMITTING PLAN: The permitting plan should identify all of the presently identified individual permits which will be required in order to construct the contemplated facility. Where there is a some doubt as to the order in which the applications are to be entered, consultation with the various regulatory bodies is indicated. For complex permitting procedures, the assistance of a consultant with experience in the area may be advantageous.

Sufficient time should be budgeted for the steps of the permit approval. Of particular note are open meetings where public objections are heard. The postponement of these meetings to assemble additional information and data can cause project delays.

A large project planned for a jurisdiction with limited manpower causes a logjam. This can be partially overcome by working with the local authority and keeping them current on timing of the permit application and subsequent information which may be requested.

Close contact and an open posture should be maintained with the regulatory boards to assure that all bases are being covered in the permitting process. This runs counter to the nature of many project managers who resent the "interference" represented by regulatory conditions. In the long run, cost and schedule disruptions will be minimized.

INTERVENERS: Public groups or private citizens who have an interest in the project can be either "pro" or "con" on the project. The full extent of any sentiment against the project cannot be properly assessed until the public meetings are held. The project manager should never underestimate the power of an aroused public. There may be instances in which he will call upon the help of a public relations expert in dealing with the situation.

SAFETY CONSIDERATIONS

From the project manager's standpoint during the design phase of the project, safety means that the facility will be designed to eliminate or at least control the risk of loss of life, health, and well-being to the employees and to the public at large. This is a heavy responsibility, especially considering that the project manager is also under intense pressure to contain costs and maintain schedule, both of which are usually objectives opposed to consideration of safety concerns.

Safety begins with the selection of the technology to be used. The feedstocks selected and the intermediate products generated have a definite effect on the inherent safety.

Earthquakes, explosions, fires, floods, human errors, lightning, spills, storms, and structural failures all are on the list of root causes of safety problems in a plant. Sabotage and terrorism cannot be ignored either. Vapor clouds, combustible dust, and toxic or hazardous materials can contribute additional safety complications. Many accidents in a plant will occur when the plant operation is not steady—when the plant is starting up or shutting down—and this fact must be taken into account in the plant design. Certain items of equipment, particularly compressors, exchangers, furnaces, reactors, storage tanks, and towers, can present higher risks.

PLANT DESIGN: The plot plan must provide for special locations and separation of hazardous equipment. Proper diking and drainage is required to keep any fires as small as possible. Special attention is needed for design of utility plants, utility distribution systems, and control rooms. The design of the plant blowdown, flare, and relief systems is a primary factor in the ultimate safety of the installation. The specification of the proper material is a very important responsibility for the design engineer. Many accidents have occurred because of faulty material specification. The process control system and all instrumentation for the emergency shutdown and interlock systems are designed to protect life and property. Care should be used in the design of the systems and redundancy incorporated where particularly hazardous conditions might prevail.

RISK ANALYSIS: In order to **identify** the types of possible accidents a "fault tree" or "event tree" analysis is conducted. This is termed a **hazards and operability analysis** or **HAZOP analysis.** This analysis is carried out by a team, the leader of which is experienced in the methodology together with others who have a technical background in the process under study.

In order to **quantify** the frequency of types of accidents and their consequences, a method of the probability assessment has been developed called **probabilistic risk assessment (PRA)**.

Very often these come too late in the design phase and protective measures have to be added to compensate for lapses. If the reviews were held earlier, there is a better possibility that the hazards themselves could be removed. Coming late in the design phase, the changes introduced as a result cause confusion and delay in the design process. Making the risk analysis for the project an on-going process and scheduling the formal HAZOP analysis earlier will alleviate many of the negative aspects of this management tool. Risk analysis has developed to a much greater degree in the nuclear plant industry than in other types of project management endeavors.

DESIGN STANDARDS: Many companies have their own safety design standards. In addition, there are industry standards such as those issued by the American Petroleum Institute (API), the Chlorine Institute, the American Society of Mechanical Engineers (ASME), the National Electrical Code, and the Chemical Manufacturers Association (CMA). Insurance groups have additional standards available such as those issued by the American Insurance Association, Factory Mutual Systems, National Board of Fire Underwriters (NBFU), and the Industrial Risk Insurers. Also important to design engineers are the National Fire Codes by the National Fire Protection Association (NFPA). Many design standards are published in local, state, and federal government regulations. In the United States many of these are promulgated in the Occupational Safety and Health Administration (OSHA).

PROJECT MANAGEMENT CONCERNS: The project manager cannot be expected to be personally cognizant of the intricacies of each of these areas; but he must understand where risks are possible and make sure that these risks are being analyzed, quantified, and managed in a manner commensurate with the objectives of the project and the policies of the firms involved.

⑨ MATERIALS MANAGEMENT

BASIC PRINCIPLES OF PROCUREMENT

Procurement in the past was a very fractured activity, split between the engineering, purchasing and construction organizations. In very recent years, all of the procurement activities on projects are being placed under the control of a manager. This combined effort effort is called **materials management.**

The major individual components of materials management shown in the accompanying summary flow chart include (1) **requisitioning,** including specifying, designing and material takeoffs, (2) **inquiry,** (3) receipt of **vendor offers,** (4) technical and commercial **bid analyses,** (5) **bid conditioning,** (6) issuing **purchase orders,** (7) **expediting vendor documents,** (8) **expediting vendor orders,** (9) **inspection** during manufacture/fabrication, (10) **shop testing/acceptance,** (11) **traffic** or transport of the material from the plant/shop to the jobsite, (12) **receipt** of the material at the jobsite, and (13) **closeout of purchase orders.**

The scheduled smooth and uninterrupted flow of material to the jobsite represents a very important determinant of project success. The cost of efforts spent to achieve this goal are well invested. Innovative ways to solve project procurement problems must be considered.

Tradeoffs are necessary. The cost of double handling material which has arrived at the jobsite early is balanced against the risk of the field forces having to wait for a delayed shipment. The cost of paying for equipment and material early has to balanced against not having the material when it is needed.

For projects with short schedules, procurement of long lead time equipment and commodities has been accelerated by:

> **Sole source, negotiated purchases** to eliminate the time required for competitive bidding

> Use of **surplus or used equipment or materials** to eliminate manufacturing fabrication time

> **Paying a premium** to the manufacturer/fabricator for extra shifts or move up in a queue

181

MATERIAL MANAGEMENT ACTIVITIES

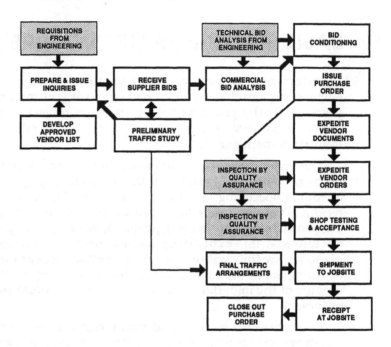

PURCHASING

PLANNING THE PURCHASING EFFORT: Because of its criticality to the success of the project, the entire procurement effort must be planned, starting with purchasing. The project itself is planned beginning with sequencing of construction. Purchasing on large jobs is usually divided into three specialties: (1) **equipment;** (2) **commodity materials** and (3) **subcontracts.** Personnel experienced in each of these areas work almost solely with their individual specialties. On smaller projects, generalists handle all areas of purchasing. The purchasing plan sets forth the strategy and program of buying for the project. It covers several aspects of the purchasing effort including these listed below:

- **The Material Coordination Plan (MCP)** is issued with the purchasing plan. The MCP is a chart that designates the organization responsible for purchasing each grouping or classification of equipment and material required for the project. The MCP is in sufficient detail to stipulate each item to be provided by the owner, a specific department of the E/C firm, the managing contractor, or the subcontractor.

- **Approved List of Vendors:** The purchasing organization is generally responsible for developing a list of those vendors which are approved to supply the various equipment items, commodity materials, and subcontracts. Approvals are based upon previous performance, reputation or track record, financial capability, appropriate facilities, and the like.

- **Modules, Preassembly, and Skid Mounted Equipment:** A definite project policy must be adopted regarding modularization and the use of preassembled or skid mounted equipment. For some projects a high degree of offsite work will be required.

- **Engineering by Vendor:** Some items of equipment and material specialties where detailed engineering might best be left to the vendor would include (1) packaged systems or skid mounted units that are customarily designed and furnished by the fabricator, (2) fire protection and sprinkler systems inside of buildings, (3) detailing of structural steel, (4) detailing of reinforcing bars, (5) detailing of pipe spools from isometric drawings, and, sometimes, the isometric drawings themselves, if the engineer is producing only piping plans and elevations, (6) prefabricated buildings, and (7) mechanical conveying systems.

- **Standardization/Blanket Purchase Orders:** It is generally advantageous from a cost standpoint to standardize upon certain equipment/commodity material items. As soon as the individual items can be identified, these can be placed early in the purchasing cycle on a blanket order without a knowledge of the exact quantities. Only a few of the possible areas for standardization would include: (1) structural shapes, (2) pipe, (3) valves, (4) piping fittings, (5) instruments, (6) motors, (7) electrical materials, and (8) small pumps.

- **Shop vs. Field Fabrication:** A general philosophy about shop vs. field fabrication should be made early in the planning process. The decisions are based upon facility location, availability and cost of skilled field labor, productivity, union regulations, and schedule. Companies use standard terms and conditions on their purchase orders; these should always be reviewed to assure that they are appropriate for the project at hand.

- **Request for Proposals:** The purchasing plan should include the format for the bid requests if the standard company format is not to be used. There should also be a schedule for sending the critical orders out for bid.

- **Receipt of Bids:** Sufficient time should be allowed for the bidders to gather the information needed for pricing the order. There should be strong insistence on the bids being submitted on time. Once you allow a bidder to deviate from the due date on one order, no vendor will give future bids the attention and priority that you desire.

- **Commercial Bid Tabulations:** Two aspects are of importance: (1) confidentiality and (2) honesty. Any penalties to be assessed to certain vendors for anticipated additional effort on the part of the buyer in expediting, inspection, and engineering for the order should be quantified prior to the bid due date and opening the bids.

- **Bid Conditioning:** The successful vendor should be called to a meeting during which loose ends or changes which have occurred since the last communication are resolved and supplementary pricing agreed to. Any doubts still existing should be clarified.

EXPEDITING

Expediting includes the activities designed to assure that the delivery terms of the purchase orders are met and that there is a steady and properly sequenced flow of information to the engineering office and equipment and materials to the job site.

TYPES OF EXPEDITING: Expediting is done using two methods. Many of the expediting activities are accomplished by routinely checking order status by **telephone**. This is also known as **desk expediting**. The other method involves **actual visits** to the plant or shop. This is **source expediting** often referred to as "**kicking iron**" — or actually seeing what has been done and what is going on. Additionally, for very critical orders, the expeditor may be responsible for **subcomponent** expediting. This consists of expediting the suppliers to the prime vendor.

Expediting by actual visits may also be classified as being of one of two types: **project oriented** or **area oriented.** A project oriented expeditor may be assigned to a specific plant or visit only specific plants to expedite orders for a single project. This would be especially true for a project on a very tight schedule and for extremely critical orders. Normally, expeditors live and work in areas with high concentrations of industry. These expeditors might cover several shops in the area expediting orders for multiple projects. The frequency of their visits depends upon the criticality of the order, the performance history of the vendor, and the magnitude and complexity of the order.

EXPEDITING INTERFACES: Expediting must work closely with project management, planning and scheduling, engineering, purchasing, traffic, inspection, and construction, in addition to the various vendors and suppliers.

The area expeditor is responsible for determining the precise individual in each vendor's organization who can effectively solve the problem at hand. He must also be able to escalate the resolution up the vendor's chain of command if it is necessary to do so. The expeditor has a great deal of power that can be used to obtain the desired results including threats to defer payments and recommend against future orders.

One factor, often overlooked, is that the expeditor must have immediate knowledge of any order, partial order, or critical component that is rejected by inspection. This is important to give as much time as possible to the shop to come up with acceptable alternatives.

Unforeseen delays to completion of orders may come from many sources.   Strikes at the vendor's shop, shops of the subcomponent suppliers, or transportation companies are often the cause of delays. Smaller vendors may have a cash flow problem leading to delays in completing the work. Lost shipments may also cause delays. Changes by the client or the design office will create havoc with the schedule. The expeditor must also be on the alert to find ways to offset the effects of these problems.

Expeditors are responsible for monitoring the flow of engineering documents to the vendor. The expeditor watches the scheduled flow of documents from the vendor to the project and expedites the return of those documents submitted by the vendor for project approval. Expediting identifies schedule and commitment problems and sees that the proper corrective action has been initiated. The expeditor must move quickly to resolve any problem that will delay delivery of any document or purchased item, which in turn will delay completion of the project. He cannot afford to wait for things to improve.

EXPEDITING REPORTS: Each expeditor prepares reports on telephone contacts or visits to shops or plants. These in turn feed information into project material status reports, which are summarized to provide cogent information for the project material manager and the project manager.

Most companies with heavy procurement responsibilities are using computerized material tracking programs, many with "on-line" information entering capabilities. These may use satellite telecommunication networks employing terminals in the design office, the jobsite and international procurement offices. These systems provide for multiple sorting capability to produce exception reports of various types.

TRAFFIC

Traffic as a project discipline is concerned with the development of appropriate and cost effective means of coordinating shipment and deliveries from the point of manufacture or fabrication to the jobsite. Planning for these activities is started early in the project as it is an integral part of the evaluating the vendors' bids.

BID EVALUATIONS: Material and equipment costs should normally be FOB at the plant or shop with the transportation costs kept separately. There are certainly exceptions to this guideline; but the project should be approached initially on this basis. Freight is a very significant portion of the total cost of much of the equipment and materials used on a project. Mass shipments to a single site invite many opportunities to save money on transport costs. Freight costs should always be considered when evaluating a supplier's bid. It often happens that the difference in freight costs will determine the successful vendor.

PLANNING: There are three modes of transport available that should be considered for almost any project: **water, land,** and **air**. In many cases the selected means of transport will be a combination of two of these modes.

Water transport include ships, smaller vessels and barges of various types. If water transport is possible, it is generally the cheapest. Land transport includes rail, truck, van, off-road vehicles and special transporters. At least a portion of the transport on most projects will be by land. Air transport for a project generally involves either a plane or a helicopter although balloons have been considered for some special applications. Air transport is usually the most expensive as well as being the fastest.

How the particular shipment will be made depends upon several factors: (1) the location of the project and its proximity to navigable waters, rail lines, highways and airports, (2) the urgency attached to delivery of the particular piece of equipment/item of material, (3) the comparative cost of the various types of transportation available, (4) the configuration, outside limits, and weight of the shipment, and (5) total quantity of material to be transported.

Transport of hazardous materials poses special problems for the traffic organization. Help is available from the vendors and from various industry sources as well as from specialists in the transportation of these materials.

Heavy lifts and difficulties in transporting modules and partially assembled systems require the intervention of safety specialists. The traffic organization should not be reluctant to call upon this resource as needed.

The traffic organization must also make route surveys where relocation of overhead lines and removal of obstructions along roadsides will be required. Identification of load limitations with regard to maximum sizes and weights is necessary. Height restrictions at over- or underpasses often dictate maximum diameter of towers and vessels.

Special attention must be given to the timing of the receipt of equipment and material at the jobsite. Timing of shipments must be coordinated to preclude having to handle demands of heavy lifts or other difficult unloading situations on the same day.

CUSTOMS DECLARATIONS AND DUTY: On international projects, the formalities of coordination with export and import regulations can be a major problem. For companies that do not do considerable overseas business, these activities might best be left to brokers practiced in handling this type of documentation. This is particularly true in situations where certain payments that must be made are better included as part of overall fees to a customs broker.

TRANSPORT OF HEAVY LOADS: With shipment of modules to the North Slope and transport of very large, heavy prefabricated towers to the jobsites, there have been very great advances in capabilities of specially designed transporters. Sometimes it pays to custom design heavy crawlers to handle a particular module or piece of equipment. Less than forty years ago the limit for an offshore lift was 200 tons. Modules for offshore platforms are now exceeding 7000 metric tons in weight and this certainly will not be the final word. The North Sea operations have been the center of offshore development.

RECEIPT OF MATERIAL

Delivery of the proper quantities of material to the jobsite at the proper time is essential to maximum field productivity. Integration of the field materials with the responsibilities of the home office materials organization promotes project efficiency. The interfaces must be clear.

The field materials organization has the responsibility for checking deliveries, on-site inspection and for making sure that the materials are correctly identified, tagged, and stored until they are needed.

SHORT SHIPMENTS: If there are shortages in the shipment when received, these must be reported to the shipper and the corresponding claims made. If there are variations from the specifications, restitution and/or substitution must also be pursued.

FIELD INVENTORY: A field inventory must be maintained of all material in stock. Inventories are increased with deliveries and reduced as the material is issued to the field fabrication or erection crews. Commonly, the warehouse will also presort and bag or bundle items which will be used together; for example all bolting and gasket material for each flanged connection would be bagged prior to being issued to the user.

MATERIAL CARE: One of the most important responsibilities of the field material organization is the proper care for warehoused equipment and materials. Materials which must be stored under cover must be segregated from those that are stored outside. All materials must be stored so that they are secure from theft and proper security measures taken to prevent this type of loss.

ISSUING MATERIALS: Using the field planning documents, the area and craft priorities, and the material status reports, the field materials organization will verify that all equipment and material needed for upcoming work is presently in stock or that it is scheduled to arrive in time for the work to be done. Any shortages will be reported to expediting for immediate action or to field purchase to complete the required stocks. Priorities for allocating material will usually have been set in the field work plans and the field material organization will issue material in accordance with these. Any conflicts in priorities must be resolved by the superintendent responsible for the work.

SHORTAGES/SURPLUSES: Short term shortages and surpluses of material will become apparent from the forecasts of material requirements. Material which is short can be expedited or field purchased, or the work can be temporarily scheduled around the missing material. These instances must be predicted as much in advance as possible in order to maintain field productivity. Surplus material stems from erroneous takeoffs or overly generous allowances for waste and losses, from installation of the wrong material and from changes made too late to cancel the shipment of the original requirements

In each case of surplus, a decision must be made as to the appropriate method of disposal. Some purchase orders call for return of surplus "off the shelf" items to the supplier, usually at a discounted price. Sometimes the owner will transfer surplus material into operating stock for replacement or for use on other projects. Most of the time, surplus material will be disposed of at the end of the job at distress prices. The risk of running short of material must be balanced against the cost of ending up with a surplus.

SPECIAL SITUATIONS: For a congested site, the warehouse is sometimes established offsite at a staging area. A separate warehouse location requires very close coordination between the crews and the materials organization in daily planning of the work to assure that the materials and tools will be available as required.

For international projects, one or more staging or marshalling sites may be established where material is received and held prior to shipment to the jobsite. Material control is particularly important at this stage as the delivery times are increased and most of the material required will not be available locally even in cases of emergency. An online computerized tracking system for equipment and materials from the material takeoff through all of the purchasing and delivery steps is very useful.

PURCHASE ORDER CLOSEOUT

Closing out a purchase order formally is an anticlimactic chore for the material organization; but it represents a potentially expensive and unnecessary risk if it is not done correctly and in a timely manner. Closing out a purchase order requires an audit of the vendor's performance and his compliance with the purchase order vis-à-vis the terms that were agreed upon.

CHECKLIST FOR CLOSING OUT PURCHASE ORDERS: Each of the following steps is necessary to properly close out a purchase order. More steps may be involved if the project coordination procedures call for them so it is always important to check for these also.

- **Quality:** Before the purchase order can be closed out, there must be documented verification that the quality of all of the material furnished is in strict accordance with the terms and conditions of the purchase order and the specifications included.

- **Quantities:** Written verification of the receipt of all of the material included by the purchase order must be at hand when the purchase order is closed out.

- **Compliance with Code Requirements:** Where code conformance is specified, a written statement should be included in the purchase order file.

- **Compliance with Delivery Terms:** The material should have been delivered in accordance with the terms and conditions of the purchase order. Adjustments should be made for any penalties set forth in the purchase order, as well as for any bonuses for early delivery.

- **Certified Vendor Drawings:** All certified vendor drawings called for by the purchase order should have been received and a written acknowledgement made to that effect.

- **Code Certifications:** Code certificates stipulated by the purchase order for material and equipment should have been received and copies placed in the purchase order file.

- **Operating Instructions:** The proper number of copies of all operating instructions specified by the purchase order should have been received.

- **Maintenance Instructions:** The proper number of copies of all maintenance instructions specified by the purchase order should have been received.

- **Spare Parts Lists:** The proper number of copies of all spare parts lists required by the purchase order should have been received.

- **Guarantees and Warranties:** All guarantees and warranties required by the purchase order should have been received. Where performance tests are required, these should have been completed and approved by the competent authority and written certification placed in the file.

- **Vendors' Claims:** No vendor claims should be left pending. All vendor claims should be resolved prior to closing out the purchase order.

- **Back Charges:** Back charges to the vendor should have been processed and accepted in accordance with the purchase order terms prior to closing out the purchase order.

- **Changes/Supplements:** All changes or supplements to the purchase order should be processed and approved prior to closing out the purchase order. This means that all of the payments to the vendor will be covered by authorizations by the proper signing authority.

- **Release from Liens:** If required by the terms of the purchase order, the vendor should furnish release from mechanic's liens and from subcomponent suppliers.

- **Negotiation:** Where there have been claims, back charges, previously undocumented changes, and variations from the guarantees or warranties, then negotiation may be required to resolve the differences prior to closing out the purchase order. It is important that the end results of any negotiation be properly documented and approved.

- **Verification of Approval Authority:** Prior to closing out the purchase order, the material manager should verify that all authorization documents have been signed by the proper authority.

- **Verification of Amount of Final Payment:** The amount of the final payment should be carefully checked to make sure that it is accurate. Unintentional overpayments are difficult and time consuming to recoup. The time required to check is a good investment.

10 CONSTRUCTION MANAGEMENT

CONTRACTUAL ALTERNATIVES

Three types of contractual configurations commonly used for engineering and construction projects are:

THE DESIGN/BUILD (D/B) OR DESIGN/CONSTRUCT CONTRACT: The contract is **directly between the owner and the contractor**. The contractor performs all of the work either with his own employees or through his own contracts with subcontractors.

- **Advantages:** Implies a single source of responsibility to the owner. The owner has one single contract with the D/B contractor. All other contracts are let by the D/B contractor. Provides the best environments for fast tracking a project.

- **Disadvantages:** Owner probably has less influence in decisions affecting the project than in other arrangements. Costs may be higher than with other contractual configurations. Conflicts can arise within the contractor's organization between engineering and construction.

THE GENERAL CONTRACTOR (G/C) ARRANGEMENT: The owner does the engineering or has the engineering performed on a fee basis, and has a contract with the general contractor for the site work. All field work is done by direct hire employees of the general contractor or by his own contracts with subcontractors.

- **Advantages:** Provides additional safeguards on cost and schedule conformance over the D/B arrangement. Owner has more direct control over the work. Provides documentation for rigorous competitive bidding for construction. This form is generally used for government work where firm-priced competitive bids are required.

- **Disadvantages:** Direct coordination with the general contractor is more difficult for the engineer/designer. This may lead to higher costs and a longer schedule.

THE CONSTRUCTION MANAGEMENT (C/M) ARRANGEMENT: The owner has a **fee basis contract with the architect/engineer for the engineering and a fee basis contract with the construction management firm for the jobsite management.** The field work is all subcontracted to specialty subcontractors. These subcontracts are let by the construction manager as agent for the owner. **The actual subcontracts are between the owner and the subcontractor.**

- **Advantages:** The owner has more voice in decision making process. This arrangement has the best features of both D/B and G/C configurations, matching the project technology capability of the construction management firm with the skills of the specialty subcontractors. This form may be most cost effective.

- **Disadvantages:** Takes more time than other configurations. Owner assumes more risk and requires more owner resources than the D/B approach.

CONTRACTUAL ALTERNATIVES

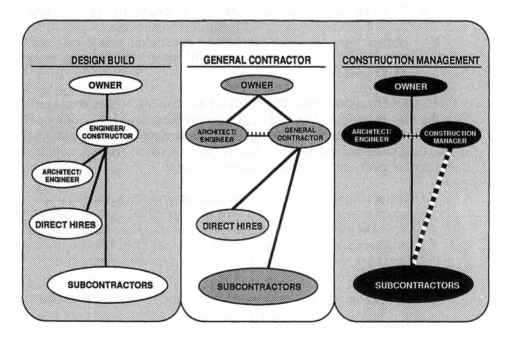

CONSTRUCTION MANAGEMENT

Construction management is sometimes used interchangeably with **project management**. Here, however, we will refer to construction management (CM) as the responsibility for **management of the site work**, including letting the construction subcontracts for the owner and coordinating and administering all aspects of the execution of these subcontracts acting as the owner's agent.

Construction management (CM) is sometimes done directly by the owner's organization; but, more often, it is assigned to a firm specializing in CM. This firm, acting as the owner's agent, may have a more positive relationship with the owner's organization than might be true with the standard general contractor or with a design/build contractor.

Construction management differs from the general contractor's role. The latter does most of the work by direct hire workers or by direct subcontracting. It also differs from the design/build relationship, where single authority is given to a single firm.

The trend today for many uncomplicated projects is toward a CM arrangement with subcontractors doing the field work, rather than using a general construction contractor.

SOME OF THE MANY POSITIVE REASONS FOR THE CM APPROACH

- By selecting three or four competent and competitive subcontractors to bid on each of the defined work scopes, it is easier to get a lower lump sum price.

- Specialty subcontractors resident in the area can normally be expected to have the best skilled and most stable craftsmen on their payrolls.

- Following the CM concept, modern planning, scheduling and cost containment techniques furnished by the construction manager may be used in conjunction with the best and most cost effective contracts with, in turn, the best specialty subcontractors using the most skilled craftsmen.

- Costs are optimized using the CM approach because bid packages are smaller, are better defined and attract more competitive bids as the smaller specialty contractors are included on the bid lists.

SOME NEGATIVE ASPECTS OF THE CM APPROACH

- Because well-defined bid packages are needed, the time required to design and build the facility is longer than for other approaches.

- In a very competitive situation, the owner can frequently offload some of the risk onto a general contractor. This would not be true in the same sense when using the CM approach.

- There is no one point of independent single cost responsibility in the CM approach other than the owner because of the way that the contracts are written.

TYPES OF CONTRACTS

There are various types of contracts which may be used with the contractual alternatives available to the project manager.

TURNKEY CONTRACT: This is a **distinction of the scope** of the contract. It does not refer to the commercial terms. There is a **single responsibility** for the work. It is used with a D/B configuration. The other types, listed below, are **commercial distinctions.**

LUMP SUM CONTRACT: This is a commercial distinction which refers to the fact that all of the work included in the contract will be done by the contractor for a predetermined and agreed to price. A great deal of risk is assumed by the contractor. A very well defined scope of work is required in order to properly use this type of contract.

- **Bid:** The lump sum contract is generally bid by three to five bidders and is based on firm scope and specifications. For a large, complicated project the preparation of the bid is an expensive proposition. The owner should not request any more bids than are absolutely necessary to achieve his purpose of getting a good competitive price from a qualified contractor.

- **Negotiated:** If getting a project completed as soon as possible is the primary objective or if there is only a single qualified contractor for the work, then a negotiated, lump sum price may be indicated.

- **Multiple Fixed Priced:** Here the contract duration is short. Small specialty subcontractor capability can be well utilized. Subcontractor coordination between several subs may be difficult.

UNIT PRICE CONTRACT: Where quantities are not well defined, but the individual operations are known, the owner may award a contract based upon firm specifications plus a fixed unit price for each type of work.

REIMBURSABLE CONTRACT: This type of contract is used when the scope is not well defined and/or the owner is willing to assume most of the risk. All of the contractor's costs are reimbursed in accordance with the provisions of a checklist of his costs. The reimbursable contract is usually bid on the basis of actual costs plus a checklist and markups. It may be negotiated if time is important as in getting a facility back on stream after an accident or if only a single qualified contractor is available in the area. A portion of the costs may be fixed where they can be defined. This type of contract is known as a **"partial fix."**

- **Cost Plus Percentage Fee:** Calls for reimbursement of all costs plus a fixed percentage of the contractor's expenditures to be paid as a fee or profit.

- **Cost Plus Fixed Fee:** Substitutes a fixed fee based upon projected expenditures rather than a percentage fee. Construction indirects are often included as a fixed price. This encourages the contractor to achieve higher productivity and reduce time in the field.

- **Guaranteed Maximum Price:** A reimbursable contact is occasionally converted at some time after award to a guaranteed maximum price (GMP). The price is based upon a new estimate prepared after additional definition has been reached. The job is executed as a reimbursable job. If the GMP is exceeded, the additional costs may be entirely for the account of the contractor. If the job underruns there may or may not be a sharing of the savings.

- **Target Price:** Similar to a GMP. A target price is set and the overruns and underruns are shared according to a set or a predetermined sliding formula. There is usually no ceiling set on a target price contract.

CONTRACTING STRATEGY

Any type of contract can be used for any type of work. Strategy involves the systematic selection of the type of contract best suited for the work under consideration. There are seven factors that will usually be the major influence on the optimum type of contract.

1. **Degree of Definition:** Increased degree of definition favors lump sum or hard money contracts. A loose definition encourages consideration of a reimbursable contract.

2. **Economic Conditions:** If the economic cycle is on the high side and work is plentiful for contractors and their suppliers, it is difficult to get bids on a hard money contract. If work is scarce then you can always find bidders for the work.

3. **Competitive Situation:** This factor ties in closely with economic conditions. If there are contractors hungry for work, this would favor lump sum contracting. If there is a lot of work, it may be difficult to find qualified lump sum bidders. There will be cases where a lack of qualified contractors with suitable experience in a particular geographic area will preclude getting meaningful hard money quotations.

4. **Anticipated Changes to Scope:** If many changes are expected on a job, it is best to let that job on a reimbursable basis. The owner will have much better control over the costs. With a hard money job, bid tightly on a competitive basis, the contractor will certainly tend to price his extras higher. This owner will have lost much of his negotiating advantage after the initial contract has been let.

5. **Schedule Importance:** If the schedule is an important consideration, a negotiated contract may be indicated. This approach can cut the schedule from one to five months or more. The longest schedule would be for a lump sum bid where bid documents have to be prepared and a minimum of two to four months allowed for bidding and bid evaluation.

6. **Total Cost Importance:** If containing cost is the most important factor, a phased project with a series of lump sum bids based on a complete bid package will probably be most appropriate. This method gives the most positive assurance of maintaining the budget.

7. **Quality Importance:**   If quality is the prime consideration, there is usually one contractor who stands above the crowd who should be chosen.   Faced with this situation, the owner can ill afford risking a contractor with less than the very best credentials.   A negotiated reimbursable contract might be the most appropriate here. Only if there are more than two excellent contractors available should other types of contracts be considered.

BIDDER SELECTION

Two of the most important decisions to be made during a project are **who should be on the bid list for work to be contracted out**, and **how should the final selection be made.** Both of these decisions can have far-reaching cost and schedule implications for the project.

PLANNING: The bidding process plan will be an extension of the execution plan. Many companies have a standardized bidding procedure, but even so, the project manager should make sure that it represents the best approach for his particular project. Sometimes corporate standards are out of date or otherwise not in tune with the economic conditions and competitive situation. How much effort the owner will spend on the bidder qualification has to be defined.

THE BID PACKAGE: The project manager must see that a great deal of care is given to the bid package to make sure that it fully describes the contemplated work, and that it prescribes a bid in the form that will facilitate the evaluation and comparison.

PREQUALIFICATION: Among the major prequalification requirements are (1) the contractor's interest in bidding the work, (2) the contractor's financial position, (3) qualified personnel to do the work and capacity for the job, (4) experience in the type of work, (5) experience with the owner on other jobs, (7) good procedures for scheduling, cost containment, and change order management, and (8) good records in labor relations, job safety, and quality work.

SELECTION OF BIDDERS: After interviews have been held with the leading contenders, the successful slate of bidders will be chosen based on their demonstration of proficiency in the above eight areas and any other areas determined to be critical to the contract at hand. The final bid list should normally consist of three to five bidders for lump sum work, and six to eight for reimbursable contracts.

THE BID PROCESS: If the bid package has been properly prepared, the bid form is clear, and sufficient time allowed for bidding, there should be few problems. Site visits and a prebid conference with all prospective bidders represented are both very helpful in getting responsible and responsive bids. Lump sum bids require a substantial amount of money to prepare. If there are too many bidders on a lump sum job, it represents a waste for the contractors and the owner will have more difficulty in evaluation. A standard bid form will expedite matters considerably.

SELECTING THE CONTRACTOR: The evaluation of the bids should be done fairly. Bid evaluation will be straightforward if the preceding work has been well done. In most cases, cost will represent the basic criterion for job award together with the prequalification factors. These will be weighted in accordance with their relationship to the project objectives. The owner, in order to place all of the contractors on the same basis, may assess penalties on certain bidders to allow for perceived differences in performance. These penalties should be determined before the bids are opened, should be fully documented with the corresponding justifications, quantified, and applied during the evaluation.

THE OWNER'S RISKS

When undertaking a capital project, the risks all lie with the owner. During the project, the owner will attempt to delegate or pass along some of these risks to the joint venture partner, co-investor, licensor, engineering and/or construction contractor, a bonding company or an insurer.

If the owner chooses to pass along a risk, he must also pass along the control of the elements which influence the probabilities that the risk will occur. Compensation will have to be provided if someone else is to assume the risk.

The probability of incurring risk is much greater when the project involves new technology. Prototype projects or **"first of a kind"** are risky. The **"largest of a kind"** presents a risk when greater than normal scaleups are required. Abnormal risks may be present when any area of the technology is unfamiliar.

Risk management involves:

1. **Identifying the area of the risk**
2. **Elimination of the risk, if possible**
3. **Consideration of transferring of the risk, if this is economically attractive**
4. **Reducing the risk, if it cannot be eliminated or transferred**

In spite of all efforts, **some risk will always be present**.

Some of the areas of risk that are of concern to a project manager include the following:

- That the scope definition will be inadequate
- That there will be inordinate changes in scope
- That the technical engineering design will be inadequate
- That there will be an inordinate escalation of labor and/or material costs
- That the technical adequacy of equipment selected will be deficient
- That the completed plant will not perform as required
- That the completion date will not be met
- That the lump sum price will exceed the budget
- That field productivity will not be as projected
- That illegal labor strikes or interruptions will occur

- That some instance of force majeure or act of God will disrupt the project
- That a fire or other disaster will occur
- That normal security will prove to be inadequate

A company that is unwilling to take risks, whether it be an owner or a contractor, always faces another risk. The risk that it will be a "no growth" company, a company that allows no creativity or innovation and, as a result, can expect no market expansion. Protection against risk does not mean the total elimination of risk, but rather the intelligent management to keep risk within allowable limits.

INSURANCE

A project manager relies on insurance experts to provide his project with adequate coverage. Insurance is a complex subject, is constantly changing and is best left to the professionals. General concepts are important to the project manager enabling him to discuss the subject intelligently with the assigned insurance representative. He must maintain this contact throughout the project.

PURPOSE OF INSURANCE: Insurance is used to transfer some of the risks of project work to others. On large projects, the insurance coverage provided by policies held by the owner, licensor, architect/ engineer, constructor and subcontractors often provides duplicate coverage. Conversely, there may be serious gaps in the coverage.

INSURANCE MANAGEMENT: The owner must take the lead in managing insurance. He must recognize exposures on the job and attempt to avoid duplicate coverage. An effective insurance model charts and assigns all of the desired coverage or a definite portion of the coverage to each of the participating parties.

Insurance costs are not the same: policies differ, rates differ, and deductibles may be modified. If the owner transfers the insurance responsibility, he must expect to compensate those parties who assume the delegated risk. The architect/engineer, the contractor, and the subcontractor must analyze the insurance plan to make sure that their firms have adequate coverage in terms of their own corporate practices.

COMMON TYPES OF INSURANCE:

- Errors and omissions insurance
- Builders' risk insurance
- Umbrella general liability
- Professional liability insurance
- Performance quarantee policy
- Consequential damages
- Consequential loss or business interruption
- Automobile insurance
- Workers' compensation

THINGS TO WATCH OUT FOR:

- The owner's project manager must obtain insurance certificates from each contractor affirming the level of coverage as stipulated by the contract.

- The owner should agree to waive all claims against the contractor in the event that   damage is done to property which is covered by the owner's existing policies.

- Some owners are providing what is called a "wrap-up" policy which is intended to cover all insurance requirements. Contractors are requested to reduce their bids accordingly. The contractor's life is complicated by having to search out those areas where he still has exposure.

- To improve coordination of insurance coverage, **contractors' all risk (CAR) insurance**, has been used in international work. This type of policy ties into the umbrella general liability, with the builders risk, and sometimes with professional liability policies. The CAR has begun to find increased use in the domestic market.

SURETY BONDS

The owner tries to reduce his overall risk on the project by transferring some of the risk to others. One of the ways this can be done is by requiring a surety bond to cover the risk in question. Surety bonds are issued by surety companies or by insurance companies. The contractor obtains the bond, but whether he is working on a reimbursable contract or on a lump sum contract, the cost of these bonds has to be passed on to the owner.

The bonding requirement provides an additional pre-screening for the subcontractors since a reliable bonding company will not bond a financially unstable contractor.

FOUR OF THE MOST IMPORTANT SURETY BONDS

- **Bid Bonds:** An owner or general contractor may suffer a loss if the selected bidder refuses to sign a contract. The owner or G/C may require a deposit, usually five or ten percent of the amount of the bid from all bidders. The deposit would be refunded to all bidders; however, the selected bidder's deposit will be retained if he decides to walk away from the bid. The bid bond is an alternative to the deposit. A bid bond guarantees that the bidder will sign an agreement to do the work at the bid price and under the conditions stipulated should he be selected to perform the work.

- **Performance Bonds:** One of the owner's risks is that the work will not be completed as called for by the contract. He may try to transfer this risk, or a portion of it, to an insurance or surety company by means of a performance bond. The contractor may be faced with a disaster or some unforeseen obstacle and insolvency may result. In this case, the surety company would take over and complete the work.

  The cost of the performance bond is ultimately paid for by the owner. The surety company, in case of the contractor's default, will normally complete the work using another contractor.

- **Payment Bonds:** If a contractor does not pay for his labor and material costs, the owner may be subjected to a mechanic's lien which imposes an encumbrance on the property. The owner can protect against this risk by withholding a part of the payments due the contractor until job completion as a fund to pay these costs. Alternatively, he may require a payment bond which guarantees that the surety company will pay the labor and supplier costs that the contractor has not paid.

* **Maintenance Bonds:** The owner runs a risk of the plant not operating satisfactorily after startup. To transfer this risk, he may withhold money from the contractor's final payment in order to assure the contractor's continued involvement during the period of the guarantee. The contractor should try to replace this withholding by a maintenance bond. Sometimes this provision would be included in the performance bond.

CONSTRUCTION SAFETY

Some project managers do not have the same dedication to running a safe job as they do toward running a job that is *on time* and *under budget*. If, for no other reason, the project manager should be concerned with safety because of the **favorable effect a good safety record has on job costs.**

Accidents are expensive, not only to the project individually, but also the the entire construction industry. The cost of construction accidents in the United States annually has approached nine billion dollars. Most accidents are avoidable, so much of this money could potentially be saved by the contractor and eventually by the owners.

SAFETY IS IMPORTANT: To be effective it needs to be seen to be of importance to top management. Safety programs must be supported form the top. Contractors' management must have a visible concern for safety. Owners should make a point of doing business only with contractors who have good safety records. If this cycle can be started, it can only have a beneficial effect on job safety and on job costs.

Worker injury insurance rates range from 15% of the field payroll down to 4%. These rates are based upon the contractor's previous claims, so a good safety record quickly pays off in reduced insurance costs.

Accidents are counterproductive not only to the affected individual and the firm, but also to the work in progress. The productivity of the workers in the immediate area is reduced; with severe accidents the entire work site is involved.

SITE SAFETY PROGRAM: The project manager should require that a formal site safety program be prepared and that one is in place on each of his jobs. He should make sure that the program has been adequately funded based upon the safety plan developed early in the project life. A single individual should be designated as being responsible for the safety program at the jobsite; but safety must be on the mind of every individual at the site— supervisors, foremen, craftsmen, laborers and visitors. There must be a comprehensive safety orientation for all workers given with the regular site induction course. The project manager must spot check to make sure that the program has been implemented, that it is being carried out and that it is effective in containing accidents.

INDUSTRIAL HYGIENE: Physical hazards are sometimes thought of as the only as the only safety concerns at a construction site. There also has to be a concern for exposure to some of the hazardous materials such as asbestos, fumes, dust, and noise.

HOUSEKEEPING: *Good housekeeping practices* throughout the construction site are a positive indication of *good safety practices*. The two generally seem to go hand in hand.

SAFETY AUDITS: The project manager should make arrangements for safety audits to be held at the jobsite to verify that the safety program is being conducted according to the plan. "Second guessing" is very evident after an industrial accident. Safety audits will help identify potential hazardous conditions. Hopefully these can be eliminated before a serious accident occurs.

SAFETY VS. PRODUCTIVITY: The project manager and the owner must be extremely careful that their insistence on safety consciousness does not interfere with the contractor's labor productivity. A fine balance must be maintained between a prudent level of safe operation and cost effective preventive measures.

On some of the larger projects, particularly those high profile jobs such as nuclear plants, the public relations programs can be very adversely affected by even a mention of construction accidents. Community relations can suffer long term serious affects from a poor safety record.

Construction Industry Cost Effectiveness Project Report #A-3 "Improving Construction Safety Performance." The Business Roundtable, New York, NY, 1982, p. 3.

LABOR RELATIONS

Over the last decade, recognition of low productivity on many union construction jobs has led to a marked increase of merit shop construction in many areas of the country. The project manager's main responsibility with labor relations is to make sure that labor relations are always carried on so that productivity is not hampered.

The Construction Industry Cost Effectiveness Project Report (1983) covers many of the problem areas seen by owners, contractors and construction unions. In the field of labor relations, the CICE task force has made important observations and recommendations.

Jurisdictional disputes were cited as being one of the barriers to more efficient construction. On a large job there may be more than a dozen craft unions represented. Exclusive jurisdiction of one craft where many jobs can be done equally well, or more efficiently, by other crafts impedes good productivity. Inefficient work assignments are sometimes condoned by contractors to avoid disputes.

CONTROL OF SUPERVISION: Craft supervisors, foremen and general foremen are often hired by agreement from the union hall. Loyalties are necessarily divided between their current job responsibilities and their union affiliations. Contractors must not bargain away their right to control work supervision. They must not condone further erosion of this right, and the owners should support the contractors on this point.

SUBJOURNEYMEN: Many tasks on a construction job do not require a great deal of skill and can be performed easily by subjourneymen. Where union agreements restrict this type of task to skilled craftsmen, productivity will suffer. More extensive use of subjourneymen on construction sites will improve productivity.

COUNTERPRODUCTIVE PRACTICES: Local bargaining agreements need to eliminate restrictive practices that interfere with efficient execution of work. Such things as pay for nonworking time (coffee breaks, etc.), requirements for excessive crew sizes, and excessive overtime payments all go against the unions' ability to compete with merit shop constructors.

Contractors and owners should present a united front in getting the unions to accept the premise that they are entitled to receive a fair day's work for a fair day's pay. The contractor must be consistent in enforcing jobsite rules without interference. Finally, the contractor should be able to maintain records on past employees, refusing to rehire those with poor performance records.

SITE AGREEMENTS: Some contractors have been very successful in negotiating **site agreements** with the construction unions. achieving many of the points listed above. When the unions and contractors are able to work together to resolve their common problems and yet maintain their own interests, they have proven to be very competitive.

MERIT SHOP: About half of all construction work is done under open shop or merit shop practices. The employer hires the workers without regard to union membership or lack thereof.

The open shop or merit shop contractor does all of the recruiting, hiring, training, disciplining, promoting, and terminating of workers rather than relinquishing these responsibilities to the local union.

Construction Industry Cost Effectiveness Project Report, "More Construction for the Money, Summary Report." The Business Roundtable, New York, NY, January 1983, p. 3.

FIELD PLANNING/SCHEDULING

Field planning and scheduling should be based on conformance to the overall job plan. It is concerned with planning the details so that the scheduled progress will be maintained. Under most circumstances, field planning will be an exercise in fine tuning and will take advantage of all opportunities to maximize the effort under changing conditions.

PURPOSE OF FIELD PLANNING: Field planning is concerned with efficient utilization of manpower, making sure that the skills of each individual are applied at all times on the most critical tasks for which all information, material, and erection equipment necessary are available. The field planning effort should be a cooperative effort between the field planner and schedulers, the construction manager, superintendents, the general foremen, foremen, and craft supervisors.

ANTICIPATED PROBLEMS: Identification of ongoing and anticipated problems becomes a significant factor in being able to maintain a schedule. Many things that happen on a construction site could not have been anticipated by the job planners working months before in the office. These new factors are considered when preparing the detailed work plans.

MONTHLY PLANNING: Monthly, for each critical area or system, work must be laid out following the current construction schedule as closely as possible. Assumptions made with regard to upcoming work will be reviewed for continued validity. The status of anticipated work necessary to start all projected activities is verified. Onsite availability of equipment to be installed and the bulk materials required should be checked. Missing items should immediately be expedited and followed very closely. Equipment required for installation should be checked to make sure it will be available. The status of crews required for work planned for the next month is reviewed. That work is expedited where delays would hamper planned crew availability.

DAILY PLANNING: This monthly look-ahead is adjusted as necessary and the shorter range planning follows in a cascading fashion. The material required for tasks is checked once again and packaged so that it is ready for issue to the erection crews on the day that it is needed. Potential conflicts between crafts or subcontractors are investigated and resolved. Day-by-day crew assignments are issued at the beginning of each week. These reflect any changes which may have occurred in the schedule from the previous week.

INVOLVEMENT IN JOBSITE PLANNING: The purpose of intensive jobsite planning and scheduling is to keep the job on schedule despite disruptions in the work and to maximize productivity of the jobsite resources. Jobsite planning needs to be more comprehensive and detailed and the short range field schedule needs to pinpoint exactly what will be done each shift by each crew. The craft supervisors must be on top of the current plan for it to be effectively translated into work.

MOTIVATION: Timely communication of the current plan will help create a positive attitude throughout the job. Construction workers are sometimes thought of as being hard to motivate, but there is probably no group of people who will take more pride in their accomplishments if only they have a sense of proper treatment.

THE FIELD START DATE

The **date that the construction effort is to be started in the field** will have a great deal of effect on all of the subsequent field operations. This date should not be fixed without a great deal of investigation.

The start date should be set only after sufficient planning has been completed to assure that the **continuity of effort can be fully supported** by the flow of engineering documentation and the receipt of equipment and materials at the job site. Few factors can demoralize the construction forces to a greater extent than that of not having sufficient work to do because of a lack of information or a shortage of materials.

PHASED PLAN: There may be instances when it is justified to start the work on a phased plan and then shut down operations for a period. Depending upon the relative costs of mobilization/demobilization, this may be an economic solution to take advantage of anticipated good weather at the start of a job. Getting site work, grading, and paving out of the way initially and then establishing a waiting period while the remainder of engineering and procurement catch up may be the proper way to go on some jobs. Experience has shown that too often the start date is set without regard to sufficient consideration about the continuity of the following work.

UNUSUAL CIRCUMSTANCES: There will be some instances in which the start date is not set by job requirements at all, but upon political or regulatory considerations. The job will pay a financial penalty, but these may be valid reasons for a premature start. The project manager should understand that, unless the objectives of the job so demand, he should not be tempted to move into the field too soon.

EFFECT ON FIELD INDIRECTS: Once the work starts in the field, the indirect costs of field construction management, temporary facilities, security, and the like will also begin. Under some reimbursable contracts, the field indirects may have been fixed, and this account may be seriously overrun if work is started too soon in the field.

AUDITS OF ENGINEERING/PROCUREMENT STATUS: The project manager and his planning staff should review that status of engineering and procurement work frequently to reaffirm the project logic and to reschedule the field start date if this become advantageous. Although it seldom happens, the field start date could conceivably be advanced if new information or better deliveries allow it and all other conditions warrant.

START DATE MAY DEPEND ON PROJECT OBJECTIVES: The project manager must sometimes make a decision about moving into the field on schedule when the early work is slightly behind schedule. It is possible that added incentive to recoup time can be given to the engineering and procurement efforts if there is added pressure from the field. In other instances, the project manager must make the tough decision to defer start of construction, which can be politically unpopular. Balancing these forces can be a delicate matter for the project manager. If he decides to start on schedule, he must be confident that engineering and procurement activities will be accelerated, and that field productivity will not suffer unduly for too long a period.

SUBCONTRACTOR COORDINATION

Every subcontractor has a right to expect that he can perform his work in an efficient manner. He also know that there will be times when the work on the site will inevitably involve problems such as when crews from two different subcontractors want to work in the same place at the same time. Problems arise when a subcontractor does not complete work needed by another according to the schedule.

When the construction manager is dealing with direct hire personnel, he faces a lesser problem because he has more direct control and more flexibility. When he is managing the efforts of subcontractors all of whom are working on a lump sum basis, equitable solutions may be more difficult.

FUNDAMENTAL CONSIDERATIONS: The easy answer is **excellent planning** and **good communication**. These two factors, coupled with **good subcontractor relations,** will make a difficult job easier. Field planning is complex, but at least it deals mostly with realities. **What** has to be done is known, and **when it can be done** and **when it should be done** are much clearer than when the job is in a more nebulous phase.

PROJECT MANAGER'S ROLE: The project manager makes certain that the planning is taking place, that the communications and the subcontractor relations are good. He is not directly involved in the day to day activities, but should plan on sitting in on a field coordination meeting occasionally to see for himself how this aspect of the job is going.

WARNING SIGNALS: The project manager should also be aware of some of the danger signs that come up during the course of the job if subcontractor relations are not being handled in a satisfactory manner.

The early warning may come with the submission of excessive subcontractor claims for delay of work, for loss of productivity, or that the contractor was not allowed to do work according to his approved schedule. This warning may come after the fact, as subcontractors are notorious for delaying claim submittal until late in the job or after job completion. Whenever there is a possibility of a claim, the subcontractor should be instructed to make an immediate evaluation and submit any claim promptly. The subcontractor should understand and the contract should stipulate that late claims for delays and loss of productivity will not be accepted. The job management should not be lulled into thinking that this type of problem will disappear.

DOCUMENTATION: If the work of a subcontractor starts to slip behind, the reasons must be established immediately. The importance of adequate documentation cannot be overemphasized. Any failure of the subcontractor to comply with the coordination planning for the site should be formally brought to his attention in the strongest terms.

Documentation is extremely important in substantiating or refuting subcontractor claims. This must be done concurrently with the progress of the work and not left until the subcontractor has completed the work and moved off the site.

IMPORTANCE OF FAIRNESS: The project manager needs to be sure that the subcontractor relations are being handled on a firm but fair basis by those with that responsibility. The project manager cannot wait too long to judge the effectiveness of the subcontractor administration on his job. If he determines that things are not going well, he must intervene to make sure they are straightened out.

FIELD CHANGES

Field changes are a fact of life. The job can be expedited or delayed depending upon how these changes are handled. Two opposing factors are involved in field changes. **Proper control** in many organizations dictates that the home office must be involved in approving any change. **Expediency**, on the other hand, says that field changes should be approved in the field.

In many cases, corporate policy and practice will dictate how field changes must be handled. The project manager will understand just what his limitations are in delegating approval authority to the field. The contract may also have provisions which limit approval of field changes.

One test seems to work well when the project manager and the construction manager are compatible in personality and style and where they enjoy one another's confidence. This says that if the change definitely does not affect the budget or the completion date, the site manager should have the authority to approve the change. If the change will probably not affect either budget or schedule, then the construction manager should make the decision and then advise the project manager of the change. If the change will definitely affect the budget or the schedule, then the project manager must approve the change. In most instances, the approval will have to be given at an even higher level of management or by the owner. The job instructions will normally specify approval limitations with regard to changes when additional costs are involved.

CHANGES IN SPECIFICATIONS/PLANS: Field changes regarding specifications or exceptions to plans should always be referred to the proper engineering or other technical authority. Any change to these documents should be completely documented as to the reasons for the change. If oral approval is given because of time constraints this should be documented as soon as possible. Any document which has required formal approval by the licensor will also require corresponding formal approval of any changes.

COOPERATIVE APPROACH NECESSARY: Many field changes are necessary and there is no standard method of approach that is without question. Much wasted effort occurs in trying to bring the home office personnel up to speed in situations with which they may be unfamiliar but which are well understood in the field. On the other hand, the field staff may be unaware of some of the complications introduced by deviations from the approved plans.

The project manager must get copies for home office cost records of all change notices approved by the site manager.

TIMING OF CHANGES: The biggest problem with field changes is the urgency with which they must be handled. For this reason local approval authority is desirable. Many times the decision to make a change does not involve a great deal of time or money unless the decision is unduly delayed. Field experience can mean a lot in knowing how to make small design modifications to make construction or erection easier. Dealing only with drawings is difficult. It is much easier to visualize how to get to the final product while standing on the jobsite.

Good ideas should be encouraged, but only when they will benefit the plant or the construction effort without affecting the cost or schedule adversely.

FIELD COST CONTROL

By the time site efforts are underway, most of the project costs have been definitely established, leaving **field productivity**, **schedule duration**, and **fine tuning the construction techniques** as three areas where the cost outcome of the project can still be affected.

PRODUCTIVITY DETERMINATIONS: Sufficient measurements must be recorded to determine productivity of the various major work outputs.

A meaningful and consistent measurement of productivity from the beginning of the site work is important to give an early indication of the validity of the estimate. Productivity should be based on output of work per unit resource used. For example, yards of foundation concrete poured per manhour actually required. Measurement should be continuous over the life of the job to reflect trends and allow more accurate predictions over the life of the job. These results will reflect trends and allow more accurate predictions of future performance.

A big problem in measuring productivity is that all time *charged* against an activity is included in the measurement rather than only that time that actually contributes to getting the job done. A great deal of apparent construction inefficiency results from time thought to be productive but which is actually nonproductive. We badly need systems of measurement which will separate this nonproductive time from that which is really required to do the work. Only that time needed to do the work should be included so that we can accurately forecast the real future requirements.

PROJECTED COSTS: Using the productivity information, the project manager can predict future performance and translate these projections into cost forecasts.

Several techniques may be used for projections of subsequent performance:

- Future performance will be the same as the past performance
- Future performance will be the same as budgeted
- A combination of the two preceding methods
- Other techniques such as the method of least squares

The actual method to be used will depend on what will work best based upon the experience of the project manager and his cost engineers.

Using the chosen method of projection, the apparent impact on the scheduled completion date may be determined. A delay in completion may have a significant effect on the project costs. Field indirect costs are extremely sensitive to construction duration.

CONSTRUCTION OPERATIONS ANALYSIS: The project manager may work with the construction manager to optimize the construction program for the remaining work. More cost effective methods of execution are always possible if sufficient thought has gone into the options for improvement.

The most profitable sector for cost containment at the jobsite could be an intensive ongoing program to review each of the major upcoming efforts to find a better, more cost effective way of doing the work. This system saves money and also leads to an improvement in worker motivation and morale.

FIELD MATERIAL CONTROL

Material control starts in engineering.

All items that will be required are defined, specifications are written, quantities are determined, and schedule requirements are set. **Control continues during the procurement cycle** when purchase orders are issued, and key fabrication and shipping dates are tracked. **Field material control** tracks the material from receipt at the jobsite to installation.

A comprehensive material control program is especially necessary for international projects, particularly for those projects located in Third World countries where shortages may not be readily filled at the last minute even for commonly available material.

The engineering firm, the owner, and the construction contractor ideally would use the same system for material control throughout the job. Unfortunately, this does not usually happen; and, if computer control is being used, there will have to be some kind of an interface setup between the programs. The current trend is toward use of a data base computer program for job material control. A probable outcome may be a separate contract for material control, when the information is input into terminals and the material control contractor processes and analyzes the information and presents reports to the engineer, owner, and the construction contractor.

On a large job, for example, there will be a field material control group and a very sophisticated computer program for keeping track of the materials. On smaller jobs, there may be a warehouseman in charge of materials. Material tracking is done manually or with a personal computer.

One of the more difficult situations from a material control standpoint involves those projects where certain materials are furnished by the owner, others by the general contractor, and the remainder by the subcontractors. This can lead to a great deal of confusion at the jobsite unless definite responsibility has been assigned for ordering, receiving, stocking, and issuing the various types of materials. The **material plan** must be absolutely clear in this respect.

Field material control emerges as being composed of all of those activities that are necessary to give full assurance that the materials needed for construction are available when required in suitable condition for immediate installation. The project manager should make certain that the objectives of field material control are understood by those in material control as well as the field superintendents and craftsmen working at the jobsite.

OBJECTIVES OF FIELD MATERIAL CONTROL

To know at all times

1. What material has been received at the site
2. That the material at the site has been properly stored
3. When the materials are scheduled for installation
4. That the material can be easily retrieved from storage
5. That commodity materials are prepackaged for issue
6. That claims are filed promptly for items damaged in shipment
7. What shortages and surpluses are anticipated

INSPECTION OF WORK

Field inspection includes those site activities designed to insure that the entire facility is faithfully constructed as specified by the engineering documents and results in work that conforms to the owner's expectations.

Failure to assign the responsibility for compliance with the specifications can lead to a confusing situation in doing inspection in the field. Contractually, the vendor may be responsible for compliance in supplying or fabrication; the subcontractor may be responsible to the prime for the subcontracted work; the general contractor is usually responsible to the owner for work covered by his contract; and the owner's project team has ultimate responsibility to the owner's senior management.

The owner may know that he has that responsibility, but often cannot staff the inspection force An architect/engineer may logically inspect the work of a general contractor. The work of a subcontractor may be inspected by a general contractor. In the case of a construction management contractor, inspection is generally one of his responsibilities. Most large D/B or E/C contractors have strong inspection groups. In many cases these inspection groups report organizationally to a senior executive as to not be unduly influenced by pressures from project or construction management. Third party inspection services are also used on D/B contracts due to their assumed impartiality.

The bottom line of these overlapping perceptions of responsibility is that there is a possiblity that duplicate inspections will be made. On some jobs that is not all bad because the initial results are not all that good. The quality assurance plan should provide the level of inspection required for each area, system, or type of work, and also assign the responsibility for the inspection. Duplicate inspection can be expensive and disruptive. However, the project manager should not hesitate to call for an increase in the level of inspection if this is required.

The project manager should make it understood that the **primary responsibility for quality is with the individual**. Followup responsibility is then with the crew which does the work, and then with the supervisor who tells what work is to be done and how. This concept is very important and will set the tone for the entire project.

Putting on more inspectors to catch mistakes may only encourage the belief that the work output of the individual is not important. An army of inspectors will not discover all of the wrongs. Depending on someone else to discover the mistakes can be self-defeating.

Inspection should never cost more than what the improved results are worth. The proper level of inspection should be determined and maintained as long as it is satisfactory. Demanding more than is specified is detrimental to the morale of the field forces. Most workers know a good job when they see it, but their perceptions of a good job will differ. That is why we have written documentation— to try to zero in on the exact requirements. Specifications and plans are still subject to some interpretation.

WHAT TO INSPECT

Content   Inspection at the site covers both the work done by the crafts and the materials used in the construction.

Scope   The site inspectors are responsible for reviewing all of the activities from the inspection of equipment and material upon receipt to the final testing and checkout of the completed plant.

Planning   Proper planning will reduce the cost of inspection and the subsequent rework. Emphasis on early detection of mistakes will minimize costly field correction.

Equipment   Inspection of equipment previously checked at the factory after fabrication should be limited to looking for shipping damage. Materials and equipment not inspected during fabrication or at the manufacturing plant should be checked for compliance with specifications.

Civil Work   Site inspection related to civil work would include soil compaction, checking of plant topographical control, form work for foundation concrete, reinforcing bars, and concrete quality control. Structural steel should be checked for surface preparation and coating. Erected steel components should be checked for out of plumb, bolting, and welded connections.

Rotating Equipment   Rotating equipment should be checked by a millwright upon receipt to determine any shipping damage and to make sure that the specified protective measures have been taken. Preservative oils and greases should have been applied to machined surfaces and all openings closed with temporary blinds.

Vessels Piping Structural   Field-erected vessels, piping and structures should be checked for proper materials, schedules and location. Completed systems should be checked against flow diagrams, P & IDs, and detailed drawings. Field inspectors coordinate the piping pressure tests and provide documentation for the system checks.

Electrical   Conformance of all of the components of the electrical and instrumentation systems and circuits to specifications must be verified.

**Field
Welding**

All field welding should be checked for being in accordance with the welding specifications and that qualified welders are used on each type of welding. Each step of the welding process and the materials used require checking. The inspectors may use both visual inspection and nondestructive testing procedures.

Insulation

Inspection of insulation is made to verify that the proper thickness and material has been installed in compliance with the specifications. Insulation almost invariably is installed under schedule pressure for plant completion. This should alert inspectors to the need for careful review of the work before the jacketing is installed.

Painting

Painting and protective coatings require careful preparation of the surfaces, correct application of the materials, adequate thickness of the completed work, and freedom from flaws or pinholes.

SITE HOUSEKEEPING

The condition of the construction site is symptomatic of the condition of the health and well-being of the project. Generally, a well-kept site indicates that the project is moving along well. This is probably not an absolute truth, but it happens often enough to be a leading indicator. Good housekeeping on the site is the responsibility of the construction manager, but its absence is a reflection on the project manager.

Good housekeeping is an indication of organization. Without the full support of the construction manager, good housekeeping will not be seen as being important. Construction sites also respond very closely to the practices of the responsible contractor. This probably means that the construction managers don't rise to that position unless they comply with the company attitudes. You can predict the condition of the site by knowing the reputation of the contractor with regard to housekeeping.

If the temporary buildings are not kept clean and orderly, there is little likelihood that the rest of the site will be. The construction office or trailer should not be cluttered with old plans, unemptied ashtrays, or broken furniture. The warehouse should be orderly and well policed. The food area and the area around the brass alley and the site entrance should be kept clean.

A well-kept site is run by people with a high regard for the material and equipment awaiting installation. On some sites structural steel, reinforcing bars, electrical conduit, and line pipe are thrown around helter-skelter. Half-unpacked equipment items are left exposed to the atmosphere. Damaged pallets of containers drip paint.

Good housekeeping also influences the operational efficiency on the job. The condition of some sites requires a major movement of material for work to be started. A well run site will demonstrate a semblance of order even during the construction of the underground systems when good housekeeping is challenging. Open trenches make job access extremely difficult. Ditches should not be opened until the pipe, conduit or cable can be laid. The systems should be checked and backfilling done as rapidly as possible.

Temporary facilities such as electrical runs, scaffolding and temporary walkways can be offenders to good housekeeping. Safety consciousness on the jobsite depends to a great extent upon concern for housekeeping. There is a need to constantly collect and dispose of metal and wooden scraps, crates and packing materials, nails, pieces of wire and cable, and wastepaper.

Housekeeping must be made an integral part of the contractual requirements at each level. Even so, there will be many instances where cleaning up will be "nobody's responsibility." The construction manager needs a "bull gang" to keep those areas of the site in order where assignment of the responsibility has "fallen in a crack."

PROGRESS MEASUREMENT

All work included in the contract should be defined in terms of the Work Breakdown Structure. The schedule and budget are developed following the same format. The planned rate of progress for each contract may be plotted on a **money/time curve** based on the applicable portions of the budget put on a time scale for the work included. The figures are adjusted for any approved modifications including the actual contract quantities covered by the current plans and the accepted work plan as proposed by the contractor/subcontractor.

Once the work at the site is underway, periodic checks on progress will be made. Measuring the work done at the jobsite serves two purposes:

1. It sets the **total amount of work accomplished** in terms that permit actual progress to be compared with the planned goals as set by the schedule and the budget.

2. It serves as a **basis for making payment** for some types of contracts.

Actual physical progress in real terms should be the basis for the measurements which should be made in the units specified by the contract. This should also make them the same as are called for in the budget. Examples of these measurements follow.

1. Total contracted length of pipe of a particular diameter, class, and material is taken from the plans. Actual installed length of pipe in measured in the field. The percent complete is the actual installed length divided by the total contracted length. Partial credit for installation may be taken for pipe in place, but not welded or tested.

2. Total contracted cubic yards of foundation concrete is taken from the plans. The actual installed cubic yards of concrete are measured in the field. Physical percent complete is the actual installed yards divided by the total contracted yards. Again, partial credit may be given for excavation, formwork in place, and reinforcing steel set.

3. For prefabricated piping spools, progress may be booked in accordance with a sliding scale taking into consideration receipt of spools moved to field location, set on supports, connected,

inspected, and tested. A percentage complete for each of these steps is assigned based upon experience.

The progress for each activity or budgeted/scheduled task is determined and weighted by dollar value. All of the individual values are then summed up to determine the percent complete of the total contract.

Field progress measurements are usually based upon physical work completed. They should not be based upon the percent of the labor budget expended. The actual physical percent complete should be compared to the planned physical percent complete. Comparing these two figures will give a reading of the performance variance.

FIELD REPORTING

Field reporting must be done before the project manager's reporting on the overall project progress. It should deal with factual material about jobsite conditions, progress, and productivity as well as cover actual and anticipated field problems. The field reports *must* be completed on schedule in order not to delay issuance of the project manager's report.

The frequency with which reports are issued is an indication as to what they should contain. Daily reports may be very detailed. A monthly report will not cover minor items that have no major effect. The interest of the intended reader must be taken into account.

THE TEN MOST IMPORTANT TOPICS TO COVER IN A FIELD REPORT

1. **Progress of work in the field compared to the plan**. Present a concise picture of the current status of the job. Graphics are ideal to help with this.

2. **Unfavorable variances in job progress: What is being done to recover position in these areas?** Don't present problems without offering a solution, preferably a synopsis of an action plan for recovery.

3. **Cost status of field work compared to the plan.** Again, graphics may be used to present this information effectively.

4. **Unfavorable variances in job costs: What is being done to recover position in these areas?**

5. **Status of material and equipment relative to promised deliveries.** Are there delivery problems anticipated during the next reporting period? What measures are being taken to alleviate these problems?

6. **Status of subcontracted work and relations with subcontractors.** Is the current performance of the subcontractors satisfactory? What measures are being taken to rectify areas where they are not?

7. **Current status of labor relations and any problems or anticipated labor relations problems**. Are there impending labor problems? What is being done to head these off?

8. **Listing of the safety statistics for the latest period and the cumulative statistics for the job.** Is the safety program deficient in any area? What measures have been taken to reverse this?

9. **Significant variances in quality and how they have been addressed.** Have there been problems in getting the specified level of quality? Is this a problem with only one subcontractor or is it general?

10. **Photographs showing progress at the site since the last report, illustrating points made in the narrative.**

PAYMENTS

Accounting practices of different companies dictate the amount of fiscal responsibility that can be exercised in the field. From a management standpoint, and with the proper controls in place, there are many areas where field handling of expenditures and payments can be cost effective.

Duplication of Effort
The project manager should be concerned with a duplication of effort. If an office manager and job accounts have been set up in the field to handle some payments, they should be assigned as many of the accounts as they can handle. Only in very special circumstances should all of the payments be handled from the home office.

Reimbursable Contracts
On reimbursable contracts, accounting services may be only partially reimbursable. If field accounting functions are reimbursable and some home office accounting is not, the contractor will move more accounting functions to the jobsite.

Jobsite Terminals
Don't tie the hands of the site manager by making it difficult for him to do what is better done in the field. Increased availability of jobsite terminals means that field processing of time charges and preparation of the payroll checks are easily done.

Field Purchases
Payment of invoices for field purchases should usually be handled at the jobsite. Less red tape is involved. Any questions pertaining to these purchases can be better handled in the field.

Home Office Purchases
Payment for equipment and for material ordered by the home office purchasing department should be paid for by the home office. The confirmation of satisfactory material receipt is furnished by the field. Damage claims and notices of short shipments are prepared by the field.

Subcontractor Payments
Subcontractor payments are often handled by the home office based upon verification by the field. If any amounts are to be withheld from the invoiced amount, the subcontractor should be advised as soon as possible and the reasons fully explained. Subcontractor

relations are frequently strained because of delayed payments and sometimes the subcontractors' operation will be impaired due to cash flow difficulties.

Field Services

Payments for temporary utilities, security services, janitorial services, and the like should be paid for in the field. There is little need for running these invoices though the home office. Keeping the payments local increases the authority needed to maintain a satisfactory level of service. The field should always have an adequate petty cash account under the responsibility of the field office manager.

Payment Timing

Payments should be made as soon as possible after receipt and verification of the invoices. Take advantage of any discounts for prompt payment. Sloppy handling of payments can lead to a negative image for both the contractor and the owner in the local area.

AUDITS

A field audit is an investigation and review of field procedures. It should not wait until the end of the job. The project manager will do well to make sure that the specified project procedures as well as the company practices are being followed. He should call for an internal auditor or an ad hoc auditing group to perform the audit.

Job accounting should be checked using normal auditing techniques. Verification is made of the records for payrolls, field purchase accounts, petty cash, and the bank accounts. In addition, time keeping practices and field assignment payments should be checked.

Although one thinks primarily of the financial aspects of an audit, verification of other performance areas can be very beneficial. Consideration should be given to the following auditable points also:

- **Progress Reporting:** Are the figures being reported valid? Are they being used properly?

- **Field Changes:** Is the documentation for field changes being done in accordance with the established procedures in a timely fashion? Are the records up to date with the proper approvals? Are the changes being incorporated into the budget and schedule so that tracking can be meaningful?

- **Safety Practices:** Is the jobsite work being conducted in the safest practical way?

- **Quality of Work:** Is the level of inspection appropriate for the job requirements and in accord with the quality plan?

- **Material Tracking:** Are material shortages being spotted in time to prevent or reduce job stoppage due to lack of materials? Is early surplus identification in place?

- **Warehouse Invntories:** Are the warehouse records being maintained properly? Are the materials and equipment being stored to minimize the effects of exposure?

- **Security:** Is security being conducted in accordance with the project plan? Is the security at the jobsite effective? Are revisions to the procedures necessary?

Audits must be very carefully handled in order not to create an adversarial relationship between the site manager and the project manager. Audits do little to improve relationships— that is not their purpose. A well-run job has nothing to fear from a good audit. A job that is not being well run can benefit from the audit recommendations. The site manager and ultimately the project manager have the responsibility for the project at this stage. They should take full advantage of the available resources to provide this important check.

No audit can offer an absolute guarantee. The audits outlined can offer **substantial assurance against loss of project control.**

11 SUBCONTRACT ADMINISTRATION

ENGINEERING FOR BID PACKAGES

Much time will be saved and a great deal of confusion will be eliminated if the division of the field work into subcontracts is decided upon at the early stages of the project.

SUBCONTRACT SCHEDULE: The project work plans and the project work breakdown structure are developed to make project execution more straightforward. An early decision must be made as to the manner in which the site work will be broken into subcontracts. The work that is to be included in each subcontract must be clearly understood. A **subcontract schedule** or **subcontract index** is prepared listing all of the subcontracts proposed. As the job progresses, it will probably be necessary to add additional subcontracts and to merge or subdivide others. **The index should be kept current.**

SUBCONTRACT SCOPE: The scope of each subcontract must be defined by means of a written work scope. It should include a listing of all of the applicable drawings and specifications governing the work to be included. The scope should be drafted before the drawing list has been finalized so that the drawings will follow the scope of the subcontracts where this is necessary and appropriate.

COMPLETE PACKAGES: The bid documents need to furnish all of the information necessary for the work included by the subcontract and, in addition, also indicate all peripheral information necessary for the bid such as existing installations and work to be done by others where this will affect the work that is included. Engineering drawings should follow division of work by subcontract in so far as possible to reduce confusion among the bidders.

CHECKING THE SUBCONTRACT: Subcontract bid packages must be checked to make sure that the bidders will have all of the information necessary to prepare their bids. If bidding requirements are not clear to those familiar with the work, it follows that the bidders will have questions. Preferably, the boundary limits of the subcontract should be clearly indicated on the plans. Alternatively, the narrative description should positively indicate the work included, as well as spell out that work tol be done by others.

DRAWING ISSUES: Preferably the plans given out with the bid packages should be sufficiently complete to be issued **"For Construction."** Because of schedule constraints, an earlier issue will sometimes be used and marked **"For Contract Bid."** Any changes made to the drawings and other bid documents will be subject to prices changes by the bidders. One last opportunity to bring the subcontract into conformance with the latest issue of plans is afforded by the **bid conditioning** process.

IMPORTANCE OF BID DOCUMENTATION: The accuracy of the subcontract bids are a function of the information provided to the bidders. If the packages are incomplete, confusing, or contradictory, the subcontractors may compensate by providing additional contingency or risk money in their bids or by taking exception to some of the provisions of the bid documents.

ISSUING THE REQUEST FOR PROPOSALS

The engineering package issued for the inquiry includes a complete description of the work to be done by means of a **written scope** together with **plans** and **specifications.** Before it is sent out to the bidders, other information must be attached including (1) **a request for a proposal,** (2) **information for bidders,** (3) **the proposed contract form,** and (4) **the commercial bid form.**

REQUEST FOR PROPOSAL: The request for proposal is the cover letter written to each of the selected bidders inviting a proposal for performing the work. In general terms, the entire bid package is sometimes known as a **request for proposal,** or an **RFP.** It may also be termed an **invitation to bid,** or an **ITB.**

INFORMATION FOR BIDDERS: This section of the inquiry is a compilation of all of the considerations to be made by each of the bidders in preparing their proposals. In it, the owner, general contractor, or construction manager provides a description of the general execution plans and identifies those factors that will be important in the subcontractor selection.

- **The general plan of execution for the work at the site.**
- **The overall schedule for the work covered by the subcontract.**
- **A listing of the additional required information from the bidders.**

  This information would include:

  a. Detailed information about the subcontractor's organization including company experience, organization charts, and the like.

  b. The subcontractor's work plan for the job including organization charts with the names and experience summaries for those employees proposed for the work, the detailed plans for the work, the subcontractor's preliminary schedule, material control plans, quality control plans, and the like.

  c. A chart demonstrating staffing capability for doing the work concurrently with other work being done over the same time period

    d. Performance assurance programs that will be used at the jobsite by the subcontractor

- **The name of the owner's representative or subcontract manager to whom questions should be directed during the bidding period.**

CONTRACT FORM: This is the draft of the agreement proposed for the work. It defines the rights, responsibilities, obligations, and the liabilities of the two parties. The subcontractor will sometimes object to some of the terms and conditions expressed in the proposed contract form. He must spell out in his proposal any changes that he wants made or upon which his commercial offering depends.

BID FORM: The form for the commercial offering should be clearly spelled out in the RFP. It is a mistake to ask for bids without specifying the format that the commercial offering is to follow. The bid breakdowns should be identical in form on all bids to simplify the process of comparison. Otherwise a great deal of time may be lost and there is a possibility that one or more items may be lost.

PREBID MEETINGS

In line with the philosophy that better understanding of the work expectations will lead to better and more responsive bids; it is helpful **to assemble the bidders at a prebid meeting.**

PURPOSE: The prebid meeting is an opportunity for bidders' representatives to ask specific questions of the owner's representative and to get an authoritative answer. All of the bidders in attendance will be able to get the same answer at the same time.

DATE OF MEETING: The meeting should be scheduled some time after the bidders have received the invitation to bid and have reviewed the documents. The meeting should be held sufficiently ahead of the bid due date so that all clarifications made can be reflected in the bids.

ATTENDANCE: There may be a difference of opinion on whether a single meeting attended by all bidders should be held or whether individual meetings with each subcontractor is better. From the standpoint of all parties concerned, it is usually better to have one single meeting. This reduces the amount of time consumed by the owner's representative for arranging and conducting the meeting and assures that all of the subcontractors will be hearing the same responses to the questions, as well as all of the questions themselves.

LOCATION: The meeting should be held at the jobsite, although for some of the early subcontracts it may be better to hold the meeting in the office where the engineering is being done. If a model has been constructed for the facility, it is certainly desirable for the meeting to be held where the model is available.

MEETING FORMAT: The prebid meeting time is given to all of the selected bidders and each is invited to send one or more representatives depending upon the size and complexity of the subcontract. The prebid meeting should be conducted by the person who will interface as the representative of the owner, general contractor, or construction manager with the subcontractor in the field.

The individual conducting the meeting should begin with an overview of the project covering any changes, modifications or clarifications which have come up since the bid packages were sent out. These should be made available to the subcontractors' representatives in written form as an addendum to the RFP. He should then ask for questions from the subcontractors' representatives. Questions should be answered simply and directly. If any questions cannot be answered on the spot, then a note should be made to obtain the answers. Minutes should be kept of the meeting including all questions and the answers as given. Unanswered questions should be researched and the proper answers provided. Copies of these minutes should be sent to each bidder, whether they were represented at the meeting or not. These minutes should be in the form of an addendum to the RFP.

IF THERE IS NO MEETING: If the project manager decides that a prebid meeting and/or a site visit is not necessary, he must be sure to handle any questions from the subcontractors on a strictly impartial basis by documenting their questions and his answers in writing to all subcontractors in sufficient time so that the correct information can be reflected in their bids for the work.

SITE VISITS

As a supplement to prebid meetings for many subcontracts, a visit to the site may be desirable to clarify points that are difficult to cover otherwise. In some cases a site visit may serve as a substitute for the prebid meeting,

DATE OF VISIT: The site visit should be scheduled after the bid requests have been sent out and reviewed by the subcontractors. Sufficient time should be left for the bidders to complete preparation of their proposals. If a prebid meeting is being held at the site, the site visit would ideally be scheduled immediately following. It is preferable to have the site visits scheduled simultaneously for all bidders unless there is some overriding reason for conducting them individually.

ORGANIZATION OF VISITS: The site visit should be conducted by the person representing the owner, general contractor, or construction manager— whoever will be the prime contact with the subcontractor after the subcontract award. This individual must be intimately familiar with the site and with all of the work to be covered by the subcontract.

OPERATIONS REPRESENTATION: If the work is to be done within an operating plant, it will be helpful to have a representative from plant operations in attendance also. There may be questions regarding applicable plant safety practices. Provisions should be made to have someone very familiar with these rules to give answers. The person arranging for the visit will need to get the names and titles of those who propose to attend the site visit so that the plant passes can be issued in advance. Also arrangements will need to be made so that sufficient personal safety equipment is available for the plant visit, including hard hats, ear plugs, masks, and safety glasses.

RECORD OF STATEMENTS MADE DURING VISIT: The person who conducts the site visit should make arrangements to record all the information given out during the visit. This information should be distributed to all of the bidders whether or not they had been represented at the site visit. All bidders should understand that the bids are to be prepared based only on the bid packages plus any written material sent to them. They should not take into account any contradictory information which might have been discussed informally at the site visit.

PLANNING FOR SITE VISITS: An itinerary should be prepared in advance so that all the areas affecting the bids can be visited during the tour. These would include the subcontractor's entry, area for parking, provisions for the time clock, any temporary facilities to be provided to the subcontractor such as temporary offices, warehouses, and utilities. It is especially important to point out exactly where the tie-ins for temporary power, water, and any other utilities will be made available to the subcontractors. Material storage and laydown areas should be indicated along with any requirements for putting these areas into shape for the work. Any constraints stemming from plant operations and specified in the bid documents should be reinforced particularly with regard to restrictions on access to the work area or permits required for burning, welding, and the like.

IMPRESSIONS IMPORTANT: The person who conducts this tour should remember that the impression that he leaves with the subcontractors' representatives will be very important to them in determining their commercial approach to the work. Their bids will depend to a large extent on their analysis and perception of his competence and capability.

QUOTATIONS

The immediate purpose of the bidding process is to obtain a price from each of the subcontractors being considered for the work. If the work has been well defined and the format for the bidders' proposals has been set, much of the work in making bid comparisons will be simplified.

Following are two problems that may arise with the proposals:

BID DUE DATE: Often the bidding period will be reduced in an attempt to recoup schedule time that has already been lost. If the subcontractors have difficulty in pricing the work in the time allowed, they will compensate by introducing additional contingency allowances. The subcontract manager should make sure that sufficient time has been allowed to get the best prices. If the majority of the bidders complain that additional time is needed, serious consideration should be given to extending the bid period for all. However, if only one expresses a problem, it may be better to retain the original bid due date.

The bid due date and the method of delivery of the bid should be strictly followed. If a bid is received late, there can be little confidence that the subcontractor will do any better with the work itself. If instructions on submitting the proposal cannot be followed, there is a question about that subcontractor's ability to follow the job specifications. Allowing extra time for one subcontractor or accepting a late bid will create problems with regard to both propriety and discipline in the submission of bids for subsequent subcontracts. The subcontract manager must scrupulously conduct the bidding process so there is no doubt about ethical conduct.

NONRESPONSIVE BID: Occasionally the subcontractors will become inventive and submit bids not in the standard format. These variations should be discouraged as this practice will create problems on bids for future subcontracts. If the guilty contractor is otherwise a quality firm and if his price is competitive, some relaxation can probably be tolerated. He should nevertheless be cautioned about deviating from the stipulated format. If there are a sufficient number of other good bids, then the faulty bid should be thrown out completely.

Subcontractors should be discouraged from taking insignificant exceptions to the agreement form. At times some provisions are stipulated by the owner which the subcontractor feels unable to assume. Unlimited liability is a frequent area of disagreement. If the subcontractor feels a need to take numerous exceptions to the proposed agreement, he should consider withdrawing from the competition before spending too much money in developing his bid. It is usually far better and more positive to make a base bid strictly in accordance with the bid documents, and provide another approach with alternate pricing to allow for the exceptions taken.

ANALYSIS OF SUBCONTRACTOR WORK PLANS

Each subcontract inquiry calls for the subcontractor **to provide a work plan**. The work plan is an important consideration in awarding the work, and on some projects may be as important as the quoted price for the work.

The inquiry should have included all of the important factors that the subcontract manager feels are important to judging the work plans. The proposals made by the subcontractors will be responsive to these particular elements.

The subcontract manager will be on the lookout for unique approaches which will give the individual subcontractors an edge over their competition. The work plan may give additional assurance to achieving the project objectives or it may be a different way of approaching the job to eliminate one or more of the owner's concerns.

- **Does the work plan envision an organization that offers an advantage to the site work?**

- **Is there a difference in the way the subcontractor will mobilize for the work to simplify it?**

- **Is there an advantage in the way the contractor plans to marshal his material and equipment for the jobsite?**

- **Is there some additional assurance of improved labor relations offered?**

- **Is the subcontractor taking advantage of proven improvements in technology to offer better construction techniques?**

- **Has the subcontractor offered work improvement methods to reduce site work?**

- **Does the subcontractor demonstrate proficiency with effective techniques of controlling schedule, cost, and quality of work?**

- **What kind of a construction safety program has been offered, and does it promise greater benefits than the competition?**

- **What kind of a program does the subcontractor offer to reduce wasteful labor practices?**

The subcontract manager and the project manager must take pains not to divulge any of the bidders' confidential work plans which they may have discussed. Corporate practice sometimes prohibits this type of discussion during the bid period precisely to prevent a breach of confidence, or accusation of such.

The subcontractor who gives a great deal of thought to better ways to do the work and demonstrates this by a superlative work plan should be given every consideration when analyzing the work plans. Sometimes provisions contained in the work plan will result in meaningful and measurable savings to the project.

BID COMPARISONS

Bid comparisons should be based on factual or well justified information. The information should be collected and each element of the bid arranged so that a direct comparison may be made among all the bidders. A radical difference in price among the bidders could be an indication of a misunderstanding of the bid documents. However, no attempt should be made to clarify any of the prices or the bidders' intent at this point. The bidders under consideration would only be contacted later, at the time of the bid conditioning.

On most proposals, the offerings should be compared based on four components:

THE BASE BID: The base bid is the cost information presented in the contractor's bid or proposal. Any exceptions which have been taken by the subcontractors to the bidding instructions or the form of agreement are noted.

SAVINGS/ADDITIONAL COSTS DERIVED FROM WORK PLAN: Apart from his quoted price, the work plan presented by a subcontractor may result in savings to the overall project. These savings should be evaluated and subtracted from that bidder's quotation. In some cases, a subcontract work plan may result in additional costs to the project. These costs are added to his quotation. Calculations and full backup are required for any additions or reductions in cost when incorporating them into the bid comparison.

SAVINGS/ADDITIONAL COSTS DERIVED FROM ALTERNATES PROPOSED BY SUBCONTRACTOR: Sometimes, a subcontractor, in addition to making a base bid, will offer an alternate approach or a different way of doing the work. Each of these alternatives must be judged as to whether it might be acceptable. If there is a valid reason for rejection, the alternative should be rejected and dropped from further consideration. All alternatives should be thus evaluated and included in, or excluded from, the bid comparison.

ADMINISTRATIVE ASSESSMENTS: This component, if judged necessary, is evaluated prior to receiving the bids. It is not frequently used. Occasionally, a subcontractor will be judged competent to do the work only if his efforts are supplemented by additional administration, supervision, or inspection by the owner, general contractor, or construction manager. This additional effort will be identified, quantified in dollars, justified and documented prior to opening the bids. It is added at the time the bid comparison is made.

As might be imagined, this may be a sensitive subject. It must be handled in a completely honest and above-board manner. It should be based on documented past experience. The assessment may be reduced if a review of the work plan shows that the subcontractor has taken concrete steps to improve his performance. Some companies do not encourage use of this "handicap" type of treatment because of the inherent dangers in its use and the difficulties in accurately quantifying the assessment. In those cases where it has been correctly applied, it represents a real cost to the project and logically should be made a part of the bid comparison.

BID CONDITIONING/ SUBCONTRTACTOR SELECTION

Bid conditioning consists of adjusting the subcontractors' base bids to comply with the conditions and to the basis of the subcontract award taking into account all of the changes introduced since the RFP. The logical steps in bid conditioning are:

- The **initial inquiry** sent to the bidders contains the original information necessary to bid the work.

- Subsequent **modifications, adjustments,** and **clarifications** are made by sending this information to all of the bidders as a result of prebid meetings, site visits, or questions which were received during the bidding period.

- The **subcontractors' base bids**, together with any suggested **alternative bids**, are tabulated. Aadjustments are made to each bid reflecting the effect of the work plan, for proposed alternates, and for assessments due to performance histories.

- A **screening** is done to determine the apparent best two or three bids.

- Any **later changes** which have been made to plans, specifications, or other contract documents are identified. The two or three apparent best bidders are asked to submit supplemental price adjustments for these additions/deletions.

- Any **clarifications** as the the intent of the bids are made with the individual bidders to make sure that there has been no misunderstanding. This the point where obvious problems with very low or very high quotations are verified. If the subcontractor discovers an error in his bid, he should be given the opportunity to withdraw his bid. Under almost no circumstances should he be allowed to change his bid at this stage or to resubmit a corrected bid.

- The **conditioned tabulations** for the two or three apparent low bidders are finalized. These bids should then be completely comparable from a commercial standpoint with the work plans evaluated and any differences in subcontract administration quantified. All work contemplated is current as of the conditioning date.

THE SELECTED BIDDER: Once the apparently best bids have been conditioned, it is a simple step to select the successful bidder.

Because of the process which has been followed, it would be a truly unusual circumstance in which the low bidder would not be awarded the subcontract. There is no longer any reason for trying to justify a reason for giving the award to anyone but the low bidder.

The steps that have been followed provide a rationale for making any of the reasonable allowances for performance differences, and, at the same time, have provided a justification for adjusting the base bid prices. This systematic process removes emotion and subjectivity and produces a logical, objective, and defensible decision open to the scrutiny of any interested party.

RELATIONSHIP WITH
THE SUBCONTRACTOR

The **subcontract manager** is that individual named to represent the contracting entity whether it be the owner, the general contractor, or the construction management firm. The **subcontractor's superintendent** is that individual named by the subcontractor to manage the site work covered by the subcontract. The relationship between these two individuals has to be based on the terms and conditions of the subcontract. The subcontractor has agreed to perform certain work that will ultimately benefit the owner in return for some financial consideration. The subcontract manager's role is to assure that all of the work is done in accordance with the plans, specifications, and other documents.

Both sides will benefit from a subcontract successfully completed. The initial intent of both sides is to achieve just that. Although the subcontract is between the contracting entity and the subcontracting firm, the most visible indication of that relationship comes from the relationship between the subcontract manager and the subcontract superintendent. Some factors that may be present will mitigate **against** harmony and unity of purpose. Typical of these are:

- **The Contract**: To provide airtight protection against all risks possible, the contract is full of language that can be described as being fundamentally adversarial in nature. As this document is generally used in resolving most of the differences, it is no wonder that the contract causes deterioration of the relationships.

- **Work Definition**: A poorly defined scope of work and poorly worded and pompous specifications will intensify problems in the relationship between the subcontract manager and the field superintendent.

- **The Organizations:** Pressures from functional departments and from senior management may be factors in worsening relationships.

- **Financial Considerations:** If the subcontractor encounters cash flow problems, these problems will manifest themselves in the field work where every effort will be hampered by a lack of the proper personnel, equipment, tools, supervision, and organization of the work.

- **Trust:** Mutual trust is essential to a good working relationship. It is most fragile and is easily destroyed by misunderstandings and misinterpretations. When this trust no longer exists, the individuals will respond by not accepting anything said on faith, but will insist on constant checking and rechecking.

- **Personality Differences:** Severe problems can result when irreconcilable differences in personality or style exist. Intervention from third parties may be the only solution other than making a change in staffing.

- **Communication Problems:** Underlying many of these other factors is the inability to communicate well. Once the ability to speak frankly and interchange concepts and ideas starts to erode, it is very difficult to reestablish communication channels.

MONITORING FIELD PERFORMANCE

The subcontractor's performance in the field is continually monitored in three different areas. Monitoring is done against the **contract documents** including the **subcontractor's work plan** as submitted to and accepted by the subcontract manager.

PROGRESS: On lump sum contracts, progress in the field is determined by comparing the total work completed with that covered by the contract. This is best done by consolidating line-to-line assessments of the completed work converted to a percentage of the contracted quantities. On some lump sum contracts, the subcontract manager must calculate design or contracted quantities as these are purposefully not given in the subcontract to avoid any responsibility for errors in takeoff.

On **reimbursable subcontracts**, the subcontract manager may be furnished with current data and performance statistics by the subcontractor as stipulated by the contract. On these subcontracts, the interest is primarily in maintaining productivity. The subcontract manager will conduct spot checks of the crew sizes to assure that the work times reported are accurate.

On **unit price contracts**, measurement of the quantities should be very straightforward if the proper definitions have been provided.

COST: Lump sum subcontracts are very difficult to monitor from a cost standpoint on an ongoing basis. The subcontractor is not obligated to furnish detailed cost information to a subcontract manager, and the jobs are generally not staffed to allow an in-depth cost monitoring program. Some contracts call for a payment schedule with a regular percentage payment stipulated. For this type of contract particularly, the subcontract manager must guard against getting into a position where more has been paid than the value of the work done.

Keeping good records of the reimbursable subcontract costs is essential. Here the majority of the cost responsibility has shifted over to the subcontract manager.

QUALITY: On some **lump sum subcontracts** there is a big incentive to the subcontractor to cut corners as all monies saved may be added to the gross profit on the job. In inspecting the work, it becomes very important to maintain a very visible presence in the field. It is less expensive to do the work right the first time rather than to do it over.

But it may be cheaper to cut corners, if there is no insistence on getting the job done right.

The incentive to perform quality work may be less on a **reimbursable contract**, as rework is generally paid for. Here the subcontract manager needs to maintain vigilance on both the work methods and the results.

As **unit price contracts** generally are written for straightforward work items, it is especially important to exercise vigilence at the beginning. This will set the stage for determining the level of inspection to maintain. It is much easier to back off from excess inspection than it is to increase inspection after off-spec work has been performed.

The subcontract manager should insist upon strict compliance with all plans and specifications. There will always be an excuse for not doing the work just exactly right. Any proposed variances from the contract should be properly documented and approved by the authorized representative.

HANDLING SUBCONTRACTOR CLAIMS

There are several areas in which the subcontractor may expect additional compensation. The subcontractor will submit claims in these instances. The claims may or may not be justified. Adequate records are alwlays the best defense against unfounded and unjustified claims.

The seasoned subcontract manager will have a sixth sense as to potential claims that may be forthcoming. He will prepare his case with contemporaneous documentation corroborating the related events.

Common claims may be put into three classifications. These are given below with typical examples for each.

DEFECTIVE PERFORMANCE BY CONTRACTING PARTY

- Incomplete plans or specifications, or those with errors
- A breach of contract by the contracting party
- Failure to allow the subcontractor to direct his own work
- Knowing misrepresentation of facts affecting subcontractor performance
- Failure to deliver sufficient information, equipment or materials as called for by the contract according to scheduled delivery dates
- Failure to properly coordinate the work of the subcontractors at the site
- Inadequate equipment or materials are supplied to the subcontractor
- Equipment or materials to be supplied to the subcontractor are not delivered by the date specified
- Failure to provide timely approvals as required by the contract

FUNDAMENTAL CHANGES IN CONTRACT CONDITIONS

- Changed site conditions, not as stipulated or described
- Changes ordered by the contracting party without compensation
- Suspension of the work

- Termination of the work
- Acceleration of the work to achieve early completion

UNCONTROLLABLE BARRIERS TO PERFORMANCE

- Abnormal delays to the work
- Severe weather conditions
- Unusual economic or physical conditions which impede the work
- An extreme change of scope of work making it impossible to continue the work under the original terms
- Strikes or other work stoppages

Every effort should be made to avoid a legal suit. These are expensive and neither of the two parties really wins. As long as both sides are sincerely attempting to resolve the claim, the first step is to try to talk out the differences. This is frequently possible, particularly if both sides approach the discussions responsibly. Quite possibly, the claim will escalate to senior management of the two firms for settlement. Here the differences will generally be less emotional as the parties are less involved in the day to day subcontract operations.

If agreement is still not possible, it would be prudent to call in a third party who might be able to assist in arbitration of the differences. If, in spite of all good intentions, a subcontract manager ends up with a litigious subcontractor who has submitted unfounded claims, he may have no choice but to fight it out in court. At this point, he must have the proper documentation and testimony to substantiate his arguments and refusal to pay the claim.

ACCEPTANCE OF WORK

The act of accepting the work covered by a subcontract should be considered a very serious matter. There are numerous legal and commercial implications which should not be overlooked.

ADVICE OF COMPLETION DATE: It is customary for the agreement to require the subcontractor to advise the subcontract manager *in writing* of the exact date when all of the work will be completed. Unless some objection is raised by the subcontract manager, this date is taken to be that on which the work done under the contract is considered as being finished and accepted.

VERIFICATION: All of the work covered by the contract must be checked to verify that it has been done in accordance with the plans and specifications. The subcontract manager will have a **"punch list"** prepared indicating any unsatisfactory, substandard, or unacceptable work. All of the items on this list must be corrected before final acceptance of the contract work.

The subcontract manager must also review the contract to ascertain that all of the other conditions required for contract completion have been met.

EQUIPMENT ITEMS: Final checkout of equipment items should be performed in accordance with the specified procedures. The equipment should be left in the proper condition as required by the contract and by the manufacturer's instructions.

SYSTEMS CHECKS: Of particular importance are the system checks where performance tests are required. Checking of these systems should be done in strict accordance with the testing procedures which were established and the results should be fully documented so that there can be no doubt about how the tests were conducted nor what the results were. Deficiencies or variances must be corrected and the tests repeated until satisfactory performance is achieved. Exceptions to this involve monetary penalties which have been set in the contract to compensate for a degree of lesser performance.

COMPLETION PRIORITIES: When projects are running on a tight schedule, it will be necessary to get some of the systems up and running early. It is reasonable for the subcontract manager to make arrangements to test and accept particular systems early. So doing can cause confusion and may also be the basis for some justified subcontractor claims. Once a system is accepted and custody has passed to the plant owner/operator, the subcontractor should not be expected to perform additional work not covered by his contractual obligations unless arrangements have been made for proper compensation. It is less trouble to get the workers who are familiar with the facility and are on the site to come back into a completed area to do minor modifications. This work is usually best handled in this manner, but additional work should not be added without considering the effect on the remainder of the subcontractor's workload and schedule. Fair compensation should be agreed on for any work above the scope of the contract.

COMPLETION DOCUMENTATION: The documentation of final inspection and tests is of considerable importance. Once a project has been finished, personnel are usually widely dispersed. A brief, well written log of the acceptance procedures used together with the results that were achieved will be extremely helpful in the case of future questions.

CONTRACT CLOSEOUT

Once the work has been accepted as being complete, the subcontract manager can proceed with closing out the contract. There are numerous items that must be done prior to finalizing the contract. As in all important phases of project work, the contract closeout should be planned in detail. The subcontract closeout plan should be followed closely.

- The subcontractor needs to provide verification that all of the bills for materials and supplies incorporated into the work have been paid for in full.

- If the subcontractor has been required to furnish "as built" drawings, these should be reviewed and verified for completeness and accuracy.

- The site must have been cleaned in compliance with the provisions of the contract; and all of the surplus material either removed from the site or returned to the proper custodian.

- All material, supplies, and equipment which have been in the care of the subcontractor for the duration of the contract should be returned as agreed in good condition.

- Any pending claims by the subcontractor should be resolved. Any credits due the contracting firm should also be closed out.

- All temporary facilities, offices, warehouses, tool sheds, and the like provided for use by the subcontractor are to be returned in good condition. All items brought to the site by the subcontractor should be removed.

- Proper disposition in accordance with the intent of the contract requirements should be made of all the surety bonds and insurance policies obtained for protection during the construction period. The insurance protection should be replaced, if required, by the policies of the owner or general contractor as appropriate.

- Finally, the subcontractor should formally acknowledge receipt of the final payment from the subcontract manager for the work covered by the contract. He should also guarantee that all work, labor, and material supplied for or used on the job have been paid for. This document will also waive all lien rights against the job. The contract may call for an affidavit from the subcontractor stating that all claims have been paid in full.

- The subcontract manager should issue a final report summariz-
  ing the significant items pertinent to the subcontract such as
  scope, conformance to plans and specifications, personnel involved, problems, and labor relations. This is usually done in
  conjunction with a subcontractor performance evaluation and is
  used for consideration of the firm for future work.

POSSESSION: Care and custody of the completed work is also a matter
for formal documentation. The subcontractor should pursue this point
to verify that, once the work has been completed, the responsibility for
care and custody has been transferred to the contracting entity or to the
owner.

SUBCONTRACTOR EVALUATION

While the performance of the subcontractor is still fresh in mind, the subcontract manager should prepare an evaluation to be used for reference in bidder selection on future projects as well as to determine if there are operational improvements that might be made on both parts on future work. Some companies have a specific format to be followed in making a subcontractor evaluation. Others leave it to the discretion of the evaluator. The following items should be considered for performance review and comments.

- **Summary:** A very brief narrative highlighting performance areas that were particularly outstanding and those that were deficient.

- **Organization/Planning of Work:** Was the work effectively planned?

- **Support from the Subcontractor's Home Office:** Was the support from the home office adequate for optimizing field operations?

- **Site Management:** Individual capability, experience and effectiveness of the superintendent, foremen, area superintendents, and other key individuals in the subcontractors organization. Turnover of top level personnel during the job.

- **Claims History:** Discuss claims quantitively and by type.

- **Quality Control:** Observations on the subcontractor's quality control for his own work and his response to advice to correct unsatisfactory work.

- **Safety Record:** The nature of the safety program if other than that for the whole site. Comparison of statistics on subcontract with total job safety record.

- **Scheduling:** Was the subcontractor proficient in scheduling his own work, especially if changes were necessary to his initial plan?

- **Cost Control:** Primarily of importance on a reimbursable contract. If the subcontract manager has had an opportunity to see how the subcontractor has handled his own cost control during the work, he should comment briefly on his observations.

- **Construction Methods:** Does the subcontractor use new and innovative construction techniques?

- **Craft Supervision:** Are the craft supervisors competent? Mention any outstanding foremen by name.

- **Crafts:** What was the general level of experience in each of the crafts? Was it outstanding, average, or poor?

- **Craftsmen:** Were there any truly outstanding craftsmen who would be valuable in future work? Was the work of any of the craftsmen unsatisfactory?

- **Labor Recruiting:** Did the subcontractor have difficulties in attracting a sufficient quantity of workers overall and in any of the individual crafts?

- **Labor Productivity:** What was the overall labor productivity in relative terms? Did the contractor have a good handle on productivity going into the job? How was he at handling labor relations? Were there problems on the job with grievances that were disruptive to the job? Were there work stoppages?

- **Material Control:** Did the subcontractor demonstrate a good capability in having the materials on the job where and when they were needed?

- **Cooperation with Other Subcontractors:** A statement as to the subcontractor's record of working out differences with other subcontractors on the site.

12 COMMISSIONING THE FACILITY

INSPECTION AND TESTING

Throughout the construction of the facility and at the acceptance of each of the subcontracts, inspection and testing have been a part of the job. For a facility with only 10,000 different components of one type or another, **a 99-percent-perfect record would still allow for 100 miscues**, any one of which could be critical to operation. The purpose of inspecting and testing is to catch as many of these mistakes as possible and to forestall that many future operational problems.

PLANNING FOR TESTING: Testing, prior to final acceptance of the facility or a portion of the facility, should be conducted following a detailed plan. This plan can be developed based on a standard checklist for equipment items and systems, but the specific plant will always have some differences or special considerations that must be taken into account.

ASSISTANCE FROM SPECIALISTS: Engineering specialists and design experts should be available to move to the site on short notice during the inspection and testing period. Delays in plant startup are very costly to the owner and the best minds should be applied to resolve problems rapidly.

MANUFACTURERS' REPRESENTATIVES: The tests of such major equipment items such as furnaces, compressors, and large pumps should be conducted by or in the presence of the manufacturers' representatives. The operating and maintenance representatives of the owner's operating department should also be present so that they can question the operating characteristics of the equipment and also verify the test results.

Field pressure tests of tanks, reactors, and piping systems are usually conducted by the constructor responsible for the work. Again this is done in the presence of representatives of the owner.

SAFETY DURING TESTING: Safety is a very important consideration during any sort of testing. Hydrostatic pressure testing can be extremely dangerous. The testing plan should indicate the specific individual responsible for safety of the personnel and the facility. All proposed testing plans and procedures should be reviewed and approved by this individual.

LINE PREPARATION FOR TESTING: Before hydrostatic testing is done, the lines must be cleaned and flushed to remove any construction debris or other foreign matter that may have been left in the vessels or lines. Screens should have been installed in suction lines before flushing to prevent debris from clogging the pumps. Blinds should be installed in compressor suction lines.

Sometimes getting water to the site in the quantities required for testing requires advance planning. Don't use service water for testing unless you are sure that any sediments will not settle out in the systems or coat the internals with mud. Disposal of the water used for testing may also require planning.

SUPPORT FACILITIES: The testing of the support facilities should not be neglected as these systems frequently cause problems during the startup of the facility. The most serious problems are encountered in the water treatment system, the steam system, and the process control systems.

MECHANICAL ACCEPTANCE

Mechanical acceptance of a facility cannot be an abstract occurence because of its extremely important legal implications. As such the definition of exactly what constitutes mechanical completion is made an integral part of the contract. Once the plant has been accepted mechanically, the care, custody and control of the facility should pass to the owner/operator.

Another significance of this project milestone is that the owner's representatives have witnessed the final inspection and testing of the facility, and they have agreed that the work has been done in accordance with the contract, plans, and specifications. Any deficiencies in the elements or systems of the plant are noted and corrections made before mechanical acceptance can be completed.

ACCEPTANCE BY SYSTEMS: At one time, mechanical acceptance meant that the entire facility was accepted. With the increasing size and complexity of the projects, facilities are being accepted by systems rather than in their entirety. Safety is certainly one of the most important considerations in setting the time for mechanical acceptance.

TANKS, TOWERS, AND VESSELS: At mechanical completion, the equipment items will have been inspected and checked to assure that all parts and pieces are properly installed. Vessels should be closed. Internals for all tanks, towers, and vessels should be in place. Fan motors for cooling towers and air fin coolers should be checked under "no load" conditions. Proper lubricants should have been introduced into all rotating equipment. Refractories should have been cured in reactors, furnaces, and incinerators. Burner piping should be connected after fuel lines have been blown out for furnaces, fired boilers, and incinerators.

ROTATING EQUIPMENT/PIPING: All pumps should be set and cold aligned with the drivers. Pumps should be coupled with the drivers after the motor has been checked for proper rotation and checks made that all vents, drains, and seals have been properly installed. All large compressors should be carefully reviewed in accordance with the engineering and fabricators' installation instructions. Piping should be chemically cleaned or pickled as specified. Temporary and permanent strainers and blinds should be in place. Air test the entire vacuum system. Calibrate all instrument and control systems and set switches in accordance with the data sheets. Check safety valve testing records to assure that checking has been properly completed.

SUPPORT FACILITIES: Support facilities should be thoroughly reviewed and readied for operation. Buildings should be ready to move in furnishings. All mechanical systems should be operational.

REMAINING WORK TO COMPLETE: The constructor does not stop work at mechanical completion. There may still be several items not essential for plant operation which are still pending. The installation of equipment and piping insulation will generally not have been entirely finished, as well as some of the painting work. Final cleanup and landscaping may also not be complete.

FACILITY TURNOVER

Following the project closeout plan, direction of the plant startup activities come under the owner's startup manager at the time of mechanical acceptance. The contractor may be involved in the subsequent activities, but they are always under the lead of the owner after the facility has been turned over to him. In any case, the contractor still must complete any unfinished painting, insulation, punch list items, and cleanup not done before the turnover.

One individual, **the startup manager**, needs to be named to assume the responsibility for commissioning the plant and for starting it up once the plant is turned over to the owner. Generally, this person will be from the production department or whatever entity will operate the plant. Infrequently the plant may be under the direction of the research and development organization until the performance tests have been run. In a few cases, the owner's project manager may be in charge of the plant startup.

Frequently, the plant may be turned over to the owner on **a system by system** basis. rather than all at one time. This may be necessary from a practical standpoint, but it can complicate the turnover process.

The first step in facility turnover is the written notification by the contractor that the plant has been completed and is ready for customer acceptance. All of the formalities of plant turnover should be checked to assure that they have been completed in accordance with the contract. The owner's project manager is responsible for assuring that all of this has been completed including the following items:

- **Documentation:** As built drawings as required by contract, latest issue of all drawings, engineering calculations, startup spare parts, operations manuals, maintenance manuals
- **Release of Liens and Subcontractors'/Vendors' Claims**
- **Site Condition:** Construction debris/site cleanup, surplus constructionmaterial disposed of, temporary facilities/construction buildings removed, construction equipment removed from jobsite

The owner must prepare a written acceptance of the work, attaching a punch list of any noncritical items that need to be completed by the contractor prior to final payment. Corporate protocol may call for additional turnover steps from the owner's project manager to the owner's startup manager. Once the facility has been accepted, it is under the **care and custody** of the owner. Some other points that need to be settled upon facility turnover are the following:

- **Insurance:** Prior to formalizing the turnover, the responsible person should make sure that arrangements have been made for the desired insurance coverage. There should be no lapse between the contractor's coverage and that being picked up by the owner.

- **Safety:** Safety should continue to be one of the most important considerations on turnover of the plant. Commissioning and startup represent a time in the project life cycle when accidents increase. The owner's representative is responsible for establishing and enforcing the safety program after turnover.

- **Security:** The security of the new facility also passes to the owner on turnover. Unless the new construction is a part of an existing plant, security will probably be an entirely new effort.

- **Maintenance:** Arrangements will have to be made for maintenance of the facility. This may be done either by the owner's own crews or by a contractor maintenance force.

- **Housekeeping:** In accepting the plant, the person in charge will need to make arrangements for plant housekeeping. This is a very mundane requirement and is often forgotten both in the plan and the budget. The contractor may have people available if he is still working at the site. A clear understanding about what is expected and what compensation will be forthcoming is necessary if the contractor is to continue with these activities after turnover. It is usually better that the owner take this responsibility from the moment of turnover.

INITIAL OPERATION

Initial operations include the introduction of the design feedstocks into the facility and the processing of these feedstocks into the specified products. Initial operations continue until a stable, safe level of plant production is reached, hopefully at or above the design capacity. There are three important aspects of plant startup: (1) the **startup plan**, (2) **equipment**, and (3) **staffing**.

AUTHORITY: In a startup situation, the owner's startup manager is in full charge of the work. The chief operators report to the startup manager and are in charge during his absence. Double coverage at the operator level is desirable during the initial plant loading. Experienced engineers who are familiar with the facility, whether from the owner's organization, the licensor, or the engineering firm, should be present during the startup. However, those outside the owner's organization act only on a consulting basis to the startup manager and his staff.

Frequent written reports by the startup manager detailing events in chronological sequence will be helpful to senior management as well as being essential in case of startup difficulties.

PLANNING: Initial operations of the facility must be planned. Once the plan has been tentatively set out in writing, it should be checked to make sure that a backup plan is available for any mishap that might occur during plant startup. Staffing is a very important consideration in initial operations. Underestimating personnel requirements for starting up a new facility is very easy to do and will inevitably lead to serious delays in getting the plant into production. Initial operations, maybe more than any other phase of the project, require **minute attention to detail.**

PHASED STARTUP: Feedstock is usually introduced into the plant at reduced rates until the reaction conditions have been established. Sometimes the minimum rate at which major equipment items can operate will determine the startup rates. The conditioning of the catalyst may dictate the facility loading rate.

SUPPORT FACILITIES: The operation of the support facilities is extremely critical during initial startup. The peak demand on some utilities may be reached before the reaction becomes self-sustaining.

FIELD/CONTROL ROOM CHECKS: Temperatures, pressures, levels, and flows are checked in the field against the remote readings in the control room. As long as there are no major problems, the component systems of the facility are gradually loaded until they reach design conditions. Acceptance of packaged equipment without proper checking has created many problems in the initial operations of numerous plants.

DOCUMENTATION: There probably have not been many startups where there was a surplus of information and data taken. There are many cases in which insufficient information had been logged to provide an insight on the problems encountered. The startup manager must insist on a level of data gathering and recording which is probably in excess of what will be needed.

PROBLEMS: Should potentially serious problems arise, the startup should be immediately aborted until the problems are resolved. In face of the risks to life and to the new facility, it is not worth taking a chance to save a little time even with intense schedule pressures. An abundance of data will be extremely helpful in analysis of any processing problem.

The **inability to design for unsteady state conditions** is the source of many of the startup problems which will be encountered.

Much can be done to ameliorate difficulties in the plant startup by reviewing those elements that have caused problems in past startups of similar plants. Once identified, checking in those areas should be redoubled. **Critical equipment** should be carefully reviewed. The **process control system** seems to be particularly prone to creating problems during startup.

PERFORMANCE TESTS

Performance tests are made in accordance with the terms of the contract. There are many occasions when exact duplications of the specified tests is impossible and mutually agreeable modifications must be made.

TIMING: The timing of the tests is important, and is generally set by the contract to be conducted within a certain period after the plant has been accepted for initial operation. A period of 120 days is normal. By contractual agreement, the 120 days will be extended to compensate for any period of time that the plant is unable to operate through fault of the contractor. Often the final payment to the contractor is tied to the successful completion of the performance tests.

STAFFING: The performance tests require a sizable number of individuals to be present around the clock to observe the tests and to take operational data. These people will come from the owner's organization and from the contractor's and licensor's firms. Representatives of suppliers may be required for critical items of equipment, or packaged systems, or from the process control system manufacturer. Additional personnel may be contracted from third parties for the test period as required. The organization of the effort should be made clear to all participants so there can be little doubt as to the proper channels of authority during the tests.

Because there is multiple firm representation, the purpose and objectives of the guarantee runs together with all of the specifications, constraints, and parameters of the tests should be made clear to all of those who participate in the performance testing. Communication is best done by putting essential information in written form, and holding a briefing for the entire staff prior to starting the testing.

DURATION: The test runs will be more meaningful if they are made at one time for the entire complex and if they extend for the full period specified. On large, multitrain facilities, performance tests may be broken into smaller pieces as a convenience and to reduce the manpower requirements. The guarantee agreement may specify a relatively long test run. If the market cannot absorb the quantity of products produced, the owner may opt for a shorter run.

LINEOUT: A period of time prior to the performance tests is required to adjust all of the streams to a normal condition. This is termed the plant **lineout**. It can vary from less than one shift to two or three days. This critical step should not be pushed, if a successful performance test is to be expected.

DESIGN OF PERFORMANCE TESTS: The performance tests should be designed to demonstrate each of those elements which are under guarantee following the terms of the agreement. Normally, these will include: (1) feedstock consumption, (2) quantity of products produced, (3) quality of products produced, (4) consumption of catalysts, steam, electricity, and treated process water, (5) quantity of by-products generated, and (6) various pressure and temperature levels.

RECORDS: The records kept of the performance tests are important as they are the basis for making monetary settlements or adjustments for less than satisfactory performance. The format of recording the test results should be standardized. Units of measurement should be consistent. The records kept during the performance tests can also provide an early indication as to bottlenecks in the plant design. Removal of these bottlenecks would allow the plant to exceed specified capacities.

TEST CONDITIONS: If specified performance test conditions cannot be duplicated, a demonstration test can be run. This is not as rigid as a performance test, but could be substituted at the owner's option. For example, if specification grade feedstocks are not available or if product storage is limited, the owner may opt for a demonstration test rather than waiting for a performance test.

The performance test results will indicate the basis for penalties in case there is an excess consumption of feedstock, catalysts, or utilities, as well as underproduction of product and overproduction of by-products. The contract may provide for the contractor or licensor to take credit for exceeding performance guarantees in one category, to be used in offsetting other categories where performance is below that guaranteed.

13 PROJECT COMPLETION

PROJECT CLOSEOUT

The project has been completed and turned over to the owner, but there is still work to be done. The beginning of a project is exciting. The production phase may be grueling, but it is usually full of problems and challenges. Completing the final details of a project might best be categorized as tedious and boring by most project managers.

A project not properly closed out loses much of its value for planning future projects. Senior management should insist on following a closeout procedure that will protect the company. Closeout should be done promptly before all of the key staff members are dispersed to their normal assignments or to other projects. Following are some of the things that need to be done to close out a project properly.

SUBCONTRACT CLOSEOUT: All subcontracts must be checked as having been properly closed out. Any remaining variances to specifications must be negotiated and compensation agreed upon. Incomplete tasks should be corrected or acknowledgement made in writing that they have been excused and any monetary differences resolved.

PURCHASE ORDER CLOSEOUT: All purchase orders should be reviewed to verify that all deliverables have been received and that any back charges settled. Certified records of fabrication and testing, spare parts or spare parts lists, maintenance recommendations and final certified drawings are among the items which are often delinquent at job closing.

FINANCIAL AUDITS: A financial audit on any of the major contracts should be ordered and completed by the owner.

WARRANTEES: The warrantee program should be implemented and turned over to the owner's operations group.

DEMOBILIZATION: Compliance with all of the contractual provisions for moving off the site is a prerequisite for job completion. Temporary facilities should be disposed of together with the return of any leased portable buildings, trailers, and the like.

CLOSEOUT REPORT: Both the owner's project manager and the contractor's project manager should prepare closeout reports for their senior management. These should both be internal reports although most of the data and statistics may be common to both. In the report, liberal use should be made of graphical presentations to review performance. Specially selected construction photographs are helpful in adequately describing job conditions. The reports should contain summaries of the job status including information on staffing, organization, schedule, costs, quality of work, and major problems, each with its indicated resolution. The report writer should conclude with recommendations for handling future work, concise critiques of the performance of the owner, licensors, contractor, subcontractors, vendors, fabricators, and other suppliers.

CLOSEOUT OF ALL CHARGES: The authorization for job charges should be sharply restricted as the end of the job nears. Only those individuals with specific closeout responsibilities should be permitted to charge time to the project. Most of the late charges to the job will be for labor and these must be rigidly controlled.

RESPONSIBILITY: On many projects, the project manager is reassigned before the project is closed out. The project manager or senior management must nominate an alternate individual who will have the responsibility for closing out the project according to the plan which has been previously developed.

14 THE PROJECT MANAGER'S ROLE AS MANAGER

MANAGEMENT SKILLS

Years ago, an individual in charge of a project had only to be technically proficient in a single discipline. The traditional disciplines themselves were more encompassing and projects generally involved only one discipline. A large building project required only a competent architect to work with several master craftsmen. Schedules were sometimes a matter of decades and labor was cheap so escalating costs were not that much of a problem.

As projects became multidisciplinary in nature, technically more sophisticated, and subject to strong schedule and cost pressures, the project managers looked for help with discipline coordination and project controls. The development of the computer together with the quantum leap in project magnitude/complexity at the beginning of the second half of the twentieth century led to the development of new project management tools. Initially many of these tools were cumbersome and unwieldy, but they have advanced project execution.

A variety of these tools and techniques are now available. The project manager can pick, choose, and adapt to fill his needs. Today's project managers know that having a strong discipline background and a knowledge of project management technical tools is not the whole answer to running a successful project. Until the late 1980s, too much emphasis was been placed on the *project* part of project management, and not enough on the *management* part.

The type and composition of projects tend to change as technology develops and economic conditions cycle. The project manager should keep an eye out for indications as to what is going on in his particular segment of industry and evaluate how that will affect future projects. We don't have to go back very far to see the tremendous changes that have occurred in the energy business and see how these changes have affected the lives of many project managers.

A project manager's potential success or failure on a project can be viewed based on three factors:

1. **A firm foundation in a discipline appropriate for the type of project in which he is involved**

279

2. **A solid technical background based on project management techniques of planning, scheduling, and cost management**

3. **Competency as a manager in a project environment**

The working project manager typically is well trained in a specific discipline. He may have been very successful in that discipline, and this fact probably contributed to his ultimate selection as project manager.

The project manager's technical knowledge and experience should include those project execution elements such as planning, organizing the work, scheduling, estimating, monitoring, controlling, and reporting.

The managerial background would ideally contain those characteristics such as:

1. Concern for performance
2. Leadership and the power base
3. Consistently high values
4. Hard worker
5. Get and keep quality people
6. Communicating skills
7. Good discipline
8. Effective work systems
9. Enthusiasm
10. Sensitivity to interpersonal relationships

The project manager's training in the techniques of the management of projects has probably been more haphazard than his formal education in his own discipline. Self-initiative will have been instrumental in acquiring knowledge through on-the-job training by schedulers, cost control personnel, and more senior project managers.

Many texts are available on the various technical aspects of project management providing a reservoir of knowledge for those willing to devote their own time and efforts to acquire it. Professional societies such as the Project Management Institute and the American Association of Cost Engineers promote the interchange of the technology of project management. This training fills a real need and it may be the best way for the project manager to gain knowledge of his profession.

QUALITY

A discussion of quality has to start with a definition about what quality is. In much engineering/construction work, quality is defined by specifications, codes, and standards. In this respect, what meets the requirements should be considered quality work, or work done as specified. *Industry standard* is frequently used, but this term is misleading. The current definition of quality is **"fitness for use,"** the result of considerable thought about what quality isn't.

To many people quality still refers to the best available. For example, a Silver Arrow is a *quality car*. This is where we get into trouble.

A recent book on quality is *I Know It When I See It* by John Guaspari (1985). The message in this book is that the product or service can meet all of the specifications, codes, and standards that are stipulated, and yet it is not a quality product unless it does what it is expected to do, or unless it meets the **expectations** of the customer.

Phillip Crosby (1975) in his book *Quality is Free* believes that there is a payout in quality because of the savings brought about by saving on rework, reject items, and the repeat business generated from satisfied customers.

There is a misconception that you can't have both *quality* and *productivity*, that these are opposing elements. We have heard the question "Do you want it fast or do you want it good?" This is countered by "We never have time to do anything right, but we always have time to do it over."

Quality is a matter of corporate survival and the entire work force must be involved. The corporate commitment to quality has to come unquestionably from the very top, but attaining quality performance must be a personal commitment of the people who actually do the work— write the specifications, perform the calculations, do the design, and do the drafting. Management at all levels must stress the importance of quality to the future of the company and to the individuals themselves.

To get acceptance of the quality work concept, the first step makes each person truly **accountable** for his own work output. Next, a **constructive auditing procedure** is used to improve existing methods and procedures. Quality circles were introduced in the U.S. some years ago. This technique has lasted where properly used. It has long since fallen by the wayside where it was just a fad, started because it was the thing to do.

The use of a technique known as **IMPROP** or **IMPR**ovement to **OP**erations (Kimmons, 1981) serves this purpose. IMPROP sessions group all levels of the organization together. At this time a product such as a drawing, a specification, a report, or a study is reviewed by a group composed of each person in the organization who was involved at any step of the process from the conceptual to the final drafting or typing. The time is equally spent between an audit of (1) **what was done** pointing out any cost, schedule, and quality variances and (2) **how it could have been done** better, faster, or more cost effectively. IMPROP facilitates communication between the levels of the organization, keeps management abreast of the work products, and serves to get people in the organization to talk to each other.

There have been corporate excesses committed in the name of quality. The prudent manager must not implement quality programs haphazardly. If the program does not have top level support, if it does not hold the producing individual accountable for quality, and if it does not result in increased customer satisfaction at a reasonable cost, then it should be scrutinized carefully before implementation.

Guaspari, John, *I Know It When I See It*, AMACOM, The American Management Association, New York, NY, 1985.

Crosby, Phillip, *Quality is Free*, Mentor Executive Library, New York, NY, 1975

Kimmons, Robert L.,"Improve Operations with IMPROP." *Hydrocarbon Processing*, Gulf Publishing Company, Houston, TX, January 1981, pp. 232-237.

LEADERSHIP

Management is concerned with accomplishing things through others by performing the functions of planning, organizing, monitoring, controlling and reporting. **Leadership** adds another dimension by introducing extraordinary motivation of the followers into the equation. Managers can manage without being leaders. They can give good direction without generating the enthusiasm and will to accomplish that a leader brings. Leaders can lead without being good managers. They can generate tremendous *esprit de corps*, but for precisely the wrong course of action.

The desired combination of a good manager and a good leader is not common. The principles of good management can be taught, but although good leaders may become better with added experience, much of their capability is instinctive.

The environment in which the business is conducted is of importance to the manager because it will tend to support or weaken his performance as a leader. A manager who is a great leader under current conditions might find considerable frustration in moving into another situation. A good example of this same phenomenon is the successful corporate executive who makes a move into government only to end up performing badly. For better or for worse, the organizational systems that are in place and the personalities of current and past senior management influence the climate in which the work is done.

This does not mean that if a manager is in a poor situation he is completely tied to it. If he **realizes** the dilemma, **analyzes** the negative effects, and aggressively sets out to **make changes,** he can take steps to mitigate the problems and make leading a much easier and more satisfying job.

One of the most important attributes of a good leader is his **credibility.** People will follow someone they can believe in strongly. Another characteristic is **consistency**. People will do more and with more willingness if they can predict the response of the leader.

Areas in which a manager may personally make a difference in the work environment by exerting strong leadership are:

- **Demand excellence in planning.**
- **Define job responsibilities that have not been well defined.**
- **Improve the flow of information by introducing innovations.**

- **Provide performance feedback on a regular basis.**
- **Make sure that unfair and unjust retaliation does not occur for honest mistakes.**
- **Assign specific responsibilities, and see that they are well understood.**

There are also areas that are more subtle where the manager can make changes which will reinforce his leadership role.

- **Assure that the contribution of each individual is seen to be important.**
- **Place a high priority on training and development of staff.**
- **Foster a unity of purpose which can be fostered by superior coordination and communication.**

A manager's reputation as a dynamic leader attracts good people.

SITUATIONAL LEADERSHIP

Effective managers understand the results of differing leadership styles on the performance of the organization and will choose the leadership style most appropriate for ultimate success in achieving their objectives. Each manager must choose the style most responsive to actual existing conditions.

The manager's leadership style may be looked on the the type of working relationship that a manager chooses to utilize with those for whom he is responsible.

Early studies of management style advanced the idea of **autocratic** or **task-related** behavior as opposed to **participative** or **relationship-based** behavior. The former was held to be best for "high pressure, short duration" situations, while the latter would work better for those of "lower pressure and longer range." There was also a general belief that each manager had a fixed style of management that did not vary.

We each tend to use a particular style of management because we are more comfortable with it and it appears to give us the best results.

Blanchard and the Zigarmis (1985) postulate that there is **no "single, all-purpose" best management style**, but that the leader's behavior should be adapted to the needs of each situation. These authors identify four basic leader-behavior styles:

- High task, low relationship **S1**
- High task, high relationship **S2**
- Low task, high relationship **S3**
- Low task, low relationship **S4**

They classify the development level of the followers from **low** to **high**. It is important to recognize that this type of development combines competence and commitment of the follower related only to the assignments at hand. It has nothing to do with the age or overall experience of the individuals.

Recognizing that people at different levels of development need to be treated differently, the authors then state that the appropriate leadership styles may be matched with a corresponding development level. The four basic leadership behaviors may be related to the development of the followers and the recommended leader behavior as follows:

Development Level of Followers	Suggested Leader Behavior
D1 - Low competence, high commitment.	**S1** - Directing
D2 - Some competence, Low commitment.	**S2** - Coaching
D3 - High competence, variable commitment. . .	**S3** - Supporting
D4 - High Competence, high commitment.	**S4** - Delegating

Leadership styles may be started at any of the four levels, but the chosen style should move only in the direction from D-1 toward D-4 in successive steps. Leadership style is extremely difficult to move in the opposite direction. The organization can accept a gradual easing off of control more easily that a tightening which is frequently less than an orderly transition.

The body of knowledge of leadership style is still evolving. Much more time will pass before it becomes a completely defined science. The style selection process requires that the manager analyze the existing situation and arrive at a positive approach based upon careful consideration of all of the known factors.

Blanchard, Kenneth, Patricia Zigarmi, and Drea Zigarmi, *Leadership and the One-Minute Manager*, Morrow, West Caldwell, NJ, 1985.

TEAM BUILDING

A closely knit group of people working together is usually **more productive** and will have a **higher morale** than equivalent people with the same level of knowledge and experience who work separately. It follows that group performance can be enhanced through building a team or teams in the work force.

A prerequisite for team building is the visible commitment of top management to the team concept. Top management must be willing to be aware of honest mistakes brought to light by team management practices without unjustly punishing individuals. Top management must give an open ear and consider objectively any honest and constructive suggestions for operational improvements that come from the organization.

To start team building, the following should be considered:

- The **environment must be open** and receptive to new ideas. Senior management must provide the conditions that will permit this.

- The **people must be brought closely together** so that they can really get to know one another. Sometimes this will have to be forced. It is easy to mistrust someone you don't know, and much more difficult to mistrust someone that you know well and with whom you can communicate easily.

- The team members must have a **commitment to a plan**. This may be fostered by insisting upon their participation in development of the plan.

- Team members must have a **defined role** in implementing the plan and have targets for which they are responsible.

- **Performance must be monitored** and **feedback furnished** to the team.

- Good performance must be visibly rewarded.

- The visible **pressure to improve poor performance** should come from the group. Managers and supervisors should discuss poor performance privately and directly with the individual responsible.

- At all levels of the organization, **creativity and innovation should be encouraged** among team members. The condemnation which says "Not Invented Here (NIH)" should be eliminated.

PROJECT MANAGEMENT BASICS: A Step by Step Approach

- **Constant feedback** tailored for the tasks at hand should be encouraged. This feedback is necessarily in three directions—up, down and sideways.

- There should be constant effort given to **improve interpersonal relationships** among team members without stifling healthy and constructive differences.

- There should be constant pressure on **"being the best that we can be."** Collective expectations should be defined and clarified to each team member.

This list must not be taken to be all-inclusive as there are other ways that contribute to the formation of a team.

Where time is of the essence, such as occurs on a project, a retreat away from the workplace can be an invaluable instrument in accelerating the team building exercise. Requirements include (1) **a challenging agenda**, (2) **advance work assignments** for the entire team, and (3) **careful and sensitive direction** of the entire program by the manager in charge.

Pincus, Claudio,"Plan Better with Team Building." *Hydrocarbon Processing*, Gulf Publishing Company, Houston, TX, November 1979, pp. 357-363.

Kavanagh, Jack T., and Barbara B. Feinstein, "Maximize Project Team Effectiveness." *Hydrocarbon Processing*, Gulf Publishing Company, Houston, TX, August 1987, pp. 71-76.

PERFORMANCE MANAGEMENT

Project time is very limited. The project manager must make use of all of the time available. All of the project planning, scheduling, and budgeting contribute to a good definition of what needs to be done. Performance management translates the global definition into specific role definition for small groups and individuals. Performance management has been characterized as assuring that the **"right things are done at the right time."**

We can all remember times of outstanding personal performance, when we were able to accomplish significantly more work. Unfortunately, these times of maximum productivity occur only infrequently. Average productivity is probably less than forty percent of peak productivity. Contributors to peak performance include the following four factors:

- **Knowing what has to be done**
- **Having all of the information necessary to do it**
- **Having all of the tools required**
- **Being excited by the assignment**

Additional factors also may affect personal productivity under many circumstances.

- An imminent deadline is a "turn on" to some.
- Visible support from management and peers can contribute.

The objective of the project management team should be to obtain the best performance possible from all of those individuals working on the project at all times. We can take the factors listed above and cast them in terms of what should be done:

- Expectations of individual results **should be made clear.**

- **Responsibility to obtain the information** should be an integral part of the assignment.

- Project management makes sure that **tools are available to the individuals to perform their assignments.** Individuals have the responsibility to advise their supervisor if there is anything lacking.

- Assignments are not always challenging, but **they can be made more interesting.** Project management has a responsibility to lean the right chords to strike in motivating each of the project people.

- The **deadline for each assignment should be clear** and there should be a reason for any extremely difficult deadlines.

- The project environment should encourage **meaningful performance feedback to each individual** and each of the groups, squads, or crews working on the project.

Performance management consists of making sure that each person knows what is expected from his work output each day and that feedback is given on his relative contribution, tying it into the total effort.

PRODUCTIVITY

There appear to be three approaches to productivity improvement. All must be utilized for maximum attainment. The first depends upon the human element; the second, the systems used; and the third involves the tools which are available.

THE HUMAN ELEMENT: Given that performance of the organization depends upon individual performance, if we are to assure good group performance, we must monitor what each person does on a regular basis.

A new term in management is **Employee Involvement (EI),** which has been demonstrated to have a very positive effect on productivity. This technique involves workers in a meaningful way in participation in the work methods and schedules, and, additionally, offers a profit-sharing formula.

We cannot monitor performance unless we have a baseline to monitor it against. Creating a baseline for technology workers is difficult and probably the techniques in use for blue collar work will not apply. But we should realize that maximum performance can only be reached when each person fully understands what is expected each hour of the day. This does not mean that assignments should be scheduled and accounted for to the nearest hour. It does mean that people are not left wondering about what they should be doing.

Five elements of white collar productivity are seen by Berglind and Scales (1987):

Focus	**Are we doing the right thing?**
Organization	**Do we have the best possible structure and integration?**
Process	**Are we doing things right?**
Motivation	**Do we want to do our best?**
Management Effect	**Are our perceptions clear? Are our interventions effective?**

THE SYSTEMS USED: The Construction Industry Institute, based in Austin, Texas has zeroed in on improving productivity by conducting research on some of the systems used including project scoping, planning, project controls, work packaging, materials management, quality, risk management, and constructability. The findings of this research are now being applied to real projects by members of the CII.

THE TOOLS: Many improvements in productivity will come about through increased use of computers with vastly enhanced capability, and through robotics and automation. In current thinking, these three areas hold more promise for doing things better than was conceivable just a short time ago.

Berglind, Bradford L. and Charles D. Scales, "White-Collar Productivity: Seeing through the Camouflage," *Management Review*, American Management Association, New York, NY, June 1987, pp. 41-46.

MOTIVATION

Some managers believe that all of their problems can be resolved by motivation. To others the word conjures up mystery and psychological mishmash. Simply stated, motivation is an **intense inner desire to accomplish**.

Abraham H. Maslow's hierarchy of needs published in the mid-1950s states that people are motivated by their inner needs to satisfy five gradations of need: (1) **physical** or physiological needs such as hunger, sleep and sex, (2) **safety** needs or protection against danger or the possibility of loss, (3) **social** needs such as the need for belonging, association or acceptance, (4) **esteem** or ego needs which involve status, recognition and respect and finally, (5) **self-actualization** or self-fulfillment needs, or the desire to "be all one can be." These needs are progressive, meaning that until a person has satisfied all his physical needs, the other needs do not really motivate him. Also, a satisfied need is no longer a motivator.

In the business world in the United States we are not primarily concerned with motivating employees by feeding them or protecting them. The two real motivators then are **social needs** and **esteem needs**. We should concentrate our efforts in these two areas.

Frederick Herzberg (1966) has divided a list of motivating factors into two categories: **satisfiers** and **dissatisfiers**. His theory states that only **satisfiers** including such things as **achievement** and **work satisfaction** can motivate. The absence of those factors listed as dissatisfiers can only demotivate. **Dissatisfiers** include **money, vacation time, insurance**, and **plush working conditions**. Salaries and benefits must be fair, and they must be justly administered.

The vast majority of people want to do a good job and to live up to the expectations of their manager as well as their own expectations. A minority of people are working just to be able to do the things they really want to do. Perhaps they are the most motivated of all.

As managers in a technical environment, we should attempt to provide an environment which will stimulate motivation in our employees. We have to create an atmosphere where there are vibrant and positive expectations. We need to assure that the hierarchical needs are fulfilled to as high a level as practicable and we need to be sure that we are **concentrating on the satisfiers** in our management efforts.

Our employees have a need for self-esteem. They need to feel good about themselves. People who are challenged in their jobs are more productive and are less likely to be dissatisfied and leave. We need to be concerned with providing recognition. People who accomplish more get more recognition which drives them to more accomplishment. People want to feel involved with the company, involved in the company operations— to identify with the company, department, or project.

We worry too much about what is important to the company, and not enough about what is important to the employee and understanding the employee's viewpoint. Motivation comes about when the employee knows you worry about his concerns. Sometimes the way company procedures are administered serves to alienate the employees. Some managers manage to turn people off. The employees get signals from above. You have to be careful and concerned about the messages that are being sent. Quality circles have been effective in bringing people into the decision making process.

Most employees are interested in the esteem of their co-workers. We must make sure that the corporate environment does not permit esteem to be given for non-productive performance. In some work environments, there is a stigma attached to exceeding the norm. Quality is a big factor in boosting pride in work. People want to be with a winning team!

In our concern for motivating our employees we must not forget that that there is really no way we can measure motivation quantitively; we can only measure results. Getting results should be our main objective.

Maslow, Abraham H., *Motivation and Personality*, Harper & Row, New York, NY, 1954.
Hertzberg, Frederick R., *Work and the Nature of Man*, World Publishing, Cleveland, OH, 1966.

CREATIVITY

In this age of increasing competition, there is a real need to discover new and better ways to do our work. There has been an explosion in technology and there is great pressure to incorporate these developments into our work methods.

It has been suggested that most employees at all levels usually function using only about one-half of their available brain power. This represents a tremendous waste of knowledge, experience and talent.

Productivity is directly related to the environment in which one works. If there is constant encouragement to improve the operation, ideas come forth and production increases.

Middle management frequently is the stumbling block to new ideas. Studies reported by Kanter (1982) indicate that middle managers who do encourage creativity among their employees share five characteristics:

1. **They are comfortable with change**. They are confident that uncertainties will be clarified. They have foresight and see unmet needs as opportunities.
2. **They have a clarity of direction**. They select projects carefully and, with their long time horizons, view setbacks as temporary blips in an otherwise straight path to a goal.
3. **They are thorough**. They prepare well for meetings and are professional in making their presentations. They have insight into organizational politics and a sense of whose support can help them at various junctures.
4. **They use a participative management style**. They encourage subordinates to put in maximum effort and to be part of the team, promise them a share of the rewards, and deliver on their promises.
5. **They are persuasive, persistent and discrete**. They understand that they cannot achieve their ends overnight; they persevere until they do.

Too many of us feel comfortable with the time tested methods and procedures. Raudsepp (1981) identifies some of the environmental organizational blocks that impede new ideas.

- Resistance to new ideas
- Resistance to change

- Negative reactions
- Lack of strength and determination
- Threat to security
- Smugness
- Private domains
- Dependency feelings
- No time
- Competition vs cooperation

Of course, no new idea should be accepted until the risks have been evaluated and the possible consequences of failure tested. You must be very careful in rejecting ideas that you do not put a damper on creativity. There should always be a dialogue with those who came up with the idea so that they fully understand the reasons behind not proceeding with implementation if that is the final decision.

Kanter, Rosabeth Moss, "The Middle Manager as Innovator." *Harvard Business Review*, Boston, MA, July-August, 1982, pp. 95-105.
Raudsepp, Eugene, "Overcome Creativity Barriers." *Hydrocarbon Processing*, Gulf Publishing Company, Houston, TX, August-November, 1981 (in four parts).

GOAL SETTING

Goal setting is a process that assures that the expectations of the supervisor are first clear in his own mind, and then that they are understood in the mind of the employee. These two assurances combine to improve the chances that the work will be done right.

People want to do a good job. If an employee understands what is wanted, he will come much closer to fulfilling that expectation. If he also has an understanding as to **why** it is wanted and **what** it will be used for, his chances of satisfying the supervisor are further increased. The responsibility for this understanding rests jointly with the supervisor and the employee.

Failure to communicate expectations adequately stems from:

1. **The supervisor assumes that the employee already has all needed information.**
2. **The employee does not question the supervisor about any uncertainties that he might have.**
3. **The supervisor may not be sure exactly what is needed and gives a fuzzy, ambiguous explanation.**
4. **Both the supervisor and the employee may have preconceived, but differing, ideas about what is wanted.**

Characteristics of goals which are used to improve performance include:

1. The goals must be defined and measurable.
2. Completion time has to be set.
3. Resources to be used are allotted.
4. Desired level of quality is determined.

DEFINITION: The work must be defined in the detail necessary to describe exactly what is wanted and the degree of detail and the format that are acceptable. Particular conditions should be explained up front. The supervisor should make known the allowable departures from standard procedures. The process of establishing goals becomes easier as the individuals become accustomed to working closely together.

COMPLETION: A full understanding of the goal implies that the completion time has been set. If review, checking or approval is required for completion, these must be taken into account so that the proper allowances are made.

RESOURCE ALLOTMENT: In addition to the time of the individual who is assigned the work, the time of others, or budgets for money, tools, and equipment may be required. The limit or budget should be stipulated. The supervisor should reach an understanding as to relative values in case that tradeoffs become necessary. The employee should understand at what point he should check back with the supervisor when additional resources are needed.

QUALITY OF WORK: The level of quality may be difficult to define. On a project, many standards and specifications are available. But these are instances where additional supplemental information is required. A rush assignment may not require the same level of quality as a critical design calculation would demand. Quality is an integral part of goal definition.

COMMUNICATION

People in an organization work best when they understand their work and responsibilities. Performance management requires good communication to be effective. Communication may take any of several forms or combinations depending upon the requirements and the situation. Three types of communication are employed in the office: **oral, written,** and **visual**. Each of these three may take various forms.

ORAL COMMUNICATION: The most frequently used form of communication It is fast, cheap, and provides immediate feedback. However, it is subject to change depending on the accuracy of the individual's memory.

- **One on One Conversations:** Most communication involves two people talking face to face. Feedback can be excellent.

- **Telephone Conversations:** Can be a real time saver. Feedback is diminished because "body language" is lost.

- **Seminars and Workshops:** Good for instructional purposes, especially when combined with written and visual forms. More structured than conversations.

- **Meetings**: The main purpose of most meetings is not to impart information to those attending, but to get something done. Communication at a meeting is primarily oral, but may involve elements of both written communication through distributed-material and visual, through films, slides, and the like.

WRITTEN COMMUNICATION: Most of the more significant communication in an office is written. Written communication, although it may be interpreted differently by different people, remains the same for each of the readers both now and in the future.

- **Letters and Memos:** The simplest form of written communication and the most used. Frequently overdone in certain office environments. Less subject to misinterpretation after the fact and to distortion than oral communication.

- **Policies, Procedures, and Standards:** Documents containing vital information for running a business. Very carefully worded and edited for maximum clarity.

- **Reports:** Present data and information gathered for a specific purpose in an orderly and structured format.

- **Newsletters** can now be produced rapidly and professionally. Extremely effective as an employee communication medium.

- **Specifications:** Generally consist of repetitive instructions or conditions used to supplement the plans and drawings.

- **Minutes of Meetings:** Should be concise but adequate for the purpose. If overly long, they will not be read.

VISUAL COMMUNICATION: Visual communication is powerful and creates a greater impact and is best at communicating complex concepts.

- **Plans, Drawings, and Sketches:** Least subject to misinterpretation.

- **Graphs, Charts , Cartoons, and Illustrations:** Powerful visual communication tool for emphasizing or comparing.

- **Video:** Cost effective complex messages presented to a large number of employees over an extended period of time. Video is used extensively in training. Multimedia presentations are rapidly making inroads in sophisticated communications as the techniques become widely available. Multimedia involve the simultaneous use of various screens, computerized selection of projected material from slides or video tape, and synchronized stereo audio, both vocal and musical.

EFFECTIVE COMMUNICATION: In selecting the type of communication to be used for each specific instance, you should analyze what needs to be communicated and to whom. The importance of accurate transmission of information and the risks that you are taking with misunderstandings and misinterpretation must be considered. Cost is often the deciding factor in the selection process.

THE COMMUNICATION PROCESS

Initially, the manager looks at communication as a very simple process. "I tell someone to do something, and he should do it." What could be simpler! In fact, communication is extremely complicated.

Communication involves at least two people who may have very different backgrounds, experience, and education. Many times these individuals come from different cultures, speak different languages, and certainly have different drives.

There are various tools for communicating. We can tell people orally what to do. We can write them letters, reports, or memos. We can produce videos showing them what to do. We gesture or use "body language," which is sometimes a powerful method of communicating.

The communication process usually involves one person (1) taking thoughts out of his head, (2) translating them into words, (3) projecting them either orally or in writing to another person; (4) these expressed thoughts are then either seen or heard, and then (5) they require translation into the brain of the receiver. The complexity of the process is evident. At each of these five steps, there are possibilities for errors and misinterpretation.

A complicating factor is that words— either written or spoken— may not mean the same thing to different people. Some of the words we rely on in the strict technical sense are adequately defined. But many words in common usage are not so adequate. The word "quality" is a good example. What does it really mean as we use it in our everyday workplace? The word "adequate" is another. In the past we used the phrase "or equal" in our specifications, causing prolonged discussions about what is really equal.

Some of the common problems with the way we communicate are as follows:

- **Unclear Expectations**: One of the root problems with communication occurs when that the manager is not clear in his own mind what he wants. Under pressure of time, he has not been able to adequately analyze the requirements and so he prematurely assigns the work. If he does not know what he expects, there is little chance that he will explain it satisfactorily to the employee. The manager is able to sort out his ideas afterward, but frequently does not go back and talk to the employee about them.

- **Unclear Definition:** Another problem may be that the manager knows precisely what he wants, but he also assumes that anything so clear to him requires no detailed explanation. The employee is sure to know exactly what is needed. But the employee may be coming from a different direction. Certainly his background is sufficiently different to cause difficulties unless the two have worked together on identical activities.

- **Inadequate Comprehension:** The manager may be very clear in his own mind and able to communicate his ideas adequately, but the employee may not have the background, technical skill, experience, or the language skills to understand the assignment.

Information in the office environment has some strange characteristics. People are hungry for it. This hunger is a void and the void will be filled. Accurate input from knowledgeable sources is preferable, but in its absence, distorted, false, and inaccurate information is born of conjecture and circulated by rumor.

Communication between two people is difficult, sometimes even for a married couple. How can we possibly expect those who only work with us to understand what we are really saying? The only answer is that we have to recognize the problems and to work at making sure our communication process is operating well.

LISTENING

Projects have failed in one or more of the critical areas because of a failure by the parties to listen to what is being said. A key complaint by the participants on a project is that there has been a lack of response brought about by a failure to listen. Let's look at some reasons for **not listening.**

1. **Not Interested:** During project execution, there are many pressures. Sometimes what the client wants to talk about does not seem as important as our own problems.

2. **Prejudgement:** When the client starts to talk about one of his concerns, we immediately jump to a conclusion or make a premature evaluation about what he is going to say.

3. **Lack of Concentration:** Maybe we are caught at the wrong time. We are thinking about things not related to the client's conversation.

4. **Material Is Too Complex:** The client may have been working on a particular topic for some time. When he springs it on us, we have not had the same amount of time to prepare and are turned off.

5. **Attention to Note Taking:** We may concentrate so much on trying to take notes that we miss half of what is being said.

6. **Pretending Interest:** Listening is work. If the listener is tired or has no interest in the discussion, he may feign interest. An inactive listener shows no energy output.

7. **Delivery Not Interesting:** Many times the speaker is not a professional and may have an annoying speech habit. We are all spoiled for listening to ordinary people by the barrage of carefully scripted, rehearsed, and presented television, radio, and theatrical performances.

8. **Listening Speed:** The average person thinks much faster than another can talk. We sometimes let our thoughts wander to other subjects while the speaker catches up with us. We should use the extra time to search for the speaker's ideas as well as the facts that are presented to us. We can also use this time to summarize the speaker's main points.

9. **Monopolizing Conversation:** If you like to dominate the conversation, you are probably a poor listener. Many managers have gotten to that position because of their ability to take charge and dominate a situation. We should not concentrate on planning what we are going to say while someone else is talking. To develop a meaningful communication there has to be a balance between the listener and the speaker.

10. **Succumbing to Distractions:** If we are easily distracted, our listening ability diminishes. This is especially evident to the speaker. A typical example of distraction is the abrupt changing of subject on the part of the listener making the speaker wonder where his former listener is coming from.

It is important that we understand the mechanics of listening since the average manager spends about eighty percent of his time either listening to someone else or depending upon someone listening to him. We can improve our listening ability by doing these things:

- **Show the speaker that you are interested** by demonstrating active, supportive attention to what he has to say.

- Even though you are busy and have your own problems, **listen.**

- **Don't constantly interrupt the speaker or try to finish his sentences** by leaping ahead with your own thoughts, and don't occupy yourself with busywork or fidgeting while you are supposed to be listening.

- **Listen for the concepts and the ideas** being presented by the speaker. Don't concentrate exclusively on the facts he is using to support his arguments.

- **Make sure that there is sufficient feedback** on both sides to assure that the points being made are clearly understood.

MONITORING INDIVIDUAL PERFORMANCE

Once individual goals or performance targets have been set, performance monitoring may start. Monitoring is a continuous process and cannot be effective without a two-way meaningful feedback.

PURPOSE OF MONITORING: Monitoring is the process of looking at the process being made toward meeting the target, as well as determining the reasons that targets are not met. Monitoring involves looking over the status of ongoing work at regular periods to assure that it has been completed on schedule or that it is progressing well.

PERFORMANCE LOOK-AHEAD: At the level of individual performance, a three week look-ahead outlining specific areas of concentration and accomplishments is a good vehicle for the monitoring program. The performance is monitored every two weeks. The supervisor and employee should agree on what is going to be monitored. Obviously there will be a difference in the material being monitored and the way in which it is monitored. The employee's experience and his capability together with the level of assigned work will determine the desired degree of monitoring. The three week period would be modified to suit the requirements of the assignment.

PERFORMANCE REVIEWS: At each review point, the supervisor and the employee will sit down briefly to review the progress on the short range targets. This review will cover the work done compared to that projected. Any shortfalls will be examined to determine the causes and then recovery programs will be developed and implemented. If additional assistance is required, it will be analyzed and measures put into motion to secure it. If information is missing, an expediting program will be imitated.

The program for the following three week period is finalized with adjustments that may arise from the current status review. Problems with the work should be discussed as soon as irregularities are discovered. People should never be permitted to continue working along the same tack on an assignment if the end product will not be acceptable.

In analyzing performance, the supervisor should take pains to make sure that his observations are specific, that they pinpoint his true concern and are not hedged in generalities.

CLIMATE FOR REVIEWS: In all cases, the supervisor should criticize the action, behavior, or the result, and not the person himself. This is extremely important in fostering a positive attitude toward accomplishment. The supervisor should encourage a feeling of confidence so that the discussion can be conducted in a frank manner. He should encourage suggestions for doing the work in a more efficient manner and give the employee wide latitude in making such suggestions. He should take the time to allow them to develop to the point where they are either adopted or where the employee clearly understands why they should not be taken on.

REGULAR SUPERVISION: This monitoring does not displace routine supervision. If the activity is critical, the supervisor will necessarily keep a tighter rein on the work.

CORRECTIVE ACTION

The purpose of a continuous monitoring program is to provide opportunity for timely correction of real or anticipated adverse effects on the project schedule or budget.

As soon as there is a definite indication of such an effect, the supervisor should work with the individual assigned the responsibility to develop a program for getting back on track.

Sometimes this can be done between the supervisor and the individual without bringing additional resources to bear. Most times it will be necessary to broaden the focus and bring in additional people to help resolve the problem.

PERFORMANCE PROBLEMS: Some problems occur repeatedly; ideas for resolution are:

- **Information Not Available:** A handy excuse for not performing is that the necessary data had not been received. The first question that the supervisor must ask is, "What have you done to expedite it?" The employee must not be let off the hook unless he has really tried to obtain the missing data. He should already have advised the supervisor of this problem before the monitoring session. If he has tried and been unsuccessful, the expediting effort must be escalated. Overtime may be a solution for recouping time after the data is received.

- **Optimistic Target Date:** Often the amount of time required to do a specific job is underestimated. A new fix must be made and its effect on the following project activities analyzed. There will be an effect on both schedule and budget stemming from an underestimate. Care should be taken that this does not create a cascading effect on subsequent work. For activities on the critical path, a delay in completion should be considered seriously to minimize the damage to downstream activities.

- **Adverse Quantity Trends:** Material takeoffs based on actual design may bring up evidence of an underestimate in quantities. The project budget may be sensitive to errors in quantity estimates. An overall evaluation is called for to determine effect of the actual design on the budget. Redesign is sometimes possible, but this is not usually an option. Far more frequently, a general trend of understanding may be brought to light. At this time   available

brain power must be brought to bear to reduce the potential
budget variance.

• **Mistakes, Errors, and Omissions:** Even with many of the calculations computerized and with an aggressive checking procedure, errors are possible. If an individual proceeds with work
based upon erroneous input, there will be complications in
completing the scheduled work on time and within the budget.
Where critical path activities are involved, serious consequences
may arise. The supervisor should make sure that the performance of the innocent employee is not jeopardized because of
something he is not responsible for. The two must work together
to get the activity back on track with as little disruption to the
project as possible.

GRAPHICAL INDICATORS

One of the most valuable tools in the project manager's arsenal is the **graphical indicator**. These charts allow him to analyze the status of the job easily and also provides one of the most powerful feedback mechanisms.

Just posting some of the charts in the task force area is sufficient to motivate many of the groups and individuals involved. A chart showing the actual progress along with the planned progress on the jobs shows accomplishment toward the target graphically and in a form understandable to the team. The importance that the project management gives to the posted results will also be a factor in each individual's assessment of the importance of reaching the goals on time. Unfortunately, the differences in planned and actual progress show up poorly on conventional charts. A need to portray status and trends in an intensified or exaggerated form is desirable. One such technique is the "QuadPlot IV" (Kimmons, 1979) which plots the current status of both the budget and the schedule as one point in a quadrant. Trends are shown by tracking the progress of the successive points. The four quadrants indicate whether the project is ahead or behind planned schedule and ahead or behind planned budget.

Pitting progress on two major work packages being done concurrently provides a competitive environment that can stimulate interest in the work and in job performance. Charting performance of individual disciplines against their plans can also help morale.

Having a posted curve showing planned progress also communicates that the project management knows where it is headed. This helps build confidence among all of the individuals working on the project. Any method capable of generating a sense of urgency and excitement can be valuable in developing a graphical indicator of project performance.

Posting a list of the critical milestones scheduled for completion during the week or the month and checking them off as they are completed adds emphasis to these activities.

Graphical indicators also serve as vehicles for individual and small group recognition. People need to feel that their own individual performance is important to the success of the project. Any way that this can be demonstrated or reinforced will benefit performance.

A graphical indicator such as one produced by the QuadPlot IV method is easily understood, readily produced, and a powerful motivator. A typical example of such a chart is shown.

GRAPHICAL PERFORMANCE INDICATOR USING QUADPLOT IV

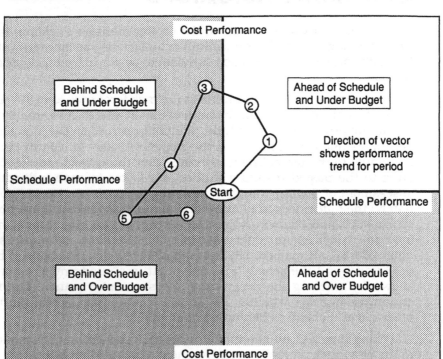

The ordinate of each performance point equals the ratio of actual cost to date divided by the budgeted cost for the work done, the abscissa equals the actual progress to date divided by the scheduled progress to date (adjusted to position the performance point in the proper quadrant).

③ Cumulative Performance at end of period 3.

Quadrant in which performance point falls each period shows cost/schedule performance to date

Kimmons, Robert L. "Track Projects with QuadPlot IV." *Hydrocarbon Processing*, Gulf Publishing Company, Houston, TX, September, 1979, pp. 301-310.

ESTABLISHING PRIORITIES

The project manager must learn to set his priorities based upon the project needs. In the simplest terms, he should spend substantially all of his time on the things that will affect the upcoming work of the majority of people working on his job. He must learn to anticipate the unexpected.

There are many techniques available to assist in setting priorities, though most of these are not particularly designed with the project manager in mind. Through analysis and modifications, one of these techniques can be selected and used. So many demands compete for a project manager's time it is necessary that he have an organized way to assign work priorities— not only for himself, but also for his key people when they need assistance in prioritizing their work.

One system used for setting sequence for tasks is to give each an "A" for highest priority, a "B" for intermediate priority, and a "C" for lower priority. To assign these priorities, all tasks are evaluated from three standpoints.

TIME ORIENTATION: The project manager should be focusing on future work. This is his area of concern. What has passed is important only with respect to how it affects the future. The project manager should analyze the task and assign it an "A" priority *for time orientation* if it concerns the future, a "B" if it deals with present activities, and a "C" if it involves the past.

NUMBER OF PEOPLE AFFECTED: If a large number of people will ultimately be affected by the task, then it should be assigned an "A" priority for *number of people affected.* If a smaller number of people, then a "B" priority should be indicated. If only individuals will be affected, a low priority of "C" is indicated.

IMPETUS: Another way to evaluate a task is by determining what is the driving force behind it. The truly high priority should be given to those tasks that are imposed by the project manager upon himself. This may seem to be contradictory in terms, but in actuality these tasks usually merit an "A" priority. Is the task imposed by the "system" or required by the organizational structure? If so, it probably deserves a "B" priority in the area of *impetus.* If it is "boss imposed," a "C" priority is assigned.

The priority actually given to the task should combine the priorities for the three areas analyzed. **This technique is valid only for**

assistance in screening and preliminary allocation of priorities. In the final analysis there will always be room for the project manager to exercise his "gut feeling" as to what needs to be done first. Experience is a great teacher.

To survive, the project manager must learn to distinguish the **important** tasks (self-imposed, involve large numbers of people, and dealing with the future) from those which are merely **urgent** (dealing, for example, with an individual action from the past and "boss" imposed activities). The project manager must respond to these urgent tasks, sometimes moving them up on his priority list, but he must find a way to minimize their number and their impact on his workday.

The project manager's selection of priorities is the first step toward efficient implementation of project execution. No technique will supply all of the answers for proper prioritizing. It is important that the project manager understand those items that are of true importance to his project and give them his first attention. The project manager who immerses himself in details better left to the assigned specialists is shortchanging his project team.

PRIORITY CUBE

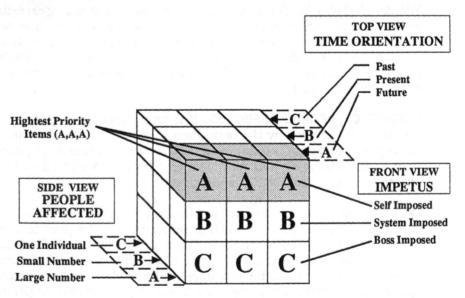

—Adapted from "A.B.C. Principle in Three Dimensions,"
by Hugh Gyllenhaal, from *PATH, an Action Planning System* (unpublished)
New York, NY,1973.

TIME MANAGEMENT

The project manager's own time may be the most limited resource on the project. Regular work habits provide a structured approach to time usage. However, even being careful, he will spend some time in situations over which he has little control.

The project manager should make use of every device available to conserve his time. Some of these techniques are described:

IDENTIFY HOW TIME IS SPENT: Many project managers do not really have a handle on how they spend their time. They rush from crisis to crisis, resolving problems on the run, and end each day without achieving some of the really important tasks. They leave the office with a large briefcase full of homework.

An indication of how your time is spent can come from keeping a daily log for a typical week. Just going though the motion of keeping track of your time tends to improve time utilization. You should be able to see some very significant **time drains** by reviewing the log at the end of the week. This information can be used to rearrange the daily schedule for more proficient performance.

PRIORITIZING: You should use a system for setting the priorities on your time. Until you can do this effectively, you cannot say that you are managing your time well. Working on the right things at all times is essential to effective use of time.

OPTIMIZING DAILY SCHEDULES: The first thing in the morning you prepare a list of those things that need to be done that day. Using the priorities that you have set for each task, group activities to (1) make sure that the most demanding activities are scheduled during the period of the day when you are most productive, (2) do like tasks concurrently or sequentially, (3) even if things are going well, devote at least a couple of hours a week to visit the current work areas of the project and talk to the workers, and (4) allot some time each day for uninterrupted thought about how the project is evolving. Don't forget to review at the end of the day your progress on completing those activities on your daily schedule.

DELEGATE: Most of us tend to want to do the things first with which we are most comfortable. For a project manager this may mean a **retreat to the familiar** or a revival of working as an engineering specialist. This can be deadly for everyone else on the project both from a productivity and a morale standpoint. Start the delegation process by making more effective use of the project secretary. In enhancing secretarial duties you can expand your own work time. Then continue to delegate other tasks that someone else can do.

ELIMINATE TIME WASTERS: Although most project managers may have an idea about where they can save time, the daily logs give a quantitative answer to this question. Once the analysis has been made, you should initiate a program to eliminate the major time wasters. **Unwanted visitors** and **unproductive meetings** are two of the most frequently named time wasters. Stern measures are necessary to reduce waste from these two sources.

DELEGATION

Delegation is the **transmission of authority to another level.** Theoretically it is supposed to work downward into the organization, but, practically speaking, some individuals are experts at delegating "upward."

There are two steps in the delegation process. At first all formal authority is vested in the individual holding the position of senior executive in the firm. Obviously for all of the decisions and individual direction to come from one person is cumbersome so, by a series of written policies and procedures, certain authority is transmitted to lower echelons in the organization.

The second step in delegation occurs within an organization when a manager gives certain of his formal authority to a specific individual or individuals in that organization. This may be done on a temporary basis, for only a short period of time, or it may be an ongoing situation in which the manager has delegated certain of his responsibilities to a subordinate for purposes of training, development, or merely as an expedient to improve the operation.

It stands to reason that when a manager delegates the less important tasks he will have more time available for the important responsibilities of his job.

Of secondary but of still vital importance is the motivational effect that delegation can have, as well as the benefit of training people for job succession.

For managers who may be unsure of their own capabilities, there is often a definite reluctance to delegate. They prefer to maintain a very tight control over all of their operations. Frequently in their organizations they stay in the same job for extended periods of time because they want to be seen as being indispensable. They train no one as a replacement.

A prudent manager delegates gradually. Delegation does not have to be absolute. Many activities preliminary to decision making can be delegated without abdicating the responsibility for the final step. The manager should also make sure that sufficient controls are in place so that the delegation process can be properly monitored.

In initiating a practice of delegation the manager can inventory his responsibilities and categorize them into three types:

- **Things that cannot be delegated**
- **Things that could be delegated provided that someone is readied to accept the increased responsibility**
- **Things that can be delegated right now to an individual who is ready**

There are certain things that *cannot* be delegated. According to Jenks and Kelly (1985) these include:

- **Fielding the repercussions of sudden changes**
- **Performing rituals when power and prestige are critical factors**
- **Reprimands, praise, resolutions of disputes and discharges**
- **Policy making decisions**
- **Final win or lose decisions**

Because of the potential risks involved, the manager must decide how much to delegate and how much to retain. He should never delegate more than he is comfortable with. By proper methods of delegation, he may be able to increase his managerial effectiveness significantly.

Jenks, James, and John Kelly, "Don't Do, Delegate!" Franklin Watts, 1985, as reported in the *New York Times*, July 1, 1985.

MAKING DECISIONS

A major responsibility of the project manager is making decisions. During the planning phase of a project there are always key decisions which have not been made. The project manager should identify these decisions, schedule a date when each decision must be made, and assign the responsibility for making it. These identifiable decisions may relate to the process selection, type of equipment, methods of contracting, or other important aspects of the project

The project manager must not be tempted to make a decisions prematurely or to make a decision when none is required. When confronted by a situation which requires a decision, the project manager should first ask these two questions.

- **Is a decision really required at this time?**
- **Is this a decision that is mine to make?**

There are some decisions that should not be made prematurely. Where these involve much dependent downstream work and there is a good chance that the decisions may have to be reversed later, a delay in making the decision should be seriously considered. The project manager must not feel pressured into acting too soon.

If the answer to the first questions is really "yes," then the second question must also be answered. The project manager's authority should have been fully defined. Repeatedly it will not be clear as to whether a decision lies within his authority. If the decision has to be made and the responsibility is clouded, then the project manager should go ahead and make it. He should immediately advise all of those who might interpret his authority differently that he has made the decision. This allows any objections to be voiced. A project manager must operate in an effective and positive way. Others involved are frequently glad that someone else has made the decision and thus assumed the responsibility.

The decision-making process should always follow along these lines: **the project objective related to the outcome should be carefully reviewed, all of the pertinent information should be assembled, the alternates should be identified and analyzed, and the outcome and potential effect of each alternate studied.** This should provide sufficient background and information for the project manager to make his decision.

If the decision is needed and the following three conditions are met, the project manager should make his decision without delay:

- **That he has as much information as can be gathered in the time period available.**
- **There is no disastrous outcome foreseen.**
- **There still is no clear-cut solution.**

Cases occur frequently in which there is a doubt as to the alternate decision that should be selected. The alternative that is selected may not be as important in some of these cases as is the **making of a timely decision.** The project manager will call upon all of the help, advice, and counsel at his disposal; but he will realize that the **responsibility for making his decisions belongs to him.**

PROBLEM SOLVING

Initially, it may appear that there is no solution to some of the many problems that come to light in running a project.   However, after due investigation, for most of these it turns out that there may be an option between two or more alternatives. The process of problem solving can be structured as follows:

DEFINITION: Clearly, the first step in problem solving is being aware that a problem exists, or better yet, anticipating that a problem is going to come up.   Sometimes the symptoms masquerade as the problem itself; some digging may be required to isolate the real problem. The problem then has to be analyzed, understood, and definitively stated. Care should be taken to make the statement of the problem specific. Too often, the problem is stated in general terms which make the approach to the solution fuzzy.

In the highly charged project atmosphere, efforts are sometimes directed solely toward solving the problem. The project manager should not neglect the alternative of choosing to eliminate the problem rather than that of solving it.

STATING OBJECTIVES: The next step is setting the desired objectives which govern the problem resolution.

PLAN FOR SOLUTION: Following a detailed analysis, a plan should be be developed outlining the approach to the investigation and arriving at a solution or alternative solutions that will best respond to the objectives set. An important part of the plan should be consideration of the probably causes for the problem.

RESOURCE UTILIZATION: Problems are best solved by calling upon the best brains available. For problems which involve meeting the objectives of the project, the project manager is well advised to muster all of the resources available to him. This is one occasion when a group meeting may be most productive. Throw down the problem and challenge the participants to "brainstorm" possible answers.

TECHNIQUES: Problem solving should involve identifying *all* of the possible solutions. If only one solution can be conceived that will solve the problem and fulfill project objectives, it must be accepted. Problem solving may end by requiring a decision between alternatives and trade-offs may have to be needed to achieve project objectives.

TESTING: Before the solution can be accepted, it should be tested. All of the adverse results or potential results of the proposed solution should be considered. If appropriate, a **"what if"** game should be employed in the testing procedure. Regardless, a backup plan should be readied in case the solution does not satisfy the project objectives.

DECISIVE RESOLUTION: Problems should be resolved in an aggressive manner. Unresolved problems on a project may lead to a very demoralizing climate for the project team. Certainly a considerable part of the perception of the project manager's performance is based upon his ability to solve problems in a timely and effective manner.

DISCIPLINE

In achieving a true results-oriented performance management environment, maintaining the proper discipline is essential. In a nutshell, maintaining discipline is knowing how to handle difficult people. In a technical environment we come in contact with all of these types. How can managers constructively deal with the problem employee so that the individual's talents are not lost, productivity is improved, and morale is enhanced? Disruptive behavior has a very detrimental effect upon the work force and it should not be tolerated.

Discipline is a difficult thing for most managers. Overcoming a lack of discipline is even more difficult. To achieve good discipline, the expectations of the company and the individual manager must be clearly defined. You have to **set high standards**, **make them known** to the employees, and then **consistently insist on compliance**. You seldom get more than you expect.

POSITIVE DISCIPLINE: Discipline normally has a very negative connotation because it is customarily associated with punishment. In a technical environment, it is probably better to try to present a positive face to correcting performance problems. Being absolutely "up front" is important. Make sure that the individuals are aware that their behavior is creating a problem.

1. Give each problem employee a chance to correct the situation by discussing it on a one to one basis.
2. If this doesn't work, put a reminder in writing.
3. The next step is to tell the problem employee to go home until the next day. During this time he must decide whether he wants to leave permanently or remain working and follow the rules.
4. The final step is to terminate the employee if he is not willing to correct his performance problem.

PROBLEM EMPLOYEES: Problem personnel may be found in any office. Their behavior is disruptive to the good performance of the rest of the staff. Typical examples of problem employees include:

- **Absent one**
- **Benedict Arnold** (the back stabber)
- **Chronic complainer**
- **Clock watcher**
- **Manipulator** (conniver)

- **Monday morning quarterback** (second guesses your decisions)
- **Omniscient being** (the know-it-all)
- **Perpetual latecomer** (for work, for meetings, for assignments)
- **Personal business first**
- **Prima donna** (everything is his way)
- **Resident clown**
- **Substance abuser**
- **Telephone addict**
- **Town crier** (gossip, rumor monger)

Management cannot sweep the problems of discipline under the carpet. Invariably, when one of these individuals is terminated, the question asked is "**What took you so long?**"

CHARACTERISTICS OF GOOD DISCIPLINE: In disciplinary actions, the manager must learn to "**despise the action, but not the individual**" He must make it clear that disciplinary action is not directed against the person, but against what that person has done. This is often very difficult.

Discipline must be fairly administered. It should be the same for all, but we must recognize that there is a difference between

- A person who comes in fifteen minutes late in the morning, but stays until late in the evening and is always ahead of schedule with his work.

- Another who comes in fifteen minutes late in the morning and leaves fifteen minutes early in the evening and consistently misses deadlines.

It is difficult to promote a sense of fairness if you do not insist on everyone arriving at work on time and staying until quitting time.

CAUTION: Most managers are not doctors or psychiatrists. They should be very careful not to try to deal single handedly with difficult cases involving possible physical or mental problems. There are some cases where professional help has to be recommended. This should always to be done in a firm and sensitive manner.

NEGOTIATION

All of us are negotiating every day of our lives. With so much practice we should be very good at it. The problem is that we don't realize that that is what we are doing. We do not go about it in an organized way; and most of the time we come away from the negotiations having done a poor job, ending up with much less than we could have gotten.

On a project, the negotiation with the client company over the contract intent is of great significance to the success of the project. The clauses that have given the most problems in past contracts have been those relating to (1) **work scope**, (2) **changes and rework**, and (3) **project controls** (CII, 1986). We should concentrate our attention on these three categories. An additional area which must be negotiated is **liability clauses**. Some contract liability clauses jeopardize corporate survival, and negotiation must procede cautiously.

Negotiation is a process which seeks to increase the probability of a favorable outcome in a difference between parties.

It is expedient to see the negotiation process as a succession of steps.

- The first step involves defining the objective that we wish to accomplish. We should also try to establish what objective the other side might have.

- The second step is establishing the strategy by which we will achieve the objective. This also involves analyzing what strategy will be used by the other side. Understand your own options as well as those of the other party. Failure to plan properly will almost certainly mean a less than successful negotiation.

- The third step is to select those tactical measures which will be employed to implement the strategy. These, of course, will have to be based upon several scenarios depending on the corresponding strategy of the other party.

Many people do not really know what they want as a result of negotiation. They have not established the limits they will settle for. For them, negotiation is merely arguing to get the better of an opponent.

In order to develop a strategy, you must evaluate your position as well as the position of the other side with respect to three factors. As proposed by Cohen (1980), these are

- **Power**
- **Time**
- **Information**

It is often difficult to make this comparison. It seems that the other side is always in a position to have more information and more time and to exert a great deal more power.

One of the most important rules of negotiating is that we must learn to concentrate on the problems or issues and not on people. We must also learn to avoid being overly emotional in our negotiations.

Negotiation used to be an "I win, you lose" situation. Today negotiators try to make negotiation an **"I win, you win"** occasion. Unless both parties come out of a negotiation feeling that they can live with the final resolution, there has not been a successful negotiation.

Study by the Task Force on Contracts, Construction Industry Institute, Austin, TX, 1986.

Cohen, Herb, *You Can Negotiate Anything,* Citadel Press, a division of Lyle Stuart, Inc., Secacus, NJ, 1980.

IDENTIFYING THE CLIENT'S OBJECTIVES

At the inception of a project in spite of careful definition, the client's project manager will probably have very different expectations from those of the E/C's project manager. The two must work together to try to bring their two viewpoints into focus early in the project. When this does not happen until the end of the project, there will probably be substantial unhappiness with the results.

The client's project manager is usually much more familiar with the background and the history of the project's conceptual development. The information contained in the inquiry documents delineates the client's latest thinking but there is generally no mention of the process followed to get to that point. The E/C's project manager normally knows little more than is contained in the bid documents. He also has a lot of information to absorb in a short period of time.

This can be shown graphically in the following three figures. The shaded circle in the first chart represents the client's project manager's expectations at the bid period. The transparent circle represents the job concept of the E/C's project manager. The portion of the overlapping circles represents concurrence of concepts. After concentrated feedback as shown in the middle chart, the area of concurrence increases. Finally, after the two project managers have had the opportunity to fine tune their concepts, the area of concurrence has increased to the practical maximum, as depicted in the third chart.

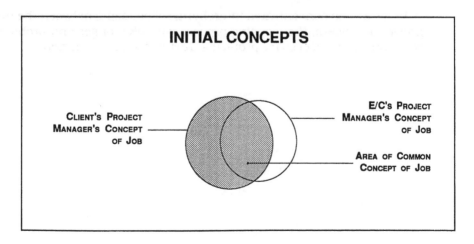

INITIAL CONCEPTS

CLIENT'S PROJECT MANAGER'S CONCEPT OF JOB

E/C'S PROJECT MANAGER'S CONCEPT OF JOB

AREA OF COMMON CONCEPT OF JOB

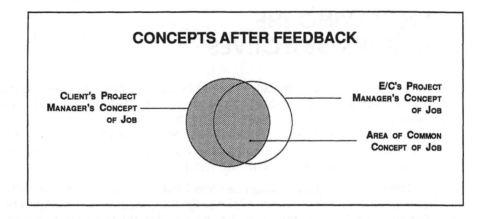

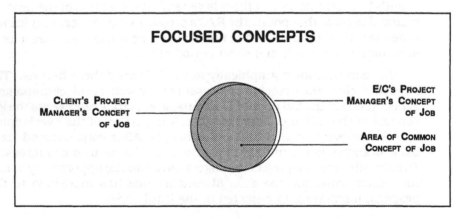

If there is no concentrated interchange of concepts between the two project managers, the focusing process will take longer and probably will result in unnecessary problems during project execution.

CLIENT RELATIONS

Maintenance of client relations is difficult. The client and the contractor frequently are the victims because they are put into adversarial positions from the very beginning. This situation may be caused by:

1. **Preconceived and erroneous ideas** about the other party

2. **Lack of mutual trust** impedes establishing a good relationship even where no adverse opinions exist

3. **Contract conditions and language** often make it impossible for the two parties to have a good relationship

4. **Insufficient funds** available for the work

5. **Irreconcilable personality differences** between the two project managers

A Construction Industry Institute (CII) study (1986) looked at 96 different general condition type clauses that appear in construction contracts and then investigated how these clauses were used on 36 different projects (21 fixed price projects, 15 cost reimbursable) on the part of both the owner and the contractor. As a basis for the study, six specific areas were considered; three were determined to be of more importance than the others:

COST	**Primary element**
SCHEDULE	**Primary element**
QUALITY	**Primary element**
SAFETY	**Secondary element**
OWNER SATISFACTION	**Secondary element**
	Very subjective
CONTRACTOR SATISFACTION	**Secondary element**
	Very subjective

The effect of the 96 clauses were evaluated as to the number and magnitude of problems that they created in each of the six areas listed. Nine of the clauses repeatedly came up as being problems—three clauses in each of three categories. It was also established that the problems were with the **administration** of the contract clauses, not with the **wording.** The three categories are:

- **Changes and rework clauses**
- **Project control clauses**
- **Work scope clauses**

Successful projects require that the parties work well together. To foster a good client relationship on a project demands that the parties pay attention to those areas that historically have caused relationship problems. Based on the information above, this implies that:

- We go into the project **without prejudices** as to the intent of the other party

- We work to establish **mutual trust** by open communication

- We **negotiate the contract carefully** concentrating on a full understanding and agreement as to what is expected on both sides and making sure that the wording that is used reflects that understanding. This is particularly important in the areas of **work scope, project controls,** and **change** and **rework** clauses

A frailty of most people is their immediate retreat to a unreasoning and defensive position when some question of performance is brought up. A quick response which involves listening to the problem, dialogue, objective investigation, and a mutually agreeable resolution is necessary to further good client relations.

Study authorized by the Contracts Task Force, Construction Industry Institute, Austin, TX, 1986.

CLIENT COMMUNICATIONS

Communication with the client affects all aspects of the work. Understanding where these communications take place, the various types of communication involved and how the effectiveness of communication may be measured are important to maintaining good relations with the client staff.

WHERE COMMUNICATIONS OCCUR: The majority of project communication with the client should take place between the two designated project managers, but the project manager who believes that all of the communication on the project flows through this channel will be in for a big surprise.

There are other project communication channels. Where the client has a large resident staff, there will probably be direct communication between the respective project engineering managers, between the construction managers, between those responsible for the various engineering disciplines, and between the project controls, procurement, inspection, and accounting staffs. In addition, there are always some very gregarious individuals from the project staff who will chat with the client's residents and may be an informal source to the latter of what is going on inside the project team.

The client's senior management will certainly have communication with the project's executive sponsor from the E/C's organization. In addition, the E/C's salesman has his own contacts within the client's organization, another valuable communication channel that should not be ignored.

If the client has a large engineering staff and if there have been previous projects done at the E/C's office, there may be several individuals who have friends and acquaintances in the other organization. Communication eminating from these contacts can be factual, but it frequently is distorted. Another communication route is through the vendor network. Vendor salesmen frequently call on both the E/C's project people and the client's home office engineering and procurement staff and thus form a channel for information which is often adjusted to serve the vendor's interests.

TYPES OF COMMUNICATIONS USED: In addition to the usual conversations, memos, letters, and reports, a few other types occur frequently in the project environment:

- **Project Review Meetings:** Some clients insist on a quarterly or monthly meeting at which time the status of the project is reviewed in some detail at a formal presentation attended by the client's senior management. These briefings may take an entire day or more.

- **Project Notes:** Where there are a number of client representatives resident in the E/C's office, it is important that all instructions be documented. This can be done most easily in the form of project notes. Whenever instructions are given which differ from the approved basis for design, involve additional work or change the work plans, schedule or costs, the individual to whom the instructions are given prepares a project note giving all of the details. The project note is directed to the E/C's project manager.

- **Social Gatherings:** A very effective way to improve communications is to have a get together away from the office for lunch or after work and involve a small group of people who work together on the project. Good results are obtained from getting people together away from the normal on-the-job conflicts.

- **Project Newsletters or Bulletins:** For a project with a relatively large staff the sense of *esprit de corps* may be enhanced with a project newsletter or project bulletin board containing timely information about project status, plans, and personnel.

EFFECTIVE COMMUNICATIONS: The effectiveness of communications cannot really be measured in an objective manner. The project manager should strive to see that he is honest in his communications with the client and with the project staff. He should project a professional image and an image of integrity. He should not be secretive, devious, or mislead the client or those with whom he works. He should establish and maintain the channels of communication necessary to operate in a matrix organization.

15 FUTURE DIRECTIONS

Developments predicted for project management in the future already have roots in current execution techniques. These changes will be concerned with:

THE NATURE OF THE PROJECTS: Future projects will continue to be technically still more demanding. We will be processing smaller quantities of high value materials through a series of complex process steps.

Increased technological complexity, involvement of new disciplines, more public attention to the projects, strange new environments will combine to make the project manager's job more demanding and to increase the need for improved management skills. There will be great pressure on the project manager and his key people to demonstrate improved productivity in all that they do.

MORE COMPUTER INVOLVEMENT: Sophisticated technology in the areas of control will take advantage of the miniaturization, broader capability, and increased speed of operation of electronic components. Advanced robotics will be added to construction activities and will complement developments in computer-aided design, drafting, and manufacturing.

Project managers will soon begin to incorporate certain elements of artificial intelligence to accelerate and enhance development of project planning. AI will also be used to verify decisions before they are implemented.

SITE CHALLENGES: As the exploitation of outer space and the deeper waters of the oceans becomes technologically and economically feasible, project sites will become increasingly more challenging.

PROJECT ORGANIZATION: The project manager will see changes in his parent organization that will cause changes to his own mode of operation. Competition will be severe whether he is with a client company or an E/C company. Many companies are turning to new business sectors to compensate for areas where business has fallen off.

A new concept of employee/employer relationship has already started to emerge and will continue to develop. The "contract employee" will be sought out and contracted for a specific project. There will be close affinity of teams who will be contracted out together, led by a project manager who picks his own key people, and who in turn select their own subordinates. Recognition of the perils of overstaffing has led to major restructuring of organizations. The trend toward "partnering" between clients and project management, engineering, and construction firms will continue, but close ties will begin to be established by the client companies with individual project managers who will have their own project teams capable of executing the work. This implies the need for "in-between" firms to handle the cash flow for these groups and service bureaus to provide computer capability.

New disciplines will have to be incorporated into the project teams. Genetic and ceramic engineering will gain importance in many new project areas.

PERFORMANCE: Individual accomplishment will become increasingly important to those who work on the projects. Performance will be monitored to a far greater extent. In turn, project jobs will become more rewarding than ever for the good performers because of increased recognition.

MATERIALS MANAGEMENT: Materials management will experience improvements in information transmittal, field inventory control, and major enhancements in procedures for requesting, receiving, and evaluating vendor quotations. Vendor prints will be received, checked, and approved electronically in a fraction of the time required today.

COMMUNICATION: Perhaps the most important improvement will be in communication and information management. Complete project planning as well as all design work will be "on-line" electronically to all of the project team. Video interchange will reduce problems with office/jobsite understanding. Communication will be made more timely and accurate with the use of modern technology in holograms, lasers, portable computers, graphics, desktop publishing, videos, facsimile transmission, and space-age portable telephones.

CONCLUSION: These changes will not take place immediately, but they are coming. We must be ready for them as soon as they do. We need to start preparing the way to utilize the new technology when it is cost effective and otherwise appropriate to do so.

Index